"First and Second Chronicles are prob[...] of the Old Testament. One king after [...] their walk with God and leadership of Israel. Yet there are important lessons for Christians today. Adam Dooley brings out the meaning and application of these Old Testament history books with verve and finesse. Solidly biblical and thoroughly practical, this work will be immensely helpful to Bible teachers and pastors alike. Highly recommended."

David L. Allen, distinguished professor of practical theology; dean, Adrian Rogers Center for Biblical Preaching, Mid-America Baptist Theological Seminary, Cordova, Tennessee

"Adam Dooley has added another important volume to this valuable series that continually reminds us that all Scripture points to Jesus, from beginning to end! With the skill of a seasoned and faithful expositor, the depth of a well-researched author, and the care and thoughtfulness of a pastor, Dooley brings 1 and 2 Chronicles to life in ways that make this a wonderful resource for every student of Scripture. You may think you know 1 and 2 Chronicles because of your familiarity with 1 and 2 Samuel and 1 and 2 Kings. Trust me, Dooley will guide you through this treasure of God's Word that summarizes all Jewish Scripture and clearly point you to Jesus Christ."

Samuel W. "Dub" Oliver, president, Union University, Jackson, Tennessee

"Jesus made clear on his walk to Emmaus, on the day of His resurrection (Luke 24:27), that the whole Old Testament is pointing to Him. This Christ-centered exposition is essential to understanding the old covenant. Adam Dooley's outstanding commentary of First and Second Chronicles gives rich insight to Christ-centered exposition. He combines his gifts as a scholar and his calling as a pastor in a way that will help every student of First and Second Chronicles to have a richer understanding of these challenging books. After all, the first nine chapters of First Chronicles can be tedious, but the sovereignty of God and His plans for His people are rich study for our faith."

Bryant Wright, senior pastor of Johnson Ferry Baptist Church in Marietta, Georgia, past president of the Southern Baptist Convention, and president of Send Relief, a Christian humanitarian and charitable organization

"I don't read commentaries merely for information, but for inspiration. I certainly want an author to help me understand the text, but ultimately, I want to know how to preach it. In *Exalting Jesus in 1 and 2 Chronicles* Adam Dooley provides the preacher precisely what he's seeking: insight *from* the text and *for* the pulpit, historical clarity within a biblical theology. This volume makes difficult biblical texts much easier to preach."

Hershael W. York, dean of the School of Theology and the Victor and Louise Lester Professor of Christian Preaching at The Southern Baptist Theological Seminary, and pastor emeritus of Buck Run Baptist Church in Frankfort, Kentucky

CHRIST-CENTERED

Exposition

AUTHOR **Adam B. Dooley**

SERIES EDITORS **David Platt, Daniel L. Akin, and Tony Merida**

CHRIST-CENTERED
Exposition

EXALTING JESUS IN

1 AND 2 CHRONICLES

HOLMAN®
REFERENCE
BRENTWOOD, TENNESSEE

Christ-Centered Exposition Commentary:
Exalting Jesus in 1 & 2 Chronicles
© Copyright 2024 by Adam B. Dooley

B&H Publishing Group
Brentwood, Tennessee
All rights reserved.

ISBN: 978-0-8054-9694-9

Dewey Decimal Classification: 220.7
Subject Heading: BIBLE. O.T. 1 & 2 CHRONICLES—
COMMENTARIES\ JESUS CHRIST

Printed in the United States of America
1 2 3 4 5 6 7 8 9 10 • 29 28 27 26 25 24
BP

SERIES DEDICATION

Dedicated to Adrian Rogers and John Piper. They have taught us to love the gospel of Jesus Christ, to preach the Bible as the inerrant Word of God, to pastor the church for which our Savior died, and to have a passion to see all nations gladly worship the Lamb.

—David Platt, Tony Merida, and Danny Akin
March 2013

AUTHOR'S DEDICATION

To my son, Brady Parker Dooley. I pray these pages will deepen your love for all of Scripture, giving you spiritual wisdom that exceeds your impressive physical stature. Words cannot express the joy being your dad brings me.

TABLE OF CONTENTS

1 & 2 Chronicles

ACKNOWLEDGMENTS

Writing a book, particularly of this kind, is a group undertaking. Before suggesting a teaching path for others, prudence requires walking through each chapter and verse in a local church setting. Because of God's providential call on my life, two congregations influenced the content of these pages significantly. The saints at Sunnyvale First Baptist Church in the suburbs of Dallas, Texas, were the first to hear the seminal lessons foundational to this commentary. Over a two-year period, we walked through each pericope together, with their questions refining and deepening my understanding of each text.

Next, the faith family at Englewood Baptist Church in Jackson, Tennessee, enhanced my grasp of these Chronicles even further by affording me a second opportunity to survey their meaning and applications. Serving as your pastor is the greatest joy of my life outside of knowing Jesus personally and helping my family to do the same. Our Bible studies on Wednesday evenings are my favorite assignment each week! Thank you for loving your pastor and for loving God's Word.

Over the years, Danny Akin has been a constant encouragement in my life. Contributing a volume to this series is a privilege tied directly to his gracious invitation, and I am grateful.

Also, working with Dave Stabnow has been a delight. Thank you for your helpful feedback and revisions, and for eliminating the drudgery of what is typically a taxing process. Finally, my brother, William Dooley, continues to be my go-to proofreader for all my projects. As always, I appreciate your help.

Lastly, but certainly not least, my wife Heather continues to be the greatest motivation and inspiration in my life. I could not teach any book of the Bible, much less write a volume about its contents, apart from your steady reassurances and support in my life. I pray the Lord gives us many more years to serve Him together.

SERIES INTRODUCTION

Augustine said, "Where Scripture speaks, God speaks." The editors of the Christ-Centered Exposition Commentary series believe that where God speaks, the pastor must speak. God speaks through His written Word. We must speak from that Word. We believe the Bible is God breathed, authoritative, inerrant, sufficient, understandable, necessary, and timeless. We also affirm that the Bible is a Christ-centered book; that is, it contains a unified story of redemptive history of which Jesus is the hero. Because of this Christ-centered trajectory that runs from Genesis 1 through Revelation 22, we believe the Bible has a corresponding global-missions thrust. From beginning to end, we see God's mission as one of making worshipers of Christ from every tribe and tongue worked out through this redemptive drama in Scripture. To that end we must preach the Word.

In addition to these distinct convictions, the Christ-Centered Exposition Commentary series has some distinguishing characteristics. First, this series seeks to display exegetical accuracy. What the Bible says is what we want to say. While not every volume in the series will be a verse-by-verse commentary, we nevertheless desire to handle the text carefully and explain it rightly. Those who teach and preach bear the heavy responsibility of saying what God has said in His Word and declaring what God has done in Christ. We desire to handle God's Word faithfully, knowing that we must give an account for how we have fulfilled this holy calling (Jas 3:1).

Second, the Christ-Centered Exposition Commentary series has pastors in view. While we hope others will read this series, such as parents, teachers, small-group leaders, and student ministers, we desire to provide a commentary busy pastors will use for weekly preparation of biblically faithful and gospel-saturated sermons. This series is not academic in nature. Our aim is to present a readable and pastoral style of commentaries. We believe this aim will serve the church of the Lord Jesus Christ.

Third, we want the Christ-Centered Exposition Commentary series to be known for the inclusion of helpful illustrations and theologically driven applications. Many commentaries offer no help in illustrations, and few offer any kind of help in application. Often those that do offer illustrative material and application unfortunately give little serious attention to the text. While giving ourselves primarily to explanation, we also hope to serve readers by providing inspiring and illuminating illustrations coupled with timely and timeless application.

Finally, as the name suggests, the editors seek to exalt Jesus from every book of the Bible. In saying this, we are not commending wild allegory or fanciful typology. We certainly believe we must be constrained to the meaning intended by the divine Author Himself, the Holy Spirit of God. However, we also believe the Bible has a messianic focus, and our hope is that the individual authors will exalt Christ from particular texts. Luke 24:25-27,44-47 and John 5:39,46 inform both our hermeneutics and our homiletics. Not every author will do this the same way or have the same degree of Christ-centered emphasis. That is fine with us. We believe faithful exposition that is Christ centered is not monolithic. We do believe, however, that we must read the whole Bible as Christian Scripture. Therefore, our aim is both to honor the historical particularity of each biblical passage and to highlight its intrinsic connection to the Redeemer.

The editors are indebted to the contributors of each volume. The reader will detect a unique style from each writer, and we celebrate these unique gifts and traits. While distinctive in their approaches, the authors share a common characteristic in that they are pastoral theologians. They love the church, and they regularly preach and teach God's Word to God's people. Further, many of these contributors are younger voices. We think these new, fresh voices can serve the church well, especially among a rising generation that has the task of proclaiming the Word of Christ and the Christ of the Word to the lost world.

We hope and pray this series will serve the body of Christ well in these ways until our Savior returns in glory. If it does, we will have succeeded in our assignment.

David Platt
Daniel L. Akin
Tony Merida
Series Editors
February 2013

1 & 2 Chronicles

Introducing 1 & 2 Chronicles

I. **Background Considerations**
   A. Authorship and date
   B. Placement in the Hebrew canon
   C. Title and purpose
II. **1–2 Chronicles as a Fulcrum**
III. **Theological Themes**
   A. God's covenantal faithfulness
   B. The Son of David motif
   C. The centrality of the temple
   D. The priority and blessing of obedience
IV. **Interpretative Challenges**
   A. Omission of material
   B. New material
   C. Numerical discrepancies

When Danny Akin asked me to write this volume, I enthusiastically agreed to do so. Soon, however, I discovered a myriad of questions that I believe function as roadblocks to our celebration of these historical collections. Why do we need these books? How are they different from 1–2 Samuel and 1–2 Kings? What strategy governs the arrangement of their abbreviated content and applications? What agenda motivated the historian to arrange his record as he did? Left unanswered, these uncertainties often force interpreters to adopt a synoptic hermeneutic that syncretizes the breadth of Old Testament history while sacrificing the particular aims of each canonical author. Tragically, doing so diminishes the Chronicles as nothing more than an addendum to the previous efforts of the Deuteronomistic historian.

Answering these questions, though, opens these books up to an interpretive feast, full of moral implications that are just as relevant for contemporary readers as they were for Jews anxious to rebuild Jerusalem. In addition, Christological shadows that anchor Christianity to its Jewish roots while simultaneously forecasting the fulfillment of promises hoped for and convictions not yet seen inspire modern believers with the comprehensiveness of the Bible (Heb 11:1). These books are not meant to contrast the distinctions between Israel and the church, though such a study is appropriate, but to highlight the overlap between the two. Overlooking these accounts, or merely using them to fill in the gaps of other historical records, is of great detriment to Jewish and Gentile Christians alike.

Background Considerations

Authorship and Date

Though the text does not identify a single author, the Jewish Mishnah traditionally celebrated Ezra as the composer of 1–2 Chronicles. Modern scholarship has departed from this view, largely because the overlap of Ezra's ministry with the events recorded is not conclusive. Richard Pratt lists three considerations that refute the traditional viewpoint:

> 1) The date of the Chronicler's composition cannot be limited to Ezra's lifetime. 2) Chronicles ties kingship and temple worship together in ways that do not appear in the teachings of Ezra. 3) Chronicles largely avoids a central issue in Ezra's ministry, intermarriage between Israelites and foreign women (Ezra 9:10-12; see Deut. 7:2-4; Neh. 10:30; 13:23-31). (Pratt, *1 & 2 Chronicles*, 9–10)

While Ezra's ministry would in no way contradict the overall message of 1–2 Chronicles, the lack of internal evidence regarding the book's composition requires more humility and less definitive claims regarding authorship.

The mystery surrounding the Chronicler's identity also creates challenges for dating the book with precision. If, for example, the same author penned Ezra–Nehemiah, the date for writing cannot precede the latest incidents in those accounts. A different historian, though, could have written as early as 529 BC or as late as 200 BC. Selman rightly points out that revisions to the genealogies of 1 Chronicles 1–9 place it approximately half a generation later than the list found in Nehemiah. From another perspective, the list in 1 Chronicles 3:17-24 is between five and ten generations after Zerubbabel (Selman, *1 Chronicles*, 73). These details seem to indicate a date between the late fifth century and the early fourth century.

Placement in the Hebrew Canon

In an effort to keep all the historical books together, English translations position 1–2 Chronicles after 1–2 Kings. The Hebrew Bible, however, ends with the Chronicler's work concluding the Jewish canon, making it the last book of what Christians call the Old Testament. Admittedly, debating placement might seem trivial at first, but broadening our appreciation for Chronicles as a summary of not just Israel's history, but of human history, is key. Doing so allows readers to interpret the exile as an expression of the fall along with its universal implications. Stated differently, these accounts are not merely records of Judah's demise but a biblical interpretation of the entire human story. Much more than an addendum to the works of others, this illustrative history forces modern readers to reckon with their similar propensity to rebel against God and to fight against his redemptive efforts.

Thus, Matthew 1, the next word in God's progressive revelation, begins with the genealogy of Jesus, recapping the starting point of the chronicle's interpretive history. Coupling the first Gospel's recap with the details of Luke's genealogy (Luke 3:23-38), the New Testament continues the exegetical survey of history as an extension of the previous story. Christ does not, in other words, compete with Israel's Old Testament biography; he fulfills it. The baby born in Bethlehem is God's answer to the fall.

Jesus's later rebuke of the Pharisees also accentuates the priority of correctly ordering the historical canon. Of note is his accusation of the Scripture's first and last death up to that point:

> *This is why I am sending you prophets, sages, and scribes. Some of them you will kill and crucify, and some of them you will flog in your synagogues and pursue from town to town. So all the righteous blood shed on the earth will be charged to you, from the blood of righteous Abel to the blood of Zechariah, son of Berechiah, whom you murdered between the sanctuary and the altar.* (Matt 23:34-35)

The martyrdom of Abel at the hands of Cain in Genesis 4 and the stoning of Zechariah in 2 Chronicles 24 bookend world history, demonstrating Satan's murderous schemes to thwart God's redemptive plan. The Pharisees' hatred grew from the same diabolical root and ultimately produced the plot to kill Jesus. The exile requires so much more than our historical observation, largely because the same carnal pattern plagues every man and woman born after Eden. The placement of 1–2 Chronicles establishes a prophetic pattern that every Christian must recognize and resist.

Title and Purpose

Originally presented as a single volume, the Hebrew name for 1–2 Chronicles is "The Events of the Times" or "The Words of the Days." Though the title clearly communicates an attempt to present an independent history, the Septuagint later titled the collection "Things Left Out," promoting the misperception that its greatest value was supplemental to the Samuel–Kings accounts. (For a history of this misunderstanding, see Kalimi, *Retelling*.) The fundamental objective of the Chronicler, though, is to interpret Judah's past failures and successes in order to form both an immediate path of renewal for the postexilic community and an eschatological vision for readers of every generation.

In addition to the unique material and the postexilic interpretation of covenantal realties, Chronicles also frames a history of the entire world in light of Yahweh's redemptive efforts—a perspective not found in Samuel–Kings. Hill astutely observes that Chronicles repeats the fall of Genesis in the sense that paradise lost sets off a journey toward paradise regained, creating a metanarrative for all of human history (*1 & 2 Chronicles*, 24). These efforts root the hope of the bewildered nation, and contemporary Christians, in the unwavering promises of God.

As Jews regathered in the province of Yehud after Cyrus broke the yoke of Babylon, the seeds of full restoration were present. The leadership of Zerubbabel signaled the renewal of the Davidic line, a recommitment to Jerusalem as the capital city restored God's promise regarding the land, and efforts to restore the temple renewed the hope of Yahweh's presence among the people again. Yet these advances were short-lived. After 490 BC the apparent absence of Davidic succession seemed to jeopardize God's eternal covenant with the nation. As the only remaining centerpieces of divine favor, rebuilding Jerusalem and the temple took on a greater urgency in the effort to regain a national identity. The cloud of foreign hegemony also loomed large, leaving the ambition for renewal much greater than the reality. A carefully arranged history anchored to Israel's covenantal promises and God's faithfulness was the Chronicler's antidote for rattled exiles.

1–2 Chronicles as a Fulcrum

The shadows of Jesus adorn the pages of Chronicles from beginning to end, inviting Christians to read with one eye on the past and one eye on the future. The absence of a descendant of David on the throne after the exile required not just a recollection of God's efforts to raise up an eternal seat in the first place but also reminders of Israel's glorious past. In this sense, David's kingdom was not just a forerunner to the Messiah but a picture of messianic strength and glory. The same principle applies to the other righteous kings who followed in the long succession of covenantal stewardship. Solomon's success in building the temple points us to a future when God will dwell among his people again in the new heaven and earth.

Reclaiming these features of Israelite identity after the exile was much more than an exercise in keeping things as they had always been. These traditions lifted the gaze of the people to a coming reality that fulfilled every previous experience. Likewise, Gentile believers separated by miles and millennia benefit profoundly from the eschatological canvas found within these historical records.

Regathering in the city of Jerusalem was not an expression of temporal ambition; it was a sign of eternal hope. Though the seat of David was a political reality, it was also a prophetic promise. Rebuilding the temple was not the end for Jews hungry for a relationship with God but the means to living with Yahweh in their midst forever. Israel's strength *among* the nations was a tangible sign demonstrating God's power *over* the nations. We cannot fully appreciate the vast purposes of the Chronicler without looking forward even as we look backward. Understanding what *was* enables us to celebrate what *is coming*.

Thus, readers of 1–2 Chronicles must continually seek to grasp the historical dilemmas of postexilic reality while also mining the implications of these accounts for the here and now. Modern believers care little about the covenantal expressions of ancient Jews, but we do cherish the future that we have in Christ. By understanding the symbols of yesterday more clearly, we can anticipate the certainties of tomorrow with greater precision.

Theological Themes

God's Covenantal Faithfulness

By summarizing and interpreting the entire Old Testament story, 1–2 Chronicles puts the faithfulness of God on full display. Tracing events that began in the protoevangelium (Gen 3:15), the Lord's determination to save sinners emerges as a breathtaking theme throughout the chronicle. Building on the promises made to Abraham (Gen 12:1-3; 15:1-21), the kings of Judah represent another crucial step toward God's restoration of creation. Because the stump of Jesse would produce a righteous branch in order to bring justice to the earth (Isa 11:1), the house of David strategically prepared the throne from which he would reign (1 Chr 17:10-14).

In his effort to remind the people that God would not renege on these assurances, the Chronicler vividly paints the nation's history in light of Yahweh's faithful efforts. The choice of David as king was not the result of accidental posturing but the divine prerogative to turn the kingdom over to him after the debacle of Saul's reign (1 Chr 10:13-14). With so many obstacles to overcome, the Lord was with David, blessing his rise and consolidating his empire (1 Chr 11:9; 14:7; 18:6,13). In the shadow of Babylon, these remembrances demonstrate not only the strength of the Lord but also his impeccable faithfulness to keep his word. The same God who raised up Israel out of nothing before was willing and able to do so again.

In addition to the encouraging implications for the postexilic community, 1–2 Chronicles admonishes contemporary believers to depend more fully on God's salvific grace. Despite our inability to live without sin, the Lord is just as faithful to keep us saved as he was to prepare a way of salvation long ago. Christians from all times and all places make up the kingdom that David received. We are the fruit of the covenantal hope, meaning that God would have to violate his promises to Abraham, David, and Christ in order to forsake his people. Israel's history buoys our security in a wonderfully unexpected way.

The Son of David Motif

The messianic heartbeat of 1–2 Chronicles rests on the eternal nature of the Davidic covenant. Even at the earliest mention of God's promise to Israel's most instrumental king (2 Sam 7:16), the abiding assurance that one of David's descendants would reign forever over the kingdom of God seemed too good to be true. Yet the consecutive kings who bore the royal blood seemed to fulfill the posterity assured to David all those years ago. Six centuries later, after seventy years of exile and an empty throne in Jerusalem, the mention of covenantal progeny seemed more like an irresponsible vision than an irreversible vow. Emerging from the ashes of God's disciplinary fire, though, was the renewal of his redemptive priorities, all of which stemmed from the house of David. The reaffirmation of God's resolve to build a house for David is an invitation to continue believing, or to believe again in the unwavering commitment of Yahweh to his people.

Consequently, the Chronicler goes to great lengths to reassure postexilic Jews that the only explanation for David's rise was God's initiative. Both Saul's downfall and David's remarkable strength reveal much more than the shortcomings of one leader and the strength of another. While the peaceful transition of power between the two men portrayed by the Chronicler eliminates a great deal of historical drama and anxiety, it provides us with the divine prerogative to establish David as a forerunner to the only King who could save his people. The frequency with which the text posits the expansion of the kingdom back to the Davidic dynasty makes it difficult to deny this major theme.

Likewise, New Testament believers can often observe the perpetual nature of the Davidic priority both before and after the arrival of Jesus on scene. The repeated title "Son of David" is an obvious indicator that Jesus is not just *a* son among many but *the* Son over all (Matt 9:27; 15:22; Mark 12:35-37; Luke 3:31; Acts 13:34; Rom 1:3; Rev 5:5; 22:16). Thus, the house/kingdom/throne of David and the house/kingdom/throne of God are one and the same (1 Chr 17:14; 2 Chr 9:8). Though the throne of David remained empty after the exile and even to this day, Jewish and Gentile believers alike look forward to the day when Jesus takes his rightful seat and commences his eternal reign.

The Centrality of the Temple

The preparation for and construction of the temple dominates large portions of Chronicles for a reason. After driving Adam and Eve out of the garden, Yahweh assured them that one day the war with the serpent would end and his remnant of people would again enjoy the freedom and blessing of his presence. Without question, the ultimate fulfillment of this beautiful promise is the new heaven and earth, but throughout Scripture God gave numerous clues that his redemptive efforts were progressing, not the least of which was his dwelling among Israel in the tabernacle and then the temple. Understanding the garden of Eden as a cosmic temple where God dwelled among his people illuminates the rich cultic language and activities surrounding Yahweh's magnificent shrine.

Rebuilding the structure after the exile was a signal of God's willingness to dwell among the people again despite their waywardness. The detail of David's planning, the execution of Solomon's construction, the centrality of worship through the leadership of Jehoshaphat, and the temple's refurbishment and restoration during the reigns of Hezekiah and Josiah were all meant to motivate the postexilic community to prioritize the restoration effort. The historical motivation continues to be a moving signal that a relationship with God was at the heart of their faith even as it is ours today. In fact, Christians today should celebrate the temple theme precisely because it beautifully foreshadows the Savior who became our temple of access to God (John 2:10-21).

For the Chronicler, Jerusalem's divine sanctuary also represents the second house promised to David, irrevocably linking the edifice to the Davidic kingdom reality (1 Chr 22:6-13; 28:2-10; 2 Chr 6:4-17; 13:4-12). Selman astutely observes, "David's dynasty and Solomon's temple together represented the 'hub of the Lord's kingdom on earth'" (*1 Chronicles*, 59). The detailed personnel and activity ascribed to the temple communicate its enduring priority as national centerpiece. In terms of their covenantal identity, the temple was just as important as the Davidic throne. Remarkably, both houses of David are but shadows fulfilled by Jesus Christ. Our Savior will assume the throne even as he functions as our eternal meeting place with God.

The Priority and Blessing of Obedience

Within the framework of Israel's covenantal relationship with Yahweh, the priority of obedience and the blessings it brings emerges. Likewise, disobedience warrants divine chastening. At the forefront of the Chronicler's purpose is to provide a better understanding of what led to the exile as well as how to avoid another catastrophic season of discipline in the future. Clearly, the nation's demise was not accidental. The narrative explicitly acknowledges that the downfall of the northern kingdom was God's design (1 Chr 5:25-26) and that Judah's vulnerability to Babylon was a consequence of their wickedness (1 Chr 6:15; 9:1).

Those who embraced holy living as an expression of worship would know the joy of divine favor and blessing. Another failure to heed Yahweh's commandments would result in additional corrective reprimands. The rise and fall of king after king in Judah's rich history proved this pattern to be true over and over. Sadly, by the time Jesus began his earthly ministry, the religious leaders in Jerusalem resembled the haughty generation preceding the exile more than the humbled remnant that returned from Babylon.

Christians today can also expect the discipline of the Lord when we stray from the Bible's commands (Heb 12:5-11). Obedience may not be the doorway into God's kingdom (Eph 2:8-9), but it remains the greatest evidence that we are in the family of God (Eph 2:10).

Interpretative Challenges

As with every book of the Bible, preaching verse by verse through 1–2 Chronicles presents numerous challenges. Though teaching these books necessitates a working understanding of the following issues, getting lost in the weeds of these complex explanations during the preaching moment is unwise and unnecessary.

Omission of Material

Even casual readers of 1–2 Chronicles will likely notice the absence of numerous details, many of them negative, when comparing these volumes to the work of the Deuteronomistic historian. Most notably, there is no mention of David's adultery with Bathsheba or the idolatrous harem that turned Solomon's heart away from God. Justifying these and other glaring omissions throughout the chronicle requires us to understand the volume as theological treatise rather than comprehensive history. As with all biblical interpretation, we must ask what the author is seeking to do with his text. Rather than asking why certain material is absent, the better question is, What does the Chronicler desire to accomplish with what he includes?

With the stench of Babylon still in their clothes, the postexilic audience of this history was all too familiar with the shortcomings of their leaders. What they were less sure of, however, was Yahweh's intentions for them going forward. Thus, with ruthless precision the Chronicler eliminates any emphases that would undermine his unwavering commitment to the Jewish people. Highlighting David's miraculous rise and his sweeping strength is a masterful attempt to remind ancient Jews and modern Christians that only God deserves glory for the birth of his kingdom, and our shortcomings cannot thwart his redemptive design. Likewise, removing the less desirable elements of Solomon's reign is less about protecting a wise leader's legacy and more about extolling how magnificent the one who is "greater than Solomon" must be (Matt 12:42)!

With all of Judah's previous kings in the grave, proving that they were not the fulfillment of the messianic hope was unnecessary. What was priority, though, was reminding readers from every generation to keep looking for the King to whom all their previous monarchs pointed, even if imperfectly. These books were more than an explanation of what led to the exile; they were also an invitation to rebuild after it was over. With the reality of God's chastening in the past, this concise history sought to turn the conversation to the future.

New Material

Equally problematic for some readers is the presence of new material in 1–2 Chronicles that is not found in the Samuel–Kings histories. Viewing these additions as fabrications is not justified, however. Merrill identified fourteen sources embedded within the various sections of the Chronicler's work (*A Commentary*, 54–55). With just one of these sources unique to Chronicles, the antiquity and reliability of these references seems obvious. The differing uses of these citations in no way undermines their veracity.

Numerical Discrepancies

Are the numerical reports within Chronicles reliable? If so, how are we to account for the discrepancies between the Chronicler and other historians? First, interpreters should acknowledge that the majority of figures are not in question. Across 629 recorded numbers, only 20 diverge from the Samuel–Kings version of events (Payne, "1, 2 Chronicles," 309). Claims that the Chronicler systematically exaggerated details are empirically false. Archer accurately observes that in seven of the disputed verses, Samuel–Kings reports larger numbers than does Chronicles (*Survey*, 454).

In the cases where approximations seem to be embellished (1 Chr 18:4; 19:18; 21:5; 21:25; 2 Chr 2:2,10,18; 3:15; 4:5; 8:18; 22:2), reasonable explanations that do not undermine the text's accuracy and inerrancy exist. Hill suggests,

> Clearly, some of the numerical discrepancies can be attributed to scribal error (e.g., 2 Kings 24:8; 2 Chron. 36:9). Others reflect a literary approach that prefers rounding off totals rather than exact readings. It is even suggested that the Chronicler may have introduced the ancient equivalent of allowing for inflation in his numerology (since he was writing some five hundred years after the time of David). Finally, it is possible that portions of the books of Chronicles may have been based on older (and perhaps more reliable?) Hebrew texts and manuscripts than the Samuel–Kings accounts. (Hill, *1 & 2 Chronicles*, 29–30)

Regardless of which explanation students of Scripture choose, the above noted differences are most likely due to transmission challenges or an intentional shift in writing style. Neither minimizes the authority of the summations in question.

What's in a Name?

1 CHRONICLES 1–9

Main Idea: A detailed genealogy reminded the people of Israel that God's redemptive plan was still unfolding and that it was not too late for them to be part his redemptive work. Remembering who we are and what we have been through is often a powerful tool for discerning God's will for our future.

I. **Recognize the Effects of Our Fall (1:1-54).**
II. **Remember the Evidence of God's Faithfulness (2:1–8:40).**
   A. The tribe of Judah (2:3–4:23)
   B. The tribe of Simeon (4:24-43)
   C. The Transjordan tribes—Reuben, Gad, Manasseh (5:1-26)
   D. The tribe of Levi (6:1-81)
   E. The Cisjordan tribes—Issachar, Benjamin, Dan, Naphtali, Manasseh, Ephraim, Asher (7:1–8:40)
III. **Reclaim the Expectation of Our Future (9:1-44).**

Have you ever wanted to be someone else? Down through history skilled imposters who were determined to exchange their real life for one that was more glamorous have fooled the unsuspecting public. Some phonies, like Christian Gerhartsreiter, were running from the misdeeds and transgressions of their past. Today, the world knows the truth about the convicted murderer, who kidnapped and killed a child in 1994. His lies did not come out, however, until after the imposter moved to New York City and identified himself as Clark Rockefeller. For years he name-dropped celebrities that he did not know, ate at private clubs for the wealthy, and boasted an expensive art collection, which was also fake. Soon, he married a Harvard executive and had a daughter, but the relationship ended in divorce and a lost custody battle. When Gerhartsreiter kidnapped his own child in 2008, fled to Baltimore, and assumed a new alias, interest in the previous abduction and unsolved homicide from the 1990s rekindled. Though it took several years to link him to the crime, in 2013 Christian received a twenty-seven-year prison sentence after being convicted of first-degree murder (Nix, "6 Famous Impostors").

Other pretenders simply crave wealth or excitement absent from their current circumstances. Brian Jackson chose to imitate members of the Pittsburgh Steelers football team. Growing up in the city, Jackson always dreamed of donning the black and gold. When it became obvious that his childhood ambitions would never become reality, he took matters into his own hands. Brian studied the players, memorizing all the important details of their lives, like where they were born, what kind of car they drove, and the names of family members. Then, he pretended to be the players. First it was Jerame Tuman, then Ben Roethlisberger. To another young lady he was Brian St. Pierre. It worked for a time, but when victimized fans began comparing Jackson to pictures of the actual players, the whole charade ended with felony charges (Geiger, *Identity*, 47–48).

The hunger to be someone else was surely a temptation for the nation of Israel while suffering in Babylonian exile. With their best days seemingly behind them and the promises of God now distant in the rearview mirror, their identity as the chosen people of God was far from glamorous. Furthermore, the sins that littered their past brought with them devastating consequences. Surely starting over as someone else was a better option than embracing their weakened reality. To counter this impulse, with ancestral precision and conciseness, the Chronicler opens his history by framing Israel's past struggles and their future significance in the context of a war as old as the garden of Eden.

Genealogies are not for the faint of heart. Chapters like these are often frustrating to Bible students motivated to learn the Bible and delightful to critics anxious to pronounce its irrelevance. With names that read like a Hebrew phone book, generational lists just aren't that inspiring, at least on the surface. Preachers looking for a sermon might skip over records like these altogether or, even worse, pull one or two names out in order to declare virtue apart from context. Allow me to suggest at least two reasons that, while cumbersome, we should mine and proclaim the message behind this roll of faith.

First, genealogies remind us that these are not fictional accounts. The history of Chronicles reveals the actions of real people with real struggles when the stakes were high. Monarchial highs and lows fit within the same patterns that preceded the time of Israel's birth. The narratives that follow remain instructive for believers today precisely because they are true, making these covenantal followers part of the great cloud of witnesses who serve as our examples (Heb 12:1-2). Even the most wicked leaders and members of the community who placed themselves outside the covenantal promises serve as powerful warnings about the dangers of abandoning our faith. In this sense, the pericope connects the realities of the past to the unfolding of the present.

Second, these records declare that the plan of God is still unfolding. By appreciating the ancestry of Israel here, we're able to monitor the full consequences of the fall as well as the divine efforts toward redemption. With similar information in Genesis 4–5 and 10, exile-weary Jews would read these details as a sign that their departure from the land of promise was evidence of the ongoing war between the seeds of the woman and the serpent, and their recent return was a powerful indicator that their past transgressions could not prevent the eventual crushing of the devil's head (Gen 3:15). When nearly the same family tree appears in Matthew 1 and Luke 3, this ancient agenda finds its fulfillment in Jesus Christ.

Inclusion of all twelve tribes in the genealogies highlights God's commitment to *all* Israel. The history of the northern kingdom is not the Chronicler's concern. Yet after Samaria fell to Assyria in 722 BC, he highlights the efforts of Hezekiah and Josiah to include them in Judah's renewal. Likewise, after the southern kingdom fell to Babylon in 586 BC, these records were a needed reminder that God is faithful to his eternal mission even when we are not. Though the Jews were battle weary, they were far from defeated. By connecting Adam to Abraham, Abraham to Israel, and Israel to David, it became empirically clear that God's intentions for his people never changed because their identity was secure. Though we look back at the Davidic hope rather than forward, Christians today find equal security in Christ, even though we sometimes stumble.

Recognize the Effects of Our Fall
1 CHRONICLES 1:1-54

The variety of forms across these first nine chapters reveals that this compilation relied on numerous sources. Drawing from the book of Genesis, the opening chapter of the pericope places the burdens of Jewish exile within the context of the greater war birthed out of the garden of Eden and its lasting effects (Gen 3:15). That the Chronicler began with God's first son, Adam, signals Yahweh's interest in the nations outside of Israel and reveals his intention of reestablishing Eden's lost paradise (vv. 1-4).

The later covenant promised to Abraham was the divine means by which everyone who was descended from Adam could receive the blessings of God again (Gen 12:3).

Before identifying the twelve tribes of promise, the Chronicler quickly traces the competing family lines after the flood, which warred on behalf of the serpent. Following the same predictable pattern as his earlier source, which lists the sons of Cain before those of Seth (Gen 4:17–5:32), the sons of Japheth and Ham before those of Shem (Gen 10:1-32), and the sons of Ishmael before those of Isaac (Gen 25:12-26), the postexilic historian highlights the theological drama by listing the wicked descendants who do the bidding of hell before celebrating the redemptive lineage. The same God who will emerge victorious over his nemesis from Eden will also bring his chosen family back into Jerusalem after the exile. In fact, both dilemmas reflect the same ongoing struggle.

In this sense, the pain of the exile, despite its severity, was not new but a continuation of the predicted enmity between competing kingdoms. And thankfully, just as God overcame the previous influences of the corrupted seed, as illustrated within the genealogy, the postexilic community could have equal confidence that he would do so again despite their past compromises. Thus, recording the descendants of Japheth (vv. 5-7) and Ham (vv. 8-16) offered evidence of God's abiding strength and faithfulness as Eden's war raged undeniably.

The sons of Japheth eventually moved into the modern regions of Europe, the Iranian plateau, and northern India (Merrill, *A Commentary*, 92). Once there, they became perpetual enemies of Israel. Though it is impossible to identify each name with certainty, Magog's descendants, most likely the Scythians north of the Black Sea, were a continual nuisance as their strength grew. These people were so wicked that they came to directly represent the shenanigans of the devil. For example, during the great tribulation Israel will be living in peace with their defenses down. The prophet Ezekiel relayed God's description of the attack that will come:

> "Son of man, face Gog, of the land of Magog, the chief prince of Meshech and Tubal. . . .
>
> "Therefore prophesy, son of man, and say to Gog, 'This is what the Lord GOD says: On that day when my people Israel are dwelling securely, will you not know this and come from your place in the

> *remotest parts of the north—you and many peoples with you, who are all riding horses—a huge assembly, a powerful army? You will advance against my people Israel like a cloud covering the land. It will happen in the last days, Gog, that I will bring you against my land so that the nations may know me, when I demonstrate my holiness through you in their sight.'"* (Ezek 38:2,14-16)

The point is not that these are the actual descendants of Japheth but that Scripture portrays the greatest enemies of God by the same name. When your behavior is so wicked that your name becomes an adjective for evil that transcends generations, it is impossible to deny the Satanic influence! Revelation 20:7-8 describes the defilement from the four corners of the earth the same way:

> *When the thousand years are completed, Satan will be released from his prison and will go out to deceive the nations at the four corners of the earth, Gog and Magog, to gather them for battle. Their number is like the sand of the sea.*

Again, the depiction has nothing to do with the identity of the enemy and everything to do with the immenseness of evil. The hostility and rebellion of Japheth's descendants lives on until the serpent is finally crushed.

Likewise, the list of Ham's sons who moved into Arabian and African regions is a reminder of known enemies outside of Israel. With no deviation from the Genesis account, the Chronicler again captures the fallen lines that oppose Yahweh's work through his chosen nation. Mizraim (v. 8) was the Hebrew name for Egypt, a nation that fought incessantly against God's redemptive agenda. Canaan (v. 8) was obviously the progenitor of the groups Scripture later identified as Canaanites, Israel's ever-present thorn, reflected in the collection of 1:13-16. From the seed of Casluh (v. 11) emerged the Philistines, Israel's most recognizable nemesis.

From Nimrod's (v. 10) progeny arose the tower of Babylon, the Assyrians, and the Babylonians. Though the Chronicler significantly reduced the record, readers would have been familiar with the idolatrous ambition of the earth's first great warrior. In fact, the first scriptural reference to a kingdom describes Nimrod's cities of Babylon, Erech, Accad, and Calneh rather than the nation of Israel (Gen 10:10). This detail may seem insignificant, but it reveals a sinful drive similar to that of Cain, whom God condemned to roam the earth under divine watch care. By building cities to protect himself instead (Gen 4:16-17), Cain sought to be his own god. Likewise, after the flood God recommissioned Noah's sons, much like Adam and Eve before them, to be fruitful and multiply as they spread out across the earth (Gen 9:1,7). Yet rather than make Yahweh's name known, Nimrod built kingdoms and strength for himself, effectively acting as his own god. Now we learn that his posterity produced the very enemies who would implement the exile of God's people—more enmity between the kingdoms of light and darkness.

The sons of Shem stand in contrast to the seeds sown by the serpent because of their messianic fruit (vv. 17-27). As with the record from Adam to Noah, ten names move the salvific progress forward to Abraham, the keeper of Yahweh's covenant (vv. 24-27). The hopeful recollection, though, is not free of spiritual casualties. Many of the names remain unidentifiable, but the two sons of Eber present another splinter away from the redemptive line. Both Peleg and Joktan lived during the time the earth was divided, likely a reference to the consequential separation resulting from the tower of Babylon (v. 19).

Even the family of Abraham is not without its compromises and distractions. Isaac and Ishmael are the primary focus (v. 28), but the log also includes the sons born to Keturah, Abraham's concubine after the death of Sarah (vv. 32-33). As in previous lists, Ishmael's family tree appears first because it is not the chosen line (v. 29). Its presence here, though not developed, was a passing indicator that from the very beginning the favored family frequently doubted the promises of God, and the monarchial adherents (vv. 43-50) dismissed them outright. Even then, God was faithful to advance his efforts through a remnant of faith. Thus, Isaac's two sons, Jacob and Esau, move the history even further (v. 34).

From Esau springs forth another competing line (vv. 35-37) that, through details we do not have, produces the Edomites (vv. 38-42; Gen 36:9). The list of Edomite kings who preceded Israel's monarchy (vv. 43-52) were Esau's descendants who reigned during the period of the judges (Gen 36:40-43). These rivalrous families fulfill the prophetic revelation that came before Jacob and Esau were born, when the Lord said to Rebekah,

> *Two nations are in your womb;*
> *two peoples will come from you and be separated.*

One people will be stronger than the other,
and the older will serve the younger. (Gen 25:23)

More importantly, though, we understand this sibling rivalry to be part of the greater struggle begotten by humanity's fall in Eden.

The point for Jews returning from the exile is that no amount of posturing by the devil could hinder Yahweh's covenantal ambitions. If that were true through so many potential hindrances previously, how much more certain was it now that the covenantal family was returning to Jerusalem? Tying their future success to the full scope of history reassured Judah's banished generation that God was not finished with them precisely because his redemptive story was still in motion. Though rebuilding the city of David was primary after the Persian resettlement, the greater aim of Yahweh was the incarnational gift of his Son, the Messiah.

Christians today should read these genealogical records with amazement over God's compassion for the whole world, much of which was a tool in the arsenal Satan used to fight against the Lord's efforts to restore the lost paradise of Eden. Jesus's rejection by his own people was nothing new (John 1:9-11) but merely the latest evidence of the ongoing war against the devil's army. Yet because of his promise to Abraham, God remains resolved to bless the whole world through his son, Israel (Gen 12:3). Furthermore, this history should increase our assurance that there is no other name under heaven by which men must be saved outside of Jesus Christ (Acts 4:12). The desperation of the serpent to substitute for the promised son of David reaffirms Jesus's exclusivity. God's first son, Adam, gave rise to the human race that fell into sin. From God's second son, Israel, rose a chosen nation that also spiraled into disobedience. God's final Son, Jesus, made redemption possible because he never disobeyed his Father, and he shares his righteousness with those who call on his name in faith. Our understanding of security in Christ soars when we realize the repeated effort necessary before he invaded the Bethlehem night.

Remember the Evidence of God's Faithfulness
1 CHRONICLES 2:1–8:40

Beginning in chapter 2 the focus shifts to the twelve tribes of Israel descended from Jacob, whom God appropriately renamed Israel. The initial survey (2:1-2), though brief, intentionally parallels the history of

Esau's opposing generations (1:35). While Joseph's name appears here, his sons, Ephraim and Manasseh, will take his place as designated tribes due to his elevation to patriarchal status by Jacob (7:14-29; Gen 48:1-6). Consequently, Joseph, who had no additional sons and daughters, joins Abraham in having offspring that outnumber the sands of the seashore. The tedious details of each generation demonstrate the continued faithfulness of God juxtaposed against the serpent's hostility.

In the verses that follow, despite being the fourth oldest son, Judah appears first in the record, dominating nearly three chapters, because God elevated him over his brothers Reuben, Simeon, and Levi due to their reckless sin. Reuben defiled his father's bed (Gen 35:22; 1 Chr 5:1) while Simeon and Levi violently avenged their sister Dinah's rape (Gen 34:25-29). Moving closer to God's redemptive goal, Judah is clearly the chosen family from which the Messiah will arrive and bless the whole world. The arrangement also prepares readers for David's prominence throughout the chronicle. Even as the nation grew, this emphasized priority remained. The logic for the order of the tribes from 4:24–8:32 is difficult to discern but should be read as an anchor for a postexilic reality.

The Tribe of Judah (2:3–4:23)

Despite providing only a brief summary of much of the Old Testament storyline, the Chronicler makes no effort to bury difficult highlights. For example, Judah's first three sons were born to Canaanite women (2:3). The move was a careless rebuttal of the practice established by Abraham, who sent his servant to find a wife for Isaac from among his people (Gen 24), and by Isaac, who sent Jacob to find a bride from the house of Laban, who was Rebekah's brother (Gen 27–28). These descendants are largely ignored and have no direct link to the birth of Christ, but their inclusion emphasizes God's intolerance of sin within his chosen lines, as well as the serpent's efforts to interrupt the mission. The text only mentions Er's sin, but Jewish believers would have been familiar with the shortcomings of Onan and Shelah that led to Judah's line through Tamar, a sordid development all its own (2:4). For the postexilic generation still reeling with the consequences of their own unfaithfulness, these examples were reminders that compromise was just as pervasive in Israel's early existence as it was just before their captivity.

Moving toward David, the genealogy emphasizes Perez, Hezron, Ram, Amminadab, Nahshon, Salma, Boaz, Obed, Jesse, and then David (2:4-15). Again, a movement of ten names carries the narrative forward to the Davidic dynasty. The tribal contributions outside of the direct line of Christ, though not surveyed within the pericope, also reveal God's comprehensive design over history. David's older siblings appear in 2:13-17; then the Chronicler returns to the descendants of Hezron (2:18-55), offering familial details found nowhere else in Scripture, focused primarily on the descendants of Caleb (2:18-24) and Jerahmeel (2:25-33). Thompson elaborates:

> The aim of the Chronicler was to attach all of these diverse elements to the tribe of Judah through Hezron and his descendants. There evidently was some prestige as well as political, economic, and social advantage belonging to the only tribe restored to its own territory by official decree. Many of those who had become attached to the tribe of Judah shared in the status by adoption, and the present genealogy served to recognize that adoption. (*1, 2 Chronicles*, 66)

While many of these names are unfamiliar to us, each reveals the intricacies involved in building a Judahite dynasty. Bezalel (2:20), for example, was a chief artisan of the tabernacle (Exod 31:1-5) whose work Solomon later sought (2 Chr 1:5). Shobal founded Kiriath-jearim (1 Chr 2:50), where the ark of God rested for twenty years until David returned it to Jerusalem. Salma established Bethlehem (2:51), where Jesus was born. Yahweh was preparing not only his Messiah but also the prophetic environment he stepped into.

Chapter 3 deals exclusively with David's family tree, organized around the birthplaces of his children, namely Hebron and Jerusalem (3:1-9). The tragedy in front of this list underscores once more both God's initiative and his preservation of the kingly line. Amnon raped his sister Tamar (3:1). Absalom killed his brother Amnon and rebelled against his father (3:2). Adonijah sought to take the throne of Solomon after David's death (3:3). The historian omits these details, though, because of his exclusive purpose of celebrating the rise and protection of the Davidic reality born through God's covenant.

Therefore, the recollection quickly transitions to the sons of David who rightfully assumed his throne (3:10-16). Despite the descriptions of idolatry and wickedness regarding these kings in Judah, the messianic route to the eternal son of David becomes clear. By tracing the rightful descendants of David after the exile through Jeconiah rather than Zedekiah (3:17-24), the historian charts a path forward for the nation even though no official king ruled from Jerusalem after the tribes regathered. The current predicament, in other words, was no threat to the covenantal promises later fulfilled in Christ. The less-than-subtle implication is that a son of David will rise and rule again.

Finally, the records of Judah conclude with a series of short genealogies unique to the Chronicler (4:1-23). The clans of Hur (4:1-4), Ashur (4:5-8), Jabez (4:9-10), Chelub (4:11-12), Othniel and Caleb (4:13-16), lesser-known groups (4:17-20), and Shelah (4:21-23) organize the chapter (Selman, *1 Chronicles*, 105–6).

Of greatest interest to modern readers is the prayer offered by Jabez (4:9-10), often presented as a formula for spiritual and material blessings in recent years. Selfish interpretations like these, however, miss the point entirely. Divorced from the context of Chronicles, we sometimes overlook that Jabez's prayer was not egocentric but a plea for an enlarged Israel. Ironically, amid a genealogy, this mysterious man, whose name reflects great pain in his family, appears with no mention of his father whatsoever. Though no details for his absence appear in the text, without a father present this son of Judah had no inheritance in the land. Yet with nowhere else to turn, Jabez humbly called out to the Lord for intervention. An enlarged border meant he would find his rightful place in God's kingdom. Jabez's prayer mirrored the open agenda of the Davidic reality; it was not a secret recipe for unlocking hidden blessings from Yahweh. Schrock rightly observes,

> Genealogies are not written to hide secrets for Bible decoders; they are given to remind us of God's unfolding of history. In 1 Chronicles, the story of Jabez doesn't give ancient hearers tips on calling down the blessings of God; it reminds post-exilic saints of God's grace, faithfulness, and sovereign rule in their history. ("Jabez")

New covenant believers quickly forget that the material realizations tied to the Davidic kingdom pointed to our blessings in Christ but were never meant to be a substitute for him. Far too often, modern Christians, whether intentionally or unintentionally, diminish the glory of Jesus by viewing him as *a means* rather than *the end* of our faith. Christ is our reward! The apostle Paul said he counted all things as rubbish

(1) "because of Christ" (Phil 3:7), (2) "so that I may gain Christ" (Phil 3:8), (3) "be found in him" (Phil 3:9), and (4) "know him" (Phil 3:10).

The Tribe of Simeon (4:24-43)

Perhaps Simeon appears next because of his shared land in the territory of Judah. Abbreviated genealogical notes compared to what comes before "indicate a decline in this tribe's land and population of which the Chronicler's readers are well aware" (Wilcock, *1 and 2 Chronicles*, 393). Jacob's final pronouncement over his sons was an abiding reminder of Simeon's egregious error and violence in defending his sister, Dinah (Gen 34:25-29). The patriarch lamented,

> *Their anger is cursed, for it is strong,*
> *and their fury, for it is cruel!*
> *I will disperse them throughout Jacob*
> *and scatter them throughout Israel.* (Gen 49:7)

Yet the intent here is not to magnify Simeon's disqualification but to celebrate his inclusion in the covenantal hope. Not only did these descendants receive the benefits of Judah's eternal throne, but God also used them to increase the benefits he would provide as they took land from the Hamites (4:38-41) and eliminated the Amalekites (4:42-43). The graciousness of the Lord was surely encouraging to Jews anxious to start over after years of waywardness, even as it is to us when we stray.

The Transjordan Tribes—Reuben, Gad, Manasseh (5:1-26)

As stated previously, Reuben forfeited his birthright by defiling his father's bed, thereby elevating both Judah and Joseph. The former received royal status by preserving the kingly line and messianic hope, while the latter, who was the firstborn of Rachel, received the birthright he would eventually share with his sons Ephraim and Manasseh, pivotal leaders in what became the northern kingdom (vv. 1-2). While these designations may seem trivial to modern ears with no cultural correlation, the practical result was that Joseph's sons exceeded Reuben in strength and influence as the young nation prospered. Nonetheless, Reuben's descendants experienced great material (v. 9) and military (v. 10) success as they grew, demonstrating their contribution to the Chronicler's theme of "all Israel." The list of Reuben's progeny extends down to the Assyrian invasion (vv. 3-10).

Continuing to move north, the genealogy next records the family lines of Gad. The brief account includes important geographical details, revealing that this tribe lived in Bashan (v. 11) and Gilead (v. 16). The note tying these lists to the time period of Jotham and Jeroboam (v. 17) not only reveals one the Chronicler's sources but also speaks to the historicity of his claims.

Before introducing the half tribe of Manasseh, the historian reports their cooperative conquests through a shared effort with Reuben and Gad against the Hagrites (vv. 18-22). The Lord's intervention in response to their humble dependence was a model for postexilic believers who faced overwhelming opposition on every side. Realizing that a large army was never the secret of Israel's strength was also instructive as the remnant rebuilt Jerusalem.

The summary of Manasseh's tribe breaks from the previous pattern by only listing the heads of households, all of which receive praise (vv. 23-24). Despite their impressive resumes, though, Reuben, Gad, and Manasseh all sought other gods repeatedly, resulting in exile at the hand of Assyria (vv. 25-26). Though the Chronicler does not hold back regarding Judah's later idolatries, highlighting the wickedness of these tribes was not only a reminder of the consequences for sin outlined in Deuteronomy 28 but also empirical evidence that even in judgment God still loved his people.

The Tribe of Levi (6:1-81)

The religious leadership of Levi occupies the center of the genealogies' chiastic structure and takes more space in the chronicle than any tribe outside of Judah. Both the location and the attention to detail speak of the priority of worship throughout the land of Israel. Positioning Levi's lineage right after the first mention of exile accentuates their devotion to Yahweh as the way home. The chapter divides around the three sons of Levi—Gershom, Kohath, and Merari—and the roles their descendants had throughout the land (vv. 1,16). As their duties unfold, we should remember that all priests were Levites, but not all Levites were priests.

The priestly line rested with Aaron; thus 6:1-15 traces from Kohath through Aaron right up until the exile when Nebuchadnezzar deported Jehozadak (v. 15). Though the list is not comprehensive, it successfully preserves the high priestly line (Thompson, *1, 2 Chronicles*, 84). Next, to demonstrate the fuller progeny of Levi, the focus returns to his three sons (v. 16) in order to establish the families of each who had varying assignments within the Levitical order (vv. 17-30). Among them were the tabernacle and temple musicians appointed by David (vv. 31-47). The three primary worship leaders, Heman (vv. 33-38), Asaph (vv. 39-43), and Ethan (vv. 44-47), represented the lines of Kohath, Gershom, and Merari respectively.

Returning to Aaron's descendants a second time and carefully articulating their cultic duties (vv. 48-53) reemphasized the distinction between a general Levite and a priest who represented the people before Yahweh by offering sacrifices and making atonement. Because God desired that his statutes be taught throughout the land of promise, the Levites received no exclusive territorial allotment. Instead, their assigned settlements, the focus of 6:54-81, spread across the eleven remaining tribes of Israel.

- Judah (vv. 57-59,65)
- Benjamin (vv. 60,65)
- Manasseh (vv. 61,62,70-71)
- Issachar (vv. 62,72-73)
- Asher (vv. 62,74-75)
- Naphtali (vv. 62,76)
- Reuben (vv. 63,78-79)
- Gad (vv. 63,80-81)
- Zebulun (vv. 63,77)
- Simeon (v. 65)
- Ephraim (vv. 66-69)

Again, these divisions are made according to the Kohathites (vv. 54-61,66-70), Gershomites (vv. 62,71-76), and Merarites (vv. 63,77-81) following the pattern laid down in Joshua 21:5-39.

For Jews returning from Babylon, this portion of the genealogy clarified the necessary credentials for their religious leaders while also offering a vivid road map for reinhabiting the land. Following these guidelines would help them lay the groundwork for worshiping Yahweh even before completing the temple rebuild. Without a sitting son of David ruling in Jerusalem after the exile, these cultic details would help preserve Israel's identity as the people of God. Believers today do not look to a designated shrine for worship because we are the temple of the living God (2 Cor 6:16) and Christ is our mediator (1 Tim 2:5). Yet the primacy of worship through the means of Scripture and music remains.

The Cisjordan Tribes—Issachar, Benjamin, Dan, Naphtali, Manasseh, Ephraim, Asher (7:1–8:40)

With the exception of Benjamin, the tribes listed from this point forward all resided in what became the northern kingdom west of the Jordan River. The descendants of Issachar were known as valiant warriors (7:1-5), as were the descendants of Benjamin (7:6-12). Strangely absent from the list is the tribe of Dan, though the inclusion of his son, Hushim, suggests he simply was not named (cf. Gen 46:23). Boda surmises that the omission was intentional due to Dan's abandonment of his allotted territory and creation of a rival religion, an incident the Chronicler returns to in 2 Chronicles 11:14-15 (*1–2 Chronicles*, 86).

In order to present a unified Israel, the Chronicler includes Naphtali in his history, albeit with only one verse due to their small size (7:13). The presence of Manasseh (7:14-19) and Ephraim (7:20-29) indicates their legitimacy among the other tribes. Homage to Joseph strategically reminds readers that his two sons, Ephraim and Manasseh, rose to tribal status because Jacob received his son as a peer (Gen 48:1-6). Finally, the tribe of Asher appears, although in a different order than previously (1 Chr 2:1-2).

Returning to the genealogy of Benjamin seems redundant initially (8:1-40), but the uniqueness of the content separates this section from 7:6-12. The chapter naturally divides between the general ancestry of the tribe (8:1-28) and the specific line of Saul (8:29-40). The goal of these verses is twofold. Selman rightly suggests that the greater reason for focusing on Benjamin again is geographical (*1 Chronicles*, 122–23). By carefully identifying the tribe's settlements, especially those in Jerusalem (8:28,32), the Chronicler underscores the continuing partnership between Benjamin and Judah that resulted in what later became the southern kingdom. In fact, the former seldom appears in the record apart from the latter. This documented cooperation would have been especially encouraging during the Persian relocation, when Judah and Benjamin were the majority of the true Israel in Jerusalem once again.

Most obviously, though, the text turns our attention toward Saul, Israel's first king, with the focus on the monarchial history beginning in chapter 10. His rise effectively demonstrates another tactic of the serpent, who not only offered rival lines to war with the seed of the woman from without (Gen 3:15) but also sought to tempt and contaminate the redemptive mission from within. Saul's spiritual apostasy, though, was not a pronouncement of Benjamin's irrelevance or demise. In fact, within the chiastic arrangement of the genealogies, Levi remains at the center while Judah and Benjamin function as protective brackets around the nation (Boda, *1 & 2 Chronicles*, 98).

Admittedly, contemporary readers often get lost in both the length and the detail of genealogies like these. Discerning the current implications or practical applications of such lists is a challenge for even the most faithful students of Scripture. In addition to the exclusivity of Jesus as the only way of salvation, allow me to suggest another theme, perhaps even more explicit, that may not be readily obvious through a cursory reading of these chapters. Behind each name recorded in this ancestry is the reminder that our past sins do not define us.

Was Israel idolatrous? Without question. Did they squander the goodness of God? No doubt. And yet, though he had every right to throw them away, God chose to forgive and restore his people. Yahweh's commitment to Israel was not due to their strength or number but to his faithful, covenantal love (Deut 7:7-9). Likewise, Christians today experience similar grace. The character of God rather than the compromises that litter our past defines who we are. Our transgressions are many, and often, they haunt us.

- Maybe the word *adulterer* keeps you awake night.
- Maybe a marriage that ended in divorce has you feeling like a second-class Christian.
- Maybe an exposed lie has you afraid to show your face.
- Maybe an abortion from your teenage years taunts your soul.

On and on we could go citing commitments we failed to keep, guilt we cannot overcome, and sin that we return to again and again. Yet where our sins abound, God's grace abounds much more (Rom 5:20). Why? Because the righteousness of Christ covers us (Rom 3:21-22); in him we are holy and blameless (Eph 1:4). Truly,

> *once you were alienated and hostile in your minds as expressed in*
> *your evil actions. But now he has reconciled you by his physical body*

through his death, to present you holy, faultless, and blameless before him. (Col 1:21-22)

The Lord remained faithful to Israel because of his holy resolve to seek and to save sinners through sending his one and only Son. And God remains just as committed to his people today, not because Jesus is coming but because he already came.

Reclaim the Expectation of Our Future
1 CHRONICLES 9:1-44

After defining "all Israel" and recalling the substance of their past while in the land, the Chronicler acknowledges the unfaithfulness that sent both the northern and southern kingdoms into exile, with a particular emphasis on Judah (v. 1). The remainder of the chapter deals exclusively with the reoccupation of the land during the postexilic period. These were God's chosen people, but their wickedness brought with it great consequence, not the least of which was proving their ancestry to reenter the land (cf. Neh 1:5). Only Judah, Benjamin, Ephraim, Mannaseh, and Levi were part of the initial restoration (vv. 2-34). The tone is conciliatory, as if the historian is admonishing,

- Look at all that you've been through!
- God isn't finished with you!
- Learn from the past without repeating it!
- Don't turn back now!

By outlining the priests (vv. 10-13), the Levites (vv. 14-16), and the gatekeepers (vv. 17-34) before the temple's reconstruction, the Chronicler prioritizes the nation's cultic identity. Israel was picking up where they left off before the exile, becoming what God chose them to be. Most importantly, the look forward reassures the postexilic community that they were still heirs of the covenantal inheritance. Despite their sins, the promises of the past were still theirs to claim.

All this means that Chronicles has taken the history of Israel a stage further than 1 and 2 Kings. Although 2 Kings ends on a note of genuine hope (2 Kings 25:27-30), it is restrained and Israel is still in exile. But now the winter is over, and these lists

are a definite sign that spring has begun to arrive. (Selman,
1 Chronicles, 129)

The hope of the final chapter is palpable as the genealogy ends
where it began. Out of all the nations on the earth, Israel came forth
as God's instrument of redemption (ch. 1). Now, after years of exile
when every seeming promise was tested, Israel came forth again, not
as the best means of cosmic renewal but as the only means (ch. 9).
Fundamentally, this actualized hope is the goal of the entire history,
which concludes,

> *In the first year of King Cyrus of Persia, in order to fulfill the word of*
> *the Lord spoken through Jeremiah, the Lord roused the spirit of King*
> *Cyrus of Persia to issue a proclamation throughout his entire kingdom*
> *and also to put it in writing:*
>> *This is what King Cyrus of Persia says: The Lord, the God of*
>> *the heavens, has given me all the kingdoms of the earth and has*
>> *appointed me to build him a temple at Jerusalem in Judah. Any of his*
>> *people among you may go up, and may the Lord his God be with him.*
> (2 Chr 36:22-23)

By appealing to Jews who have yet to return to the land that they might
do so, the Chronicler simultaneously admonishes Jews already living in
Jerusalem to accept those who will come later as the fulfillment of God's
unfolding plan (Boda, *1–2 Chronicles*, 101). All is not lost. Dead genealogies that surveyed nothing but wasted potential during their captivity
now resonated with life as historical demonstrations of God's faithfulness again and again.

Contrary to 1–2 Kings, which offers a sliver of hope for the future in
the release of Jehoiachin from prison (2 Kgs 25:27-30), 1–2 Chronicles
again refocuses Israel on the reestablishment of their covenantal community and the arrival of their Messiah. Realizing that these books are
the final testament of the Hebrew Old Testament further accentuates
the tremendous anticipation they bring. After reassuming their place
in the land and reconstructing their temple, the next major event in
the history of the nation is the birth of Christ in Bethlehem. Or, as
Selman so eloquently states, "But now the winter is over, and these
lists are a definite sign that spring has begun to arrive" (*1 Chronicles*,
129). It was time for the Jews to actively participate in building God's
kingdom again.

Before doing so, postexilic Jews needed a deeper appreciation for all that led to their exile in order to avoid repeating it in the days ahead. Returning to Saul's genealogy (vv. 35-44), at the very least, offered a transition to the narrative history of the nation in 1 Chronicles 10 through 2 Chronicles 36. Perhaps, by using the names Eshbaal and Merib-baal for Ish-bosheth and Mephibosheth, there is also a subtle clue to the explicit idolatry of Saul that gave way to David's leadership. Regardless, the Chronicler had many lessons to teach the chosen people as they sought to reclaim their previous expectations for the future. By reemphasizing the Davidic covenant, recalling the detailed plans and construction of the temple, and celebrating the blessed realities of the nation during times of faithfulness, this history charts a path forward in the renewed hope of a coming Messiah.

Clearly, God's plan for Israel included a future and a hope (Jer 29:11). After years in Babylon patiently enduring the consequences of their sins, finally it was time to resume the purpose for which they existed. But how is this relevant for believers today? Like our Jewish forefathers, there are times that we, too, will need to learn from past mistakes. During seasons of chastening, we should trust God's discipline as a gift from the hand of a loving Father (Heb 12:4-11). And as the Lord gives us opportunity, we should return to our places of disobedience and resume walking with him without delay. Seasons of waywardness and the outcomes they bring should not prevent us from reclaiming the future God designs for us.

Reflect and Discuss

1. How does having a list of names designated as inspired Scripture teach you about the love God has for his children? For you in particular?
2. Discuss the numerous ways Satan tried to prevent the coming of Christ.
3. What does Satan's war with Israel teach us about his agenda for our lives today?
4. What do the shortcomings of Israel teach us about the faithfulness of God?
5. What do these genealogies teach us about our own vulnerabilities before the Lord?

6. What does the exaltation of some tribes over others teach us about the consequences sin sometimes brings?
7. What does the centrality of Levi within the genealogy teach us about the priority of worship for the church? The practice of worship?
8. How do the sins of our past sometimes prevent us from walking with God today?
9. What evidence will be present when we learn from and yield to God's discipline in our lives?
10. List practical ways we can reclaim the future God desires for us after a season of repentance.

Sovereign over Our Mistakes

1 CHRONICLES 10:1–11:3

Main Idea: The devastation surrounding the death of King Saul is a vivid reminder that God's purposes for our lives cannot be thwarted, even when we face the consequences of our sinful actions.

I.   God Sovereignly Redeems Our Sinful Path (10:1-6,13-14).
II. God Sovereignly Reveals His Salvation Plan (10:7-14).
III. God Sovereignly Reaffirms His Supernatural Promises (11:1-3).

Agitated does not begin to describe how I felt that evening. I was just a week shy of graduating from Bible college. With finals behind me, all that remained on my to-do list was a series of farewell lunches and informal gatherings with friends that I would no longer see each day. A couple from my home church (also students) planned to take me and a few others out to dinner to celebrate. Much to my surprise, however, the entire group left me behind at the prompting of a classmate who insisted that I would catch up later. Because I had no car on campus, I was unable to do so, and the celebrative evening occurred without me!

In my frustration, I roamed the campus looking for anyone I knew. While doing so, I met a young pastor who, one year later, invited me to speak before his congregation. It seemed unremarkable at the time, though, and I ended the evening sulking in my room. Soon, I forgot about the disappointment of that moment, but it all came flooding back when I finally showed up to preach at a small, country church twelve months later. Yet, on that Sunday, I met the young woman who would soon become my wife.

None of it ever would have happened apart from the lackluster night that seemed like a complete failure. Had I been at that dinner table with friends, I never would have met my new friend. Apart from our brief interaction, he never would have invited me to his church. And if I had not walked through those church doors that morning, I never would have laid eyes on the mother of my children. God's sovereignty over our lives is the common thread that holds everything purposeful and meaningful together.

Despite its parallels to the histories of 1–2 Samuel and 1–2 Kings, readers must resist the temptation of viewing 1–2 Chronicles as an abbreviated or even supplemental history of Israel. Instead, understanding what the writer is doing with his historical recollections should be our primary consideration. (For further discussion of the text as a means to the author's intention, see Kuruvilla, *Privilege the Text*, 51.) Whereas the narratives of Samuel and Kings offer a fuller story from the human perspective, these chronicles pull back the curtain to reveal the divine viewpoint. In an effort to encourage Israel to pick up the pieces after the Babylonian exile, the reality of God's sovereignty over the nation emerges as a dominant theme.

With the temple desecrated and the wall around Jerusalem in ruins, remembering God's faithful intervention in the past proved to be helpful for the struggling remnant. The catastrophic repercussions surrounding King Saul's fall are difficult to overemphasize. As the first king over Israel, Saul had all the outward qualifications of a noble ruler (1 Sam 9:2). His ascension to the throne brought with it hope and ambition for the future. His prominence within history, however, was nothing more than a footnote from the perspective of God. What the world applauds seldom garners the same attention and enthusiasm in heaven. Thus, the only detail recorded here regarding Benjamin's leader is that of his demise.

The account is intentionally dark, precisely because it mirrored the demoralizing realities that plagued Israel immediately after their banishment to a foreign land ended. Yet this previous moment of apparent defeat on Mount Gilboa catapulted Israel toward the fulfillment of God's promise rooted in Genesis 3:15. What initially appeared as irreparable devastation actually rallied the nation around a new king chosen to establish the throne of their Messiah. The Lord's determination to save his people was not shaken by their stubborn resolve to crown their own leader (1 Sam 8:4-9).

Likewise, in the days after their exile, Israel again needed to rest in the Lord's sovereign determination to keep his word. The careful placement of the incident is God's way of reminding the people that their present difficulties were no threat to his eternal agenda for them. If the promise of a coming Messiah remained secure after Saul's debacle, its certainty could not be undone by the ruins of Jerusalem upon their return. Grappling with the despair surrounding their first king helped Israel grasp the importance of their true, coming King in light of their new hardship. The same word of consolation continues to edify today, reminding believers that no personal shortcomings can shake God's purposes in Christ. When we limit our focus in the same manner, the Chronicler admonishes us to interpret reality in light of the promises of God rather than merely what we see with our eyes. God's purposes for our lives cannot be thwarted, even when we face the consequences of our sinful actions.

God Sovereignly Redeems Our Sinful Path
1 CHRONICLES 10:1-6,13-14

The prominence of Saul's sin in these opening verses is rivaled only by the carnal ambition that drove Israel to demand a king in the first place. Despite the Lord's intention to be their leader, they rejected their true sovereign in order to be like other nations (1 Sam 8:5). Even then, God graciously resolved to work through the people's sinful choices in order to accomplish his plan. Doing so, though, required a king after his own heart rather than the compromised monarch who first sat on Israel's throne. Still, the Lord would have honored Saul had his faithfulness not been lacking so severely (1 Sam 13:13-14). These verses are a reassurance that neither Israel's unseemly request nor Saul's disappointing reign could undermine God's covenantal commitment to his people. Instead, he sovereignly worked through their shortcomings in order to establish the eternal throne of David.

Because the emphasis here is more theological than historical, the details of the circumstances precipitating the battle on Mount Gilboa are unimportant. These opening verses contain four declarations of Saul's death (vv. 5,6,7,8). The ancient Philistine nemesis is a jarring reminder that the battle between the seed of the woman and the seed of the serpent continues to rage (Gen 3:15). Lest readers conclude that Saul is a victim to be pitied due to his plight, the Chronicler reveals that the whole scene is an act of judgment from the Lord (vv. 13-14). In addition to disobeying the law of Moses by usurping the priestly prerogative when he sought the Lord's favor through a burnt offering (1 Sam 13:8-12; Num 18:7), Saul recklessly sought divine revelation by means of a medium at En-dor (1 Sam 28). These lapses in judgment are part of the larger problem: he generally did not seek or inquire of the Lord as a pattern. Thus, his ties to Israel's throne ended even more abruptly than they began.

By conflating Saul's death with the demise of his household (v. 6), the writer celebrates the divine outcome of these events rather than their detailed unfolding. Though three sons died in battle alongside their father that day, a fourth son, Ishbosheth, sought the failed leader's throne by means of Abner's proclamation (2 Sam 2:8-9). Because Judah never recognized him as their leader (2 Sam 2:10), and due to his ultimate surrender to David and untimely death after his failed campaign (2 Sam 4:1,5-8), there is no mention of Ishbosheth anywhere in these verses.

Any mention of Saul's only living son would distract from the main reminder driving the pericope. The goal here is to mark the passing of one dream in order to give birth to another. What might appear to be a glaring oversight is actually an intentional omission to communicate Yahweh's sovereign agenda. Saul's brief, tumultuous rule was more of a hindrance to the promises of God than a means for their fulfillment. As is sometimes the case, the lack of spiritual leadership the chosen nation endured was more a reflection of their self-centeredness as a people than evidence of their abuse at the hand of another. Thus, the God who puts down one and exalts another intervened in order to accomplish his plan (Ps 75:7).

Why was this particular historical recollection essential for Jews returning to Jerusalem after years in Babylon? And why is this account still relevant for modern believers in places that know nothing of kings or exile? Considering the former is necessary in order to fully comprehend the latter. Contextually, the purposeful despondency elicited here is the effort of the Chronicler to identify with Israel's present predicament. Just as the future seemed lost immediately after the death of their king, returning to the ruins of Jerusalem after years in exile made the forfeiture of covenantal glory seemingly inevitable.

But God. As he often does, the Lord intervened to set his people on an alternate course. God had worked around and even through the sinful aberrations of his people before, and he was more than capable of doing so again. With the hindsight of a Davidic dynasty, the Jews receiving these words certainly would have recalled how God not only overcame their carnal impulse to be like other nations but also how he soothed their assailing fears by building a kingdom for them and *despite* them. The cloud surrounding Saul's plight was nothing but a distant fog for postexilic Jews. Nonetheless, remembering how the Lord overcame their past iniquities in order to accomplish his divine purposes was surely an encouragement as they reeled from the lingering effects of the depraved missteps that sent them fleeing a besieged Jerusalem in the first place (Jer 25:8-11).

This not-so-subtle comparison was the Chronicler's way of insisting that Israel's current lament would become a faint memory as well due to God's continued sovereignty over their sinful choices and actions. Imagine how consoling this was for the remnant in Jerusalem who saw nothing but ruin and despair all around them. Though it was true that they had no one to blame but themselves, dwelling on that fact here would only guarantee irreparable decline rather than spiritual renewal. For the Israelites who wondered if God could overcome their past grievances, this strategic trip down memory lane was the lifeline they needed.

Just as the overthrow of Saul was the means God used to hand the kingdom over to David and, therefore, establish the throne of the Messiah, Israel could now trust that the Lord was just as capable of using the consequences of sin surrounding the exile as a means to a similar end as well. With King David now in the grave and his throne vacated, the people would need to believe God again as they waited for an heir from Judah who could solidify the kingdom forever (1 Chr 17:11-14). The Messiah of whom the prophets spoke would soon rise from the ashes of their pain, just as David had so long ago. Their years of banishment in a foreign land did not invalidate God's covenant; instead, they revealed his unwavering loyalty to them, just as Saul's downfall had so many years prior.

And how should modern believers see this passage? What reassurances are applicable for Christ followers now? God is not frustrated by our disobedience. His plans are not thwarted. His agenda is not changed. His resolve is not diminished. His love is not quenched. His grace is not exhausted. God remains sovereign over any sinful path we choose, and in ways that are difficult to comprehend, he charts our course in order to accomplish his plans. The ramifications here are manifold and beautiful.

First, realize that **the consequences of our sin are evidence of God's love and activity in our lives** (Heb 12:5-11). Not only is our heavenly Father caring enough to correct us when we stray, but he is also wise enough to redirect our paths in ways that are consistent with his intentions. Neither is he agitated enough to write us off nor dumbfounded so that he does not know how to help us.

Next, trust that **God roots our eternal security in his redemptive plan, not our daily performance**. The Lord initiated the work of salvation in each of us; therefore, he vows to see it through to completion (Phil 1:6). Failure to do so would diminish God's commitment to give Abraham spiritual descendants that outnumber the stars in the heavens and the sand on the seashore (Gen 22:17). More problematic, however, would be the implication that Christ's righteousness is not sufficient to secure those who belong to the family of God (1 Cor 1:30).

Finally, while managing the daily dilemmas of living in a fallen world, **we dare to believe that God can bring good out of our hardships, even those we directly cause**. Just as Joseph rested in the providential purposes behind every difficulty he faced, we should live with faith that God will use for good what we, or others, mean for evil (Gen 50:20). If God works all things in our lives together for his noble purposes, we should repent quickly and yield to his mysterious designs and guidance. When our faithfulness is lacking, our confidence is that that he remains faithful, unable to deny himself (2 Tim 2:13). Thank the Lord that he sovereignly guides our sinful paths.

God Sovereignly Reveals His Salvation Plan
1 CHRONICLES 10:7-14

While Israel was previously eager to be like other nations, the God who called Abraham (Abram) out of Haran had a different plan altogether. In order to fulfill the protoevangelium (first gospel) of Genesis 3:15, the Lord chose the Hebrew people as his special possession despite their unremarkable status (Deut 7:6-8). It all began when the Lord called the first patriarch to leave his homeland for a territory revealed later. The father of Israel received the threefold promise of land, descendants, and divine blessing.

> *The Lord said to Abram:*
> *Go from your land,*
> *your relatives,*
> *and your father's house*
> *to the land that I will show you.*
> *I will make you into a great nation,*
> *I will bless you,*
> *I will make your name great,*

and you will be a blessing.
I will bless those who bless you,
I will curse anyone who treats you with contempt,
and all the peoples on earth
will be blessed through you. (Gen 12:1-3)

Both the Mosaic and Davidic covenants that followed are further testimonies of God's efforts to fulfill the assurances first given to Abraham.
Each historical progression reveals new details of the Lord's sovereign
protection over his salvation plan. Likely, the former duress surrounding Saul's shameful fatality revealed the perceived jeopardy his death
posed to the Abrahamic covenant. Close examination of these verses
reveals how thoroughly the king's fall undermined each of the patriarchal promises.

First, consider the abdication of the promised land. As Saul lay
dead, Israel's army fled for their lives, forfeiting their God-ordained
territory (v. 7). With the throne of their anointed king, their messiah,
seemingly overturned, any hope for spiritual heirs seemed lost. Finally,
the Israelites watched in horror as the Philistine pagans desecrated the
former king's corpse and mocked their God, challenging the notion that
cursing the sons of Abraham brings with it dire consequences (vv. 8-10).
The whole scene appeared to be the unraveling of the Abrahamic future
before their eyes.

Worse still is the apparent triumph of the serpent over the seed of
the woman here. While no mention is made of hanging Saul's body on
the wall of Bethshan (1 Sam 31:10), the text focuses on the fallen monarch's decapitation and the display of his skull in the temple of Dagon
(v. 10). In a dramatic role reversal of the enmity revealed in Genesis 3,
the bruised heel of the Philistines has effectively crushed the head of
their Israelite foe. All seemed lost and the Lord appeared defeated. Yet
as is always the case, God was perfectly in control, and his promises were
secure during this dark moment.

The first clue appears in the form of honorable men from Jabesh
Gilead who retrieved the body of Saul, along with those of his fallen sons
(vv. 11-12). Certainly, these comrades owed their lives to their king after
he rescued them from the Ammonites (1 Sam 11:1-11). Their presence,
however, signals more than gratitude for one of Saul's better moments.
By looking back at the early inspiration they felt from their leader, these
servants were a reminder of the hopes tied to Israel's throne. Seeking

to preserve a form of decency despite their shattered ambitions, these faithful men also lift our gaze to look for another who will occupy the throne. Stated simply, Saul was not the promised seed who would deliver God's people from the wiles of the devil. So, like postexilic Jews forced to pick up the pieces of their national identity after years in Babylon, these early followers of Yahweh pressed on despite the diminished realities of their surroundings. Their inclusion in this carefully assembled history of Israel is just as instructive for Christians today as it was for ancient Jews as they reoccupied Jerusalem.

A more vivid indicator of God's protective sovereignty, though, is the clarification that the Philistines were merely the instruments of Yahweh's holy judgment (vv. 13-14). Toward that end, the painful consequences our sinful choices bring could rightly be viewed as a subtheme of the text. Lest we believe his one act of recklessness elicited excessively harsh punishment from the Lord, the Chronicler presents Saul's disregard for the law of God as a thoroughly predictable pattern. Thompson rightly notes,

> Failure to inquire of the Lord on this occasion was a further indication of Saul's whole attitude. Godly leadership is characterized by complete obedience to the Lord and by seeking guidance from him in faith. Saul failed on both counts. (*1, 2 Chronicles*)

Yet the greater implication here is the relentless pursuit of God's redemptive goal. Despite the appearance of the serpent's victory, Israel's God is merely subjecting himself temporarily in order to establish the throne of David. The "son" of God who survived exodus from Egypt (Exod 4:22-23) would now watch the perceived death of the monarchy so that it could be resurrected again. Replacing Saul was not a threat to God's salvific plan; it *was* the plan. Much like the eternal Son who later fulfilled the Father's expectations in ways they could not, Israel needed to humble themselves to the point of death in order to taste the glory of what lay ahead (Phil 2:8).

The loss of this single battle is but a determinative step toward the outcome prescribed for the war in Genesis 3. Because of God's previous commitment to place the Messiah's scepter within the tribe of Judah, what appeared to be total devastation was really a divine means to the promised redemptive end (Gen 49:10). Likewise, years later when the people lamented the fallout of their Babylonian existence, the prophet

Jeremiah reminded them again that a Righteous Branch for David would spring forth from Judah, saving all of Israel (Jer 23:5-6). The ultimate fulfillment of their faith was not the temporary reconstruction of Jerusalem, as important as it was, any more than the useless preservation of Saul's throne would have been. Instead, their faith will not be fully sight until the eternal son of David reigns forever in the city of God. Saints today must anchor their salvation to the same truth.

Much like our spiritual forefathers who endured weeping for a season, contemporary believers rest knowing that the havoc of our sin cannot break the gracious resolve of our heavenly Father to save us. During those dark hours surrounding his cross, it appeared as though God was defeated. The sinless lamb of God swallowed the jeering of those he came to save; he grimaced from the piercing sting of the whip; he gasped as his bones popped out of joint; he cried as his Father cursed him under the weight of our sin. As water and blood flowed from his side, it again seemed as if the hiss of the serpent was a permanent victory declaration. But again, just as when Saul fell, and just as when Jerusalem lay in ruins, the agony was over a bruised heel, not a crushed head. What appeared to be defeat was actually part of the divine narrative, for the glory of resurrection would not come until after Jesus drank from the bitter cup of death. And it was all part of the plan.

Think for a moment about how this seemingly insignificant turning point for Israel's throne is intricately linked to the salvation God would later offer all people. Had Saul remained at the helm of Israel, and had his sons and grandsons followed him to the same post, the redemptive efforts of Jesus would have been a futile exercise not worth noting. Apart from David's ascension, the birth of Jesus bore no significance. Yet as it stands, Gabriel announced to Mary,

> *You will conceive and give birth to a son, and you will name him Jesus. He will be great and will be called the Son of the Most High, and the Lord God will give him the* throne of his father David. *He will reign over the house of Jacob forever, and* his kingdom will have no end. (Luke 1:31-33; emphasis added)

With sons from the tribe Benjamin on the throne, the miracles of Jesus bore no implication beyond the physical realm, his preaching was nothing more than moral platitudes, and the future he promised was unattainable. But, as the son of David, the Messiah resolves to steady the government on his shoulders.

The dominion will be vast,
and its prosperity will never end.
He will reign on the throne of David
and over his kingdom,
to establish and sustain it
with justice and righteousness from now on and forever.
The zeal of the LORD of Armies will accomplish this. (Isa 9:7;
          emphasis added)

God is serious about saving sinners. While the contemporary relevance of this ancient milestone from Israel's history may not be initially obvious, the whole scene is a concrete depiction of how God often repurposes our worst moments to keep us on the path of redemption or to help us take our first step. Temporary setbacks do not equal eternal consequence precisely because history is marching toward his kingdom. It was true for an infantile nation as they grieved the passing of their first king. It was true for weary exiles who sought to make a home in a Jerusalem void of its former glory. And it is true for Christ followers now who endure the daily intrusions of a world that loves the darkness more than the light. The redemptive plan of God remains unshaken no matter the circumstances of the moment. Even as David assumed the throne despite incredible odds against him, one day his eternal Son will do the same; and he will be our God, and we will be his people (Rev 21:3).

God Sovereignly Reaffirms His Supernatural Promises
1 CHRONICLES 11:1-3

To the avid historian, these verses leave much to be desired due to additional omissions that, at first, seem inexcusable. We read nothing of David's grief over Saul and Jonathan, no mention of Abner's anointing Ishbosheth or the brief reign that followed. Likewise, David's shortcomings are largely absent, though Jewish readers would have been well aware of them. The portrayal of a peaceful transition of power might even seem misguided apart from our affirmation of the Chronicler's primary aim for his record. Remember, the goal is not a comprehensive chronology of events but a word of comfort to a people with splintering faith. Because the bloodshed of 2 Samuel 1–2 was already documented, those details were an unnecessary distraction from the main message—namely, providing a messianic picture as proof that God always keeps his word.

Therefore, these opening verses of a new chapter present a unified Israel under the leadership of King David. The entire nation already knew David as a great warrior after his numerous exploits on behalf of Saul (v. 2). By this point it is also clear that, through the prophet Samuel, God set David apart as the next leader over Israel (v. 3).

> *The LORD said to Samuel, "How long are you going to mourn for Saul, since I have rejected him as king over Israel? Fill your horn with oil and go. I am sending you to Jesse of Bethlehem because I have selected for myself a king from his sons."* (1 Sam 16:1)

This, even before Saul's death, was a clear sign that God had a greater purpose for the son of Jesse, born in Judah. Like the eternal Seed who will one day reign from his throne, the Lord chose David because of his heart rather than his appearance or stature (1 Sam 16:7,13; Isa 53:2). Reading these verses in light of the Davidic covenant recorded in 1 Chronicles 17 is important. Better still, seeing this portion of Israel's history as the runway that made their eternal throne promise possible brings even greater understanding. David was not the Promised One who could save Israel eternally, but he was the forerunner who stewarded the pledge of a Messiah by inaugurating the seat from which he will rule.

This carefully summarized narrative is not only a guarantee that God will keep all of his promises but also a demonstration that he was already doing so! For the Jews still washing the scent of Babylon out of their wardrobes, this consoling reminder would have been the motivation they needed to keep looking for the promised son of David. If the Lord unilaterally removed Saul in order to launch David's throne, there was no way he would be content to leave it empty after such efforts. With Jerusalem in ruins, surely this reaffirmation of the divine promise bolstered the returning remnant to keep believing God. By this point, neither David nor any of the kings who followed him had met the qualifications of the one foretold. Yet the point remains clear: *the problems of our present are no threat to the promises of our God.* Looking back compelled God's people to keep looking forward.

As the world grows increasingly perilous and wicked, remember the lesson found here (2 Tim 3:1-5). Contemporary believers join their Jewish brothers and sisters in looking for the chosen Seed who will reign eternally from David's throne (17:11-14). The second advent of Christ will consecrate the kingdom sought by Jews and Gentiles alike (Dan 7:13-14). His coming not only provides the security of his promise to save us from our sin but also guarantees the glory first disclosed to King David and Abraham before him.

Why should we trust Jesus with our souls? Because our salvation was securely prepared before we were born; it was sacrificially purchased on the cross; it is supernaturally preserved by means of the Holy Spirit; and it is safely protected by the coming of our Lord. No wonder Christ assures us that we have eternal life (1 John 2:24-25), that no one can snatch us out of his hand (John 10:28), and that nothing can separate us from his love (Rom 8:35-39). To renege on these commitments would violate not only his covenant with us but also his oaths to Abraham and David.

So, just as the first patriarch looked for a city prepared by God (Heb 11:16), we, too, are anxious to see the place Christ is preparing for us (John 14:2-3). Just as the king after God's own heart believed he would receive an heir to reign from his throne forever (John 17:23-24), we, too, look for the one who boldly declares that he is the seed of whom the prophets spoke (Rev 22:16). His promises are sure. His word is true. His testimony is clear.

Reflect and Discuss

1. Why should we view these collections of Israel's history as more than lessons for therapeutic morality?
2. In what ways can you identify with the Babylonian exiles who returned to a Jerusalem devastated by ruin? Have you ever drawn strength from God's previous activity in your life or in the lives of others?
3. How does God's sovereignty over all things, including your sin, shape your understanding of repentance?
4. Are there instances in your life where it was obvious that God redeemed your sinfulness in order to accomplish something good? If so, what?
5. Give an example of how you witnessed God's overcoming the disappointments we face by means of a greater good. How do such examples encourage you?

6. If God forgives our sins and even uses them for good, how should we view consequences for our waywardness?
7. Do you typically think of salvation as God's singular commitment to you? How does viewing your redemption as a fulfillment of God's promises to Abraham or David change your perspective?
8. What do God's promises reveal about his character? How do his promises tie believers together?
9. In what ways does King David point to Jesus? How is Jesus better than David?
10. What current discomforts in your life can only be remedied by the ascension of Jesus to David's throne?

Still Looking for the Kingdom

1 CHRONICLES 11:4–12:40

Main Idea: By remembering David's initial siege of Jerusalem, Jews who previously lived outside of the covenantal location found needed confidence that God would rebuild his kingdom after they returned from Babylon. Likewise, the eternal shadows behind these historical events compel us to keep looking for the kingdom David so vividly inaugurated.

I. **The Success of the Kingdom Is Certain (11:4-9).**
II. **The Security of the Kingdom Is Clear (11:10–12:40).**
III. **The Savior of the Kingdom Is Coming (Isaiah 11:1-12; Acts 7).**

Country music fans are likely familiar with the 1972 hit single, "Delta Dawn," first recorded by Bette Midler but popularized by the rendition of Tanya Tucker at the age of thirteen. The song is about a woman from Brownsville, Tennessee, who is so beautiful in her youth that she is given the name Delta Dawn. Unfortunately, she falls for the wrong man, and he promises to make her his bride. Though he deserts her, he assures the young girl that one day he will return. As time passes, it becomes obvious to everyone in the little town that she was deceived. Sadly, Delta Dawn grows older and more cynical as each day passes, waiting for a bridegroom who is never going to come. Can you imagine the sad scene of a bride who throws her life away walking the streets, waiting for the husband who is never returning? The chorus evokes images of pity and concern.

I hear the song differently since moving to west Tennessee, where many residents have told me they knew the woman described in the lyrics. Can you imagine having someone so foolish within your community? And yet, just as quickly as having these thoughts, I realize that many consider the church of the Lord Jesus to be just as duped and misguided.

- What's all this talk about being the bride of Christ? Awaiting his physical return?
- You think he's prepared a mansion in the sky for you?
- Are you really scanning the skies and watching the clouds?
- You Christians are so heavenly minded you're no earthly good!

Much of the world laughs at and ridicules the notion a new heaven and earth, which constitute the kingdom of God. Discussions of a future son of David ruling as our eternal king are quickly dismissed as outrageous. More hostile critics might even scorn,

> *Where is his "coming" that he promised? Ever since our ancestors fell asleep, all things continue as they have been since the beginning of creation.* (2 Pet 3:4)

So allow me to ask the hidden questions that plague all believers at some point. Are we crazy? Are we throwing our lives away? Should we be looking for the return of the Lord? Should we just stop living and wait? These were the same type of doubts that likely plagued the nation of Israel as they rebuilt their lives after leaving Babylon. With promises of a future descendant of David ruling again in Jerusalem growing thin, the Chronicler wanted to shore up the nation's confidence in Yahweh's future kingdom. By reminding the people of God's miraculous works to raise Israel up, he intentionally pointed them, and us, to a coming kingdom that was just as certain.

Though the religious significance of the temple would not come until much later, David's conquest of Jerusalem was a vivid recollection of God's unwavering resolve to build his kingdom through the chosen monarch. Like a healing tonic for the despairing souls of postexilic Jews, this pericope elucidates the theme that God and God alone raised his people into a mighty nation previously; and now, despite the grim circumstances that loomed, he was more than capable of doing so again. The passage functions like a highlight reel proving that the Lord is strong and determined for the sake of his people.

Because the Chronicler's emphases are more theological than historical, missing material from Samuel's record should not concern us. Instead of assuming that deleted material is evidence of an attempt to elevate David above the glaring contradictions that plagued his life, we should appreciate that the precise selection of necessary details is a means to protect readers from falsely positioning David as the focal point of the narrative (for a detailed harmony of 1–2 Samuel, 1–2 Kings, 1–2 Chronicles, see the *ESV Study Bible*, 702–3). Stated differently, Israel's God, not their king, is the real hero of these verses.

Carefully arranged generalizations leave us less infatuated with the Davidic resume and more appreciative of the Architect who built and sustained the kingdom. By magnifying Yahweh's past covenantal efforts, the belittled remnant, as well as contemporary believers, would grow in their confidence of the kingdom's present and future expansion. Both the structure and the language employed underscore Yahweh's faithfulness to his promises, as well as his relentless pursuit of his glory.

The Success of the Kingdom Is Certain
1 CHRONICLES 11:4-9

The chiastic structure of this pericope highlights God's efforts to establish Israel as a united monarchy under the direction of their greatest leader. David's rise and anointing as king serve as book ends (11:3; 12:38) that establish the clear effort and initiative of the Lord for his people. Practically, these verses admonished postexilic Jews to remember that the God who established the kingdom did so by means of his unparalleled strength, and despite their weakened existence, all hope was not lost. Simply put, no logical explanation for David's rise or Israel's prominence will suffice. Only a divine agenda could accomplish these miraculous feats.

Recalling the capture of Jerusalem represents the Chronicler's explicit effort to encourage those who now saw the city of David lying in ruins, with its walls torn down and its temple desecrated. Though the focus of the parallel text (2 Sam 5:1-10) is more historical, the emphasis here is pastoral. The significance of David's move from Hebron (where he reigned for seven years) to Jerusalem should not be understated. This geographically centered location deepened solidarity among twelve tribes because none of them had any unique claim on the territory (*NIV Biblical Theology Study Bible*, 667).

The Chronicler reminds the struggling Jewish remnant that, not unlike the situation in their current plight, Jerusalem was previously fortified by the Jebusites (v. 4), who occupied the territory despite former attempts to take and hold the city (see Josh 10:10,16-27; Judg 1:8). And in similar fashion, the antecedent that made the battle necessary was the disobedience of the Benjaminites, who failed to drive out the Canaanite inhabitants who lived there more than four hundred years ago (Judg 1:21).

No wonder these enemies exuded confidence that David would never overtake them (v. 5)! And that is precisely the point. These incredible odds against God's budding nation should not be lost on contemporary readers. A victory of this magnitude was not only unlikely, but its success also required supernatural intervention. Numerous clues throughout the narrative elucidate this theme:

11:3—"in keeping with the LORD's word"
11:9—"the LORD of Armies was with him"
11:10—"according to the LORD's word"
12:18—"your God helps you"
12:22—"there was a great army, like an army of God"
12:23—"according to the LORD's word"

Jerusalem's inaugural rise was the direct result of God's determination to bless his people. Their past success and growth were not a consequence of their personal strength or skill. Imagine how comforting this must have been to those struggling to hold on to the covenantal assurances of old. The demise of their beloved city loomed large over their aspirations to trust God. Their eyes betrayed what they sought to believe by means of visionary faith. By emphasizing this strategic historical moment, the Chronicler assures his weary audience, and us, that the success of the kingdom is certain because the God they serve is just as strong as ever.

David's elevation to the throne then required the unlikely siege of the very place that now seemed damaged beyond repair. Yet the former stronghold of the enemy soon became home to Israel's king, bearing his name from that point forward. These postexilic believers would also make a home in Jerusalem again, even if it appeared improbable. If God gave Israel this city initially, how could he not restore it now that his people were returning from Babylon? The same God who was with David years before was still with them as well, following the same pattern of victory they had previously known.

The language of divine activity governs the entire passage in order to reassure the present and future success of the Jerusalem kingdom. The overthrow of the Jebusites is little more than a narrative footnote with no superfluous details largely because we should assume nothing less when Yahweh is the focal warrior leading the charge. The text even treats Joab more favorably than Samuel's account (2 Sam 3:22-39) due to the precise goal of celebrating the sacred agenda surrounding the city. Likewise, the subtle nuance away from David naming a city after himself (compare 2 Sam 5:9 to 1 Chr 11:7) is not meant to deny the king's role but to acknowledge that God was working through him to accomplish a greater agenda.

The reason for including this military flashback may be increasingly obvious for postexilic Jews desperate to reclaim their resolve as citizens of God's kingdom, but what value do these verses possess for believers today? How should contemporary Christians understand the significance of this incident?

Generally, in moments of weakness, we are likely to fall into the same trap of unbelief that plagued these ancient Jews. Our senses betray us as the burdens of the immediate diminish the realities of the eternal. When undesirable circumstances pull us down, it is difficult to trust in promises that seem improbable. Yet merely reminiscing over God's past faithfulness can powerfully remind us that "we are more than conquerors through him who loved us" (Rom 8:37) in large part because "the sufferings of this present time are not worth comparing with the glory that is going to be revealed to us" (Rom 8:18).

More specifically, though, this pericope should drive us to celebrate the eternal city of God that we will one day call home. Not only does a messianic throne govern our vision of Jesus as our eternal Lord (Phil 2:9-11), but the concept of a messianic kingdom also shapes our appreciation for heaven and the life we will enjoy there. For the Jews, God's established kingdom headquartered in Jerusalem forged their national identity. Likewise, our hope should never be rooted in the realities of this world but in the city that is to come (Heb 13:14).

Because the intended realties of God's kingdom were never fully realized for the followers of Yahweh who returned from Babylon, we join our Jewish brothers and sisters in anticipating a heavenly Jerusalem inhabited by all believers from all ages. The earthly Jerusalem we read about here was but a shadow of the eternal fulfillment that is coming in God's heavenly kingdom. Jerusalem will remain the focal point of God's work as we gather in one accord. Revelation 21:1-2 describes the scene:

> Then I saw a new heaven and a new earth; for the first heaven and
> the first earth had passed away, and the sea was no more. I also saw
> the holy city, the new Jerusalem, coming down out of heaven from God,
> prepared like a bride adorned for her husband.

Why should this strike a chord of hope in our hearts? Because the Jerusalem these Jews longed to see reestablished is the same city we are looking for! And our assurance that God's kingdom is coming rests on the same foundation the Chronicler used as encouragement here. Namely, seeing God's work through David is a sure sign that God will succeed again. Our exile on this earth cannot diminish the covenantal promises to the king whose reign inaugurated the kingdom we seek. We endure with confidence that the Lord is preparing a place for us just as he did for the Jews so many years ago.

The Security of the Kingdom Is Clear
1 CHRONICLES 11:10–12:40

The military detail contained here is a deliberate reminder of the inexplicable wonder around the kingdom if considered apart from divine intervention. Both the gathering of this army and its many exploits are intended to serve as further testimony of God's hand orchestrating these events. One evidence that David grew more powerful (11:9) was the assembly of an unlikely cast from across all Israel (v. 3), some of whom represented Saul's most ardent supporters. Placing these lists here rather than at the end of David's reign (2 Sam 23:8-39) accentuates the swell of support contributing to the overall security and well-being of the kingdom as it rose from nothing (Olley, *1–2 Chronicles*, 984–85).

These verses cover decades of victories that span from the time David was on the run from Saul to the end of his reign as king. The underlying theme is that only God could have established David's throne and secured it so profoundly. All these occurrences were "according to the Lord's word about Israel" (11:10). Again, the applicable backdrop to these recollections is that God worked powerfully before and he can do it once more for the floundering remnant.

In addition to improbable alliances are the many improbable triumphs that reveal God at work. Both Jashobeam (v. 11) and Abishai (v. 20) killed three hundred enemies with a single spear in a single encounter. Eleazar, along with David at Pas-dammin, defended a field against the Philistines resulting in a great victory attributable to no one but the Lord (vv. 12-14). Benaiah slew two sons of Ariel from Moab, a lion on a snowy day, and a giant from Egypt standing over seven and a half feet tall (vv. 22-25). The Chronicler even adds details reminiscent of Goliath's fall at the hand of David that are noticeably absent in 1 Samuel 17 in order to reinforce the unearthly success of the exchange (Olley, *1–2 Chronicles*, 985).

Clearly, the Lord was consolidating the kingdom under King David through the hands of Israel's most skilled warriors. Yet equally important is that God aligned the hearts of his people under his chosen ruler.

In a dramatic display of loyalty and devotion, three of David's men broke through the ranks of the Philistine army encamped in the Rephaim Valley for the sole purpose of securing their king water to drink from the well at the gate of Bethlehem (11:15-19). Only God could foster support so deep and comprehensive. Apparently, David was overwhelmed by the Lord's goodness here, choosing to offer the water as libation to the God who continued to promote his leadership.

The names that follow in verses 26-47 mean little to modern readers, but their geographical significance boasts again of the encompassing coalition the Lord furnished his monarch. The presence of soldiers from Judah (vv. 26-30), northern tribes (vv. 31-37), and even non-Israelite territories (vv. 38-47) demonstrates that David's support was both deep and wide (see Selman, *1 Chronicles*, 143). Indeed, the presence of all twelve tribes here is a less than subtle validation that *all Israel gathered to David* (vv. 1-3).

Next, the focus shifts to four groups most unlikely to offer allegiance to David due to their association with his predecessor. Even more remarkable is that the realignment of these soldiers took place while Saul was still king. Their early recognition of God's anointed leader may be the most dramatic confirmation that God was working supernaturally to secure and unify the kingdom.

First, ambidextrous archers from Saul's own family came to David's aid (12:1-7). Second, valiant warriors from Gad defected in order to fight for the messianic king (vv. 8-15). Third, more soldiers from the tribe of Benjamin as well as the tribe of Judah vowed allegiance to David (vv. 16-18). In view of the king's suspicions, God confirmed their sincerity as the Spirit spoke through Amasai. Finally, a group from Manasseh joined with David in his efforts against Saul (vv. 19-20). Throughout, the emphasis is on the exceptional skills and effectiveness of each battalion.

Daily, more and more came as further evidence that God was building a great army to secure David's kingdom (v. 22). The sheer magnitude of their numbers was astounding (vv. 23-37). They were "wholeheartedly determined" and "of one mind to make David king" (v. 38). The unified vision and the joy it brought (v. 40) leave the reader with no doubt that God was orchestrating these events. Despite every potential hurdle and the relational fragility of this cooperation, God seated his leader and secured his kingdom.

The meticulous nature of this galvanized alliance exuded confidence for Babylon-weary Jews who boasted no army at all. Neither

David's skill nor his integrity was the basis for Israel's rich history. God had always been their protector, even when he raised up a regime like Babylon to do his bidding. Though their circumstances were dramatically different after the exile, the Lord who previously walked with them was still the same. He secured the kingdom once, and he was ready to do so again.

The same is true for believers today. Even as we pray for his kingdom to come, we know that God is a shield to those who take refuge in him (Ps 18:30). Furthermore, just as God raised up an army to secure Jerusalem during the reign of King David, one day he will again assemble an army from heaven to overcome the forces of hell once and for all in order to secure his kingdom forever (Rev 19:11-16).

The Savior of the Kingdom Is Coming
ISAIAH 11:1-12; ACTS 7

The Christocentric themes build while working through this passage. The earthly Jerusalem points to the heavenly city of God. The mighty men of the king foreshadow the coming army of the Lord. But, perhaps most importantly, the kingship of David points to our eternal ruler. Stated simply, David is a type of Christ who foreshadows the Messiah we receive by faith. Israel's first shepherd (1 Chr 11:2) beckons us to follow the good shepherd who is God's Son (John 10:11). Furthermore, the lack of a Davidic monarch after the exile compels us to look forward with hope that a son of David will, by the same sovereign initiative, not only assume the throne of God's kingdom again but also fulfill the covenantal promise of a perpetual reign (2 Sam 7:16). The increased usage of David's name (fifty-four times more than 2 Kings) also communicates the messianic fervor of the Chronicler (Merrill, "1 Chronicles 17," 435, footnote 34).

David's dramatic rise is a descriptive portrayal and assurance that the scepter will not depart from Judah (Gen 49:10). As predicted, a shoot from the stump of Jesse will one day spring forth to inhabit the throne vacated by David. The same striking occurrence observed here will be repeated, lauding the sovereign strength and design of the Lord as the nations are drawn to the coming son of David. With the Spirit of the Lord resting on him, his throne will be glorious, and his reign will be full of righteousness, security, and peace. The Lord's banished tribes will assemble again in Jerusalem, and the nations will be drawn to his light (Isa 11:1-12).

In addition to the clarity of this typological scene, the holistic composition of David's kingdom points us to the ministry impact of our Savior. Consider, for example, the movement of Stephen's sermon in Acts 7. Using Joseph and Moses as illustrations, the church's first martyr recounts Israel's history of rejecting those whom God sent to deliver his people, causing the following pattern to emerge: (1) God raises up a deliver; (2) the Jews reject him; (3) the Gentiles receive him; (4) the deliverer brings salvation to the people. The obvious implication of Stephen's glaring rebuke is that these historical grievances accurately foreshadowed the Jewish rejection of Christ.

God raised up his only begotten Son to be our deliverer from sin (John 3:16). Yet remarkably even if not unpredictably, though Jesus came into the world, neither did the world know him, nor did his people receive him (John 1:10-11). Due to the repudiation he endured from his Jewish family, however, and because of the transgression committed against him, Jesus turned to the Gentiles who were hungry for grace (Rom 11:11). But the Lord will not discard his people forever, and ultimately, salvation will come to all Israel again (Rom 11:25-26).

Of note here is that the life and reign of David followed the same trajectory. Clearly, God raised him up as a deliverer by transferring the kingdom away from Saul. Acts 13:22 explains,

> *After removing [Saul], he raised up David as their king and testified about him: "I have found David the son of Jesse to be a man after my own heart, who will carry out all my will."*

Initially, though, David faced the scorn of the very people God prepared him to lead. Saul resented the notion of David's reign. Nearly all of the tribes (except for Judah) jettisoned his reign in favor of his predecessor and that dynasty. Ishbosheth even fought to replace David as ruler over God's people. As a result, the shepherd of Israel lived among the Gentiles (1 Sam 27) while fleeing for his life. Yet despite the hardship he faced, David became king over Israel, presiding over a kingdom the people could have only dreamt about under Saul.

It is fitting that the first king from the tribe of Judah would so beautifully capture the life and ministry of Judah's final, eternal King. Lurking in the shadows of better days was a reminder to postexilic Jews, and to us, that the kingdom is still secure because the Savior is still coming.

Reflect and Discuss

1. In what ways have you previously understood King David to be a type of Christ?

2. How does the concept of the kingdom in these verses better shape your understanding of heaven and eternity?

3. What practical responses should we have to the reality that Jesus is coming again?

4. How do current events shake your confidence in God's kingdom, and how does this passage renew it?

5. In what ways do these verses solidify a kingdom ethic?

6. What does God's determination to establish David reveal about his commitment to believers today?

7. How should these verses inform the way we worship God?

8. How has God protected you in the past? How does that memory strengthen you when you face trials in the present?

9. How does our understanding of the community of faith protect us from individualistic extremes?

10. In what ways does David's rise to leadership increase your hope in God?

The Center of It All

1 CHRONICLES 13–16

Main Idea: Returning the ark of the covenant to Jerusalem was less fundamentally about its placement and more about the priority of worship among God's people. Although it was neglected during the reign of Saul, David understood that without seeking the Lord as a nation Israel was destined to repeat the sins of the past. The same is true for Christians today.

I. **We Should Fear God's Holiness (13:7-14).**
II. **We Should Seek God's Will (14:1-17).**
III. **We Should Obey God's Word (15:1-26).**
IV. **We Should Celebrate God's Presence (15:27–16:43).**

I will never forget that day. It was my second year of Bible college, and I was attending our spring campus revival. Neither the songs we sang nor the sermons I heard are still with me. What I do remember, though, is that God seemed to show up in an unusual way as we gathered for worship that morning. Students began confessing sin. Professors repented publicly for secret transgressions. Our president stood to apologize to the faculty for a grievance between them. Pockets of prayer and reconciliation broke out around the room. There were no miraculous signs or gifts, but God's presence seemed so tangible that you could cut it with a knife. No one fought for the microphone. In fact, most who were present later said they wanted to hide themselves under their chairs. In that moment, the greatest desire of my heart was to be right with God and with those around me. The Lord was nearer in that moment than at any other before it.

When I left the meeting, the single question that dominated my thoughts was, "Why isn't it like that all the time?" I doubt I am alone. Most Christians, I suspect, have had one or more experiences along the way that left them longing for more of God's presence in their lives. How do we explain how God seems so close at times and then so far away at others? To answer, we need to appreciate the distinction between the omnipresence of God and the manifest presence of God.

There is a sense in which God is always present among us. Wayne Grudem explains,

> God does not have size or spatial dimensions and is present at every point of space with his whole being, yet God acts differently in different places. (*Systematic Theology*, 173)

We refer to this reality as the omnipresence of God, which simply means he is in all places at all times. Psalm 139:7-8 illustrates:

> *Where can I go to escape your Spirit?*
> *Where can I flee from your presence?*
> *If I go up to heaven, you are there;*
> *if I make my bed in Sheol, you are there.*

The challenge, however, is that God's omnipresence doesn't guarantee our awareness. Because the Lord chooses to work differently depending on the circumstances, Christians may remain oblivious to his company.

If you ask congregants, for example, if God is present in an empty worship center, most will say yes. But if you then consider whether God is present in the same way when the room is full of congregants praising the Lord, we instinctively know there is a difference. The explanation for the distinction is the manifest presence of God, or those moments when God makes his nearness known.

- Adam and Eve experienced it in the garden of Eden.
- Moses encountered it at the burning bush.
- The people of Israel witnessed it at the tabernacle and then the temple as God dwelt among them.

Thus, remembering the ark of the covenant would have brought Jewish believers great joy as they recalled God's unique presence among them, but it would have also caused despair due to its absence after their Persian captivity ended. Thankfully, the Chronicler reframes their understanding of his willingness to dwell among them.

Though not obvious initially, this pericope culminates in chapter 16 with a decisive call to revel in the substance of God's grace rather than in the symbol that had impressed it upon Israel's hearts for generations. Indeed, David's passion to relocate the ark from Kiriath-jearim was more about establishing a liturgy of worship than its precise placement (Japhet, *I & II Chronicles*, 276). Michael Wilcock correctly maintains,

"What matters is not so much the thing itself . . . as the truth which the thing enshrines" (*Message of Chronicles*, 71).

This delineation is critical for interpreting these chapters because the description and celebration of the ark found here overshadow the historical situation for modern readers. Jews returning from Babylon no longer possessed the relic, nor would they ever again. The goal of the passage is not for God's people to find or replace the ark's physical structure but for them to rest in the reality it pointed to. Namely, God would be present among them and gracious to them even after the exile.

Likewise, these verses reassure contemporary believers that God will never leave us or forsake us. Grace is still available by means of Jesus's substitutionary sacrifice if only we will respond to it. His cross is the doorway through which the presence of God floods our souls. While religious expressions can be helpful tools to remind us of God's redemptive work, they should never become hindrances to our active recognition of how the Lord deals with us continually.

Nevertheless, we must submit to the hard work of grasping and appreciating an ancient symbol that is largely foreign to us in order to pick up its significance. We cannot unlock the substantive truths of the Chronicler's message if we do not understand the symbols God used to reveal them. Just as the ark of the covenant was rich in implication for postexilic Jews, its application to our lives should be just as meaningful in the twenty-first century.

These verses continue to demonstrate how the Lord established David as king, but the emphasis here is on his spiritual leadership. In addition to his military prowess, David catalyzed religious renewal in the kingdom. In contrast to King Saul (13:3), this ruler sought the Lord with his whole heart while leading his people to do the same. Verses 1-4 are unique to the Chronicler, emphasizing the national consensus that God continued to afford David (see previous section). Intrinsic to these expanded details is the invitation for all the people to gather for the purpose of worshiping Yahweh. Thus, we read that David "consulted with all his leaders" (13:1) and "the whole assembly of Israel" (13:2).

As a result, the proposal seemed fitting, and the people determined to spread the call to action throughout the nation (13:2). In fact, the "Shihor of Egypt" was a brook to the south and "Hamath" was a city on the northern border of Israelite territory (13:5). The idea is that from top to bottom the people assembled with the unified goal of reclaiming the ark (Boda, *1–2 Chronicles*, 126–27). Obviously, consensus building of this kind was unnecessary for the king to accomplish the ark's relocation, but David's agenda is more about the heart of the nation than the geography of this artifact.

Though outside of Jerusalem, Kiriath-jearim was still within the boundaries of Judah (13:6). The issue at hand was a renewed emphasis on seeking the Lord. Possessing the ark was foremost a commitment to connect with the Lord in a way that was foreign during the reign of Saul. Geography was secondary to the primacy of worship in the nation (Japhet, *I & II Chronicles*, 276). The movement of the ark and its reception in Jerusalem teach us four governing principles about worship.

We Should Fear God's Holiness
1 CHRONICLES 13:7-14

Lest we be taken aback by the abrupt display of God's judgment in these verses, a brief reminder of how the ark was previously dislocated is in order. Before David's efforts to reclaim this centerpiece of Hebrew worship, the sign of God's presence among the nation had already taken quite a journey. The Philistines were responsible for capturing the ark initially, after the elders of Israel recklessly assumed strategically placing it on the battlefield would guarantee their victory (1 Sam 4:1-11). Over the next seven months, Israel's pagan enemy bounced the ark from Ashdod to Gath to Ekron, wreaking fear and causing plagues in each location due to God's anger against the Gentile antagonists (1 Sam 5:1-12).

To rid themselves of the burden, the Philistines placed the ark on a cart, accompanied by a guilt offering, and sent it to the village of Beth-shemesh (1 Sam 6:1-18). Once there, God struck down seventy of his own people who were brazen enough to peek inside the golden box in order to see its contents (1 Sam 6:19). Before sending the relic to Kiriath-jearim, the people of Beth-shemesh lamented, "Who is able to stand in the presence of the LORD this holy God? To whom should the ark go from here?" (1 Sam 6:20). With Eleazer as its caretaker, the ark remained at the house of Abinadab until David initiated the relocation recorded by the Chronicler.

Even before the Lord's hand comes against Uzzah in these verses, the ark's pilgrimage teaches us profound lessons about the blessing and the danger of God's presence. We worship God not only because he is loving and gracious but also, and primarily, because he is holy. The protective cloud that covered Sinai and that surrounded the Lord's throne in Isaiah's heavenly vision helps us understand that we cannot look on the holiness of God, much less treat it flippantly, and live. We dare not enter the presence of God without caution and reverence. His holiness is breathtaking. His strength is frightening. His majesty is unparalleled. His glory is unstoppable. If this incident regarding Uzzah seems excessive to us, it says more about our mischaracterization of God than about who he actually is.

Immediately, transporting the ark on a cart rather carrying it with poles is more reminiscent of heathen strategies than the required Levitical decorum for such an occasion (contrast 1 Sam 6:11 with Exod 25:10-15). As a result of this procedural oversight, the ark nearly fell when the oxen stumbled amid the festive chaos, causing Uzzah to steady it with his hand (13:8-9). Whether this action was due to the familiarity brought on by the previous twenty years of exposure to the ark (1 Sam 7:2) or something more sinister, we can only surmise. Regardless, this act of irreverence was fatal.

Of note is a subtle albeit significant nuance in the description of the scene. Whereas Samuel's record reports that Uzzah "died there next to the ark of God" (2 Sam 6:7), the Chronicler explains that "he died there in the presence of God" (13:10). The change highlights the contextual aim of the pericope—namely to remind postexilic Jews that God was still among them. This act of sacrilege was never about the ark itself but about transgressing God's holiness.

Here we learn much about the divine mission to redeem us as well as the consequential nature of God's holiness. As far back as the garden of Eden, the Lord demonstrated his desire to be among his people. Not only did he walk with Adam and Eve in the cool of the day (Gen 3:8), but God also reigned over them after creation. His rest on the seventh day has little to do with recuperation and everything to do with his active reign over all that he made. John Walton correctly sees the Lord's resting place as "the equivalent to being enthroned" or "taking up his role as sovereign ruler of the cosmos" (*Genesis,* NIVAC, 148). No wonder Isaiah 11:10 declares his resting place to be glorious.

Men and women made in God's image were given the task of ruling over all the Lord created even as they filled the earth. In fact, the language of cultivating (*abad,* "work") the ground (Gen 2:5,15) is later employed to communicate cultic expressions ("serve" in Num 4:37). Likewise, the notion of watching over (*shamar*, Gen 2:15) the garden will later correspond to the priestly duties within the tabernacle (Num 1:53) (Kuruvilla, *Genesis*, 59). Added to this, the creation narrative presents the earth as a cosmic temple belonging to the Lord. In Isaiah 66:1-2, God declares,

> *Heaven is my throne,*
> *and earth is my footstool.*
> *Where could you possibly build a house for me?*
> *And where would my resting place be?*
> *My hand made all these things,*
> *and so they all came into being.*

With this background, the garden of Eden functions as a divine sanctuary, housing the presence of God enjoyed by the first man and woman. Yet because of God's holiness, the fall of Adam and Eve necessitates their expulsion from the place where divine access was common. The cherubim stationed outside of Eden will appear again as images in both the tabernacle and the temple, as well as a covering over the ark we read about here (Kuruvilla, *Genesis*, 58). Numerous other commonalities exist between the garden and the tabernacle/temple narratives (see Wenham, "Sanctuary Symbolism").

But how does this background illuminate the implications of Uzzah's untimely death? God made us to worship in his presence, yet our sin prohibits us from doing so. Since the fall, however, clues emerge that God is determined to lift Adam's curse. The presence of the tabernacle and temple points us back to Eden's garden where God dwelt among his people even as they lift our gaze to the new heaven and earth where God will again make this earth his home. In the meantime, Adam and Eve were driven from the garden that was then guarded by cherubim, lest they offend God's holiness and die immediately. Uzzah approached the presence of God, enthroned by the cherubim on the top of the ark. But he did so without reverence or concern for his sin, and the consequence was severe.

In both instances, the presence of these angelic beings is a warning and admonishment that we must not approach the holiness of God without fear. Worship, before anything else, is coming before God with a proper awareness of his person. Yet as A. W. Tozer explained, this is precisely where we often fail:

We know nothing like the divine holiness. It stands
apart, unique, unapproachable, incomprehensible, and
unattainable. The natural man is blind to it. He may fear
God's power and admire his wisdom, but his holiness he
cannot even imagine. (*Knowledge of the Holy*, 111)

How holy is our God? So much so that he requires our perfection
before we enter into his presence. Knowing this, Jesus suffered and died
on a cross, facing the full wrath of God for us. Through his sacrifice he
not only wipes our sins away, but he also clothes us in the righteousness
of God, leaving us free to enter God's presence again (2 Cor 5:21). The
death of Jesus is, if nothing else, a dramatic display of God's holiness.
The Lord was pleased to crush his own Son as guilt offering so that we
might be reconciled to himself (Isa 53:10).

Indeed, reverential fear is foundational for biblical worship. Without
a sincere appreciation for how holy God is, we are unable to grasp fully
the magnitude of our sins. And without the correct awareness of our
guilt before God, we will lack the genuine humility necessary to call out
to Christ for forgiveness and grace, rendering true worship impossible.
Even worse, approaching the eternal presence of God apart from Christ
will result in our eternal death.

Confused, even bewildered, David is so angered by the incident that
he names the place to reflect the Lord's outburst against Uzzah (v. 11).
Uzzah's offense is not unlike ours today. At first glance, this seems to be
a major overreaction on God's part. Death for what appears to be an
unintentional blunder leaves us cringing with questions. Far too often,
the God of Scripture embarrasses our contemporary sensibilities. We
view any talk of holiness as curmudgeonly, and the notion of eternal
punishment for sin seems to go entirely too far. The concept of a literal
hell is uncouth to modern ears bound up by equity and opportunity.

Yet in his grace God demonstrates that though his presence is ter-
rifying, it is life-giving as well. Unwilling to move forward with the ark's
retrieval, David grew in his fear of the Lord (13:12). Remarkably, leaving
the ark in the house of Obed-edom for three months resulted in tremendous blessing for its caretakers. The whole scene is a reminder that
the fear of God's holiness is to our benefit and blessing, while approaching the Lord flippantly is both reckless and dangerous. God's presence
may cause us to tremble, but he invites us in nonetheless.

In his Chronicles of Narnia, C. S. Lewis created a fictional world depicting God as a majestic lion named Aslan. In a lesser-known scene from *The Silver Chair*, a selfish young girl named Jill Pole has an encounter with Aslan, who saved a traumatized boy she pushed off a cliff. Much to Jill's relief, the kingly lion simply walks back into the forest after the ordeal. As time passes, though, the girl grows thirsty, and the sound of a stream in the forest beckons her. Proceeding with caution, Jill moves through the trees, closer and closer to the rushing water. Once there, the girl freezes as soon as she sees Aslan sitting beside the river. Because of her indecisive fear, several minutes of silence pass before Aslan finally calls out to her.

"Are you not thirsty?" said the Lion.

"I am dying of thirst," said Jill.

"Then drink," said the Lion.

"May I—could I—would you mind going away while I do?" said Jill.

The Lion answered this only by a look and a very low growl. And as Jill gazed at its motionless bulk, she realized that she might as well have asked the whole mountain to move aside for her convenience. The delicious rippling noise of the stream was driving her nearly frantic.

"Will you promise not to—do anything to me, if I do come?" said Jill.

"I make no promise," said the Lion.

Jill was so thirsty now that, without noticing it, she had come a step nearer.

"Do you eat girls?" she said.

"I have swallowed up girls and boys, women and men, kings and emperors, cities and realms," said the Lion. It didn't say this as if it were boasting, nor as if it were sorry, nor as if it were angry. It just said it.

"I daren't come and drink," said Jill.

"Then you will die of thirst," said the Lion.

"Oh dear!" said Jill, coming another step nearer. "I suppose I must go and look for another stream then."

"There is no other stream," said the Lion. (*The Silver Chair*, 26–27)

The depiction captures the magnitude of Yahweh's holy presence. Ours is a God who does whatever he chooses without apology. Sometimes he frightens us. Sometimes it seems as though he might hurt us. But he is our only option. You will not find living water apart from him. You will not find direction and purpose in life apart him (John 6:68). You will not find the forgiveness of your sins apart him. But coming to him is always costly. We must yield to whatever he wants to do, trust that what he desires is best, and submit our future to his control.

Before leaving this theme, we should also consider the identity of Obed-edom as a matter of meaningful importance. The designation here that this man is from Gath (13:13) seems problematic if this is the same individual mentioned as a Levitical gatekeeper in 1 Chronicles 15:18, 21. The most likely solution is that "he was ethnically a Philistine, a Gentile who was adopted into the Levitical clan after successfully caring for the ark" (Leithart, *1 & 2 Chronicles*, 51). Of greater significance, though, is the implication that a reverential Gentile found peace and blessing from the presence of God while the efforts of King David were rejected outright.

The principle in front of the text remains as instructive today as it was to postexilic Jews long ago. God invites all people, Jew and Gentile alike, into his holy presence. Yet we dare not come on our own merit or wisdom. Religious pedigree and performance do not qualify as exceptions. We must humble ourselves before God and trust his sacrificial work on our behalf or else be destroyed by his holiness. God reserves the joy of his presence for those whom he covers with the righteousness of his Son.

We Should Seek God's Will
1 CHRONICLES 14:1-17

What at first appears to be an unnecessary excursus is more properly understood as a meaningful demonstration of maturation for David. The chronological break with Samuel here in no way undermines the efforts of the Chronicler, whose focus is on interpreting these events rather than ordering them. Also of note is the glaring absence of numerous failures that litter David's past. His adultery with Bathsheba, murder of Uriah, and subsequent strife are notoriously absent in this recollection. Rather than assume a coverup, however, we should realize that Jewish readers would have been well aware of these events. Furthermore, the Chronicler's efforts to encourage his audience are rooted in the kingdom wrought by the Davidic covenant, not in the moral deficiencies of the king.

Thus, the pericopal focus shifts to the unilateral nature of the divine blessing. Consequently, verses 2 and 17 read like headlines that govern the chapter. God exalted David's kingdom and caused terror among the nations because of him, resulting in the king's growing fame. These remarkable developments signaled God's unwavering commitment to his people, a reality that would have been especially encouraging to the former Babylonian exiles. As clearly indicated in verse 2, David's rise was "for the sake of his people Israel." Nevertheless, as the historical face of the kingdom, David grew in his worship of the Lord underneath the broader movement of the chapter's theme.

Notice the threefold progression of David's ascent. First, King Hiram offers supplies and workers to construct the royal palace (v. 1). Consequently, we should not interpret David's blunder at Kiriath-jearim as an indicator that his kingdom is no different from Saul's. Contrary to his predecessor, whom the Lord refused to build up (10:13-14), God established David by securing a clear capitol and a throne for the monarchy (14:2), all for the benefit of the nation as a whole. Emphasizing the exaltation of David in this way, while the ark remained outside of Jerusalem, would have been extremely heartening for the postexilic community, whom the Lord expected to live in light of the Davidic promise despite the absence of the ark and palace. The Lord's purpose to care for his own had not changed even though the realities that preceded the present generation had greatly deteriorated. In addition, the support these distressed believers received from King Cyrus of Persia was not unlike the inexplicable support of King Hiram of Tyre. If God worked so miraculously at the outset of their climb to significance, perhaps it was not foolish to believe he would graciously do so again.

Second, the growth of David's family is a sign of the throne's continued viability for future generations (vv. 3-7). Despite the clear violation of God's law regarding multiple wives (Deut 17:17), the Lord is gracious to establish what will become a perpetual messianic throne. Unlike Samuel's account, there is no mention of children born at Hebron; the Chronicler instead focuses on the divine progeny after David entered Jerusalem. Two names, Elpelet and Nogah, are missing from Samuel's account, but this is likely due to the untimely deaths of these children (Hill, *1 & 2 Chronicles*, 232). The posterity of the king's home is an additional dissimilarity between David and Saul, whose house died with him (10:6).

Finally, two victorious battles against the Philistines also mark stark contrasts with the failed leadership of Benjamin's king while also providing messianic images rooted in David. Both instances reveal David, unlike Saul (10:13), inquiring of the Lord before moving into battle (14:10,14). And in both the Rephaim Valley to the southwest of Jerusalem (v. 9) and the Gibeon valley to the north of the city (vv. 13,16), Israel defeated their bitter rivals behind the leadership of their favored king. The wonderous sound of marching in the trees was an indicator that God was leading the way for Israel (v. 15). Under Saul, whose disastrous military operations ended with his armor and skull in the house of Dagon, it appeared that the head of Israel's savior was crushed forever (Gen 3:15). Now, with a new king leading the way, Israel was finally able to crush the head of their Philistine enemy and burn their idols in the fire (v. 12; Deut 7:5).

As the fame of David spread throughout the surrounding lands, the conclusion is that only God could have done this. Even as the nations were drawn to David (as King Hiram was) or terrified by him (as the Philistines were), our gaze lifts to another who would be just as polarizing. The hatred of the Pharisees and religious leaders could not prevent the fame of Jesus from spreading (Matt 4:24; Mark 1:28; Luke 5:15). Still today, the promised son of David leaves fathers divided against sons and mothers against daughters (Luke 12:53). Yet despite the pain they cause, the failures of his saints and the schemes of his enemies remain impotent to prevent Jesus from ruling over heaven and earth as our eternal king.

By arranging his record this way, the Chronicler aims to teach us that God is the main character of the drama. Neither the demise of Saul nor the deficiencies of David could impede the birth and growth of the kingdom. God, often working despite his chosen vessels rather than because of them, raised up David to provide a shadow of the King who is to come. By anchoring our hope to the latter, we can lean on the promises these events represent rather than falling victim to the contradictions each narrative participant poses. We are also free to learn from the mistakes and successes we observe.

For instance, already David has taught us much about worship through his failed effort to transport the ark. Now, through his determination to seek the Lord, we learn that walking with God is impossible without a genuine concern for God's will. Likewise, *how* we worship is just as important as *whom* we worship. We must approach God on his terms if we are to render him the exaltation he deserves.

Against this backdrop, we also observe the Lord breaking out *for* David rather than *against* him. Nine times in chapters 13–15 the Hebrew noun *perets* (outburst) or its verb form appears, intentionally contrasting the work of the Lord *against* David while moving the ark and *for* him as he waged war against Israel's enemies (Johnstone, *1 and 2 Chronicles, Vol. 1*, 169). David's failure to consult the Levites for guidelines necessary to transport the ark was no small matter, resulting in the Lord's outburst against Uzzah (13:11). Now, on the battlefield David wins a decisive victory after seeking the Lord. Thus, *parats/perets* appears four times in 14:11 as David celebrates that the Lord burst out on his behalf. In other words, "David learns his lesson. If he wants the Lord to burst out against the enemies and not the servants of the Lord, he needs to ask according to his ordinance (15:13)" (Leithart, *1 & 2 Chronicles*, 51–52). May the Lord break out on our behalf in a similar way as we learn to worship within the boundaries of his will.

We Should Obey God's Word
1 CHRONICLES 15:1-26

With material unique to Chronicles, 15:1-3 reaffirms David's efforts to transport the ark back to Jerusalem, but this time according to the scriptural guidelines prescribed during the time of the exodus (Exod 25:13-14). The scene is altogether different from the king's first attempt, primarily because of his meticulous diligence to honor the Lord's presence. "Reverence for the ark," says Michael Wilcock, "means not respectful feelings, but practical obedience to God's Word" (*1 and 2 Chronicles*, 396). The narrative holds forth the biblical discernment necessary for worship that pleases God. Ultimately, our efforts to seek the Lord must be governed by the liberties and restrictions of Holy Writ. Worshiping God on our own terms is fundamentally idolatrous and equally as dangerous as not worshiping him at all.

The stakes laid out by the Chronicler are eternally high. In addition to building a house for himself, 15:1 indicates that David prepared a tent for the ark of God. The verb "prepared" (*kun*) appears again in 15:3 in reference to the determined location where the temple will ultimately rest. Often translated "established," this word remarkably makes the point that "what was done by David and his legitimate successors was firm and final" (Merrill, *A Commentary*, 192). For postexilic Jews, this meant that though the ark was now absent, God's presence among his people remained due to the promises of the Davidic covenant.

David's admission of failure to obey Mosaic procedures while relocating the ark was twofold (v. 13). Because the ark was God's throne among the people, using a cart rather than carrying it with poles was offensive (Exod 25:13-14). In addition, the absence of the Levites during the previous exercise was a clear violation of God's revealed intent (Num 4:15; Deut 10:8; 31:25). To right these wrongs, the king insisted that only God's chosen servants would move the shrine from that point forward. He assembled the descendants of Levi and commanded their consecration for what was ahead (vv. 4-12).

Doing so was a return to what "Moses had commanded according to the word of the LORD" (v. 15). Following the pattern of 6:1-81, the Chronicler grouped the priestly servants according to the three sons, Kohath, Merari, and Gershom (vv. 5,6,7). Leithart astutely observes that there were 862 total Levites, which was the gematria of *tabnit*, the word for "pattern" found in tabernacle and temple texts. He contends, "The priests form the pattern for the house. Under Yahweh's inspiration, David forms a human temple of living stones" (*1 & 2 Chronicles*, 53). In other words, David was not only obedient to what God revealed previously through Moses; he also became the channel through which God brought new revelation to light.

Arranging Levitical singers and instrumentalists went a step beyond Torah requirements, yet these expressions were foundational to the permanent worship structure of the temple priesthood. While verses 16-18 name specific leaders in charge of musical worship, verses 19-24 clarify the roles they will assume. Once the ark finds its final resting place in Jerusalem, codifying these new responsibilities will serve as a testimony of Yahweh's eternal enthronement. Because the number of gatekeepers listed (70) corresponds to the number of Gentile nations (Gen 10) and the number of Israel among the Gentiles (Exod 1:5), this expansive celebration is a reminder that the nations will be drawn to the light of their heavenly King (Rev 21:24-26) (Leithart, *1 & 2 Chronicles*, 53).

Though the canon is now closed, twenty-first century believers would do well to emulate the thoroughness of David's eagerness to comply with the Lord's commands. As a result, God helped the Levites as they worked, a clear indicator that he honors our submission to divine instruction (v. 26). The descriptive shift from "the ark of God" to "the ark of the covenant" seems to be a nod to the Ten Commandments housed within the sacred chest, pointing again to the resulting harmony and blessing of obedient worship. After refusing to seek the Lord during the days of Saul and then failing to seek him correctly despite David's pure motives three months earlier, Israel finally learned to seek God as prescribed in Scripture.

The shifting contexts of modernity do not prevent Christians today from similar obedience to the Word as they worship the Lord. Olley helpfully observes,

> David followed Moses' commandments but also developed new forms to accompany kingship and the new capital, Jerusalem. Jesus both affirmed the past and also pointed to new patterns of faith and obedience (e.g., Matthew 5–7), while the early church, now comprising Jews and non-Jews, grappled under the guidance of the Spirit with what it meant to follow God and worship him among the nations (Acts 10–11; 15). (*1–2 Chronicles*, 1001)

Likewise, believers today must grapple with the nature of biblical faith far outside the realities our Jewish forefathers knew. The illuminating work of the Spirit promises to guide us as we articulate the faith once for all delivered to the saints in an ever-changing world (Jude 3).

We Should Celebrate God's Presence
1 CHRONICLES 15:27–16:43

As the ark's movement comes to a conclusion, the joy of the Lord's presence and our right response are on full display. With the wooden box now in the tent David prepared, the people made offerings "in God's presence" (16:1). David's distribution of food harks back to the meal shared by the elders of Israel, also in the presence of God (Exod 24:9-11). This distinguishing reality of the Lord's intention to dwell among his people is why David worked so hard to retrieve the ark in the first place. And for those Jews looking to start over after the exile, God's presence remained the single greatest indicator that the future was not lost to their adverse circumstances. Despite losing the ark tradition after the exile, the presence of God remained among his people. Like a healing balm, these words were a reminder that God himself, not their cherished traditions, is the great reward of faith. The same is true for us.

After affirming Samuel's record of David wearing a *linen ephod* (2 Sam 6:14), the Chronicler enhances the detail by highlighting that the Levites and singers wore the same attire (15:27), suggesting that the majesty of the moment is more in play here than the priestly function of the king. Juxtaposed against the joyous, musical celebration of the ark's return is the devastating rejection by David's wife, Michal, who showed similar disrespect to the presence of God as her father Saul. Her resentment toward her husband is clear (v. 29), but neither their tenuous past nor their defunct future is mentioned.

Instead, the issue is one of royal succession (Merrill, *A Commentary*, 195). By identifying Michal as the daughter of Saul rather than the king's spouse, the text equates her rejection with the failure of David's predecessor. This further establishes the exclusivity of David's throne, debunking claims to the contrary as illegitimate. Though Samuel interprets the scene as evidence of the divine prerogative to exalt David while vacating Saul's throne (2 Sam 6:20-23), the curt dismissal here communicates that such matters do not warrant any further attention or clarification. In fact, the nature of David's throne is so obvious that diverting attention to Saul is more insulting than helpful. Michal, like her father, was unwilling to seek or celebrate the presence of the Lord, caring more about her perceived dignity.

Assigning permanent worship leaders under the direction of Asaph (16:5-6,37) further indicates David's commitment to honor the presence of the Lord. The practice continued in Solomon's temple when these musicians were joined by the Levites charged to serve the tabernacle at Gibeon (vv. 39-43). What follows is a microcosm of the praise that became a normal part of worship during the reigns of David and Solomon. In fact, Olley notes,

> By prominently placing this psalm (the only such song in Chronicles) at the beginning of worship in Jerusalem, the chronicler unmistakably shifts his hearers' attention from the ark itself (which for the hearers had ceased to exist) to what the ark symbolized, the sovereign Lord who had made an everlasting covenant with Israel. (*1–2 Chronicles*, 1005)

The basic division of David's compilation is threefold: verses 8-22, 23-33, and 34-36. The patterns are just as inspiring as they are instructive. By assembling portions of Psalms 96, 105, and 106, these verses remind us that part of honoring God's presence is remembering his works and offering him praise as result (16:4).

Focused exclusively on Israel, David uses the words of Psalm 105:1-15 to offer both imperatives and covenantal reminders. We are told to thank the Lord, call on his name, proclaim his deeds to others, sing to him, boast in his name, rejoice in him, seek him, and remember his deeds and covenant (16:8-14). The sheer frequency of these instructions leaves no room for praise among God's people to be optional. Next, the text roots Israel's covenantal life to the patriarchal period, specifically Abraham (v. 15). When they were few in number and without a land to call home, God established Israel with a permanent promise of land, descendants, and blessing (Gen 12:1-3). These words would have been especially comforting for a nation desperate to reclaim their land despite the lack of a temple for worship or a Davidic king on the throne. Though the visible realities of a Davidic community appeared to be shaken, this psalm reminds the hearers, and us, that the substance of God's commitment to them preceded their beloved king.

Turning to Psalm 96:1-13, the focus broadens to include Gentiles, who are always in the background as recipients of Israel's testimonies about Yahweh (16:8-9). Again, worship directives drive the emphases. The glory of Yahweh is such that "the whole earth" must sing to him, proclaim his salvation, and declare his splendor (vv. 23-24). He should be feared above the worthless idols of the heathens (vv. 25-26). The God who made heaven and earth should receive the glory due his name, offerings of tribute, worship for his holiness, and trembling reverence (vv. 27-30). Ultimately, all creation will join the chorus of praise, from the heavens to the seas to the fields to the forests, because the Lord reigns and he will judge the earth (vv. 31-33). As yet another sign of their future viability, this progressive reassurance upholds the Jews as the means God will use to bring the whole earth under his glorious reign. Even today, Christians rest knowing that no matter the depth of the world's fallenness, creation will ultimately bow before the eternal son of David.

Finally, an appeal to Psalm 106:1,47-48 concludes Israel's celebration with a petition to the Lord himself. In light of his goodness and love, which are well documented throughout the psalm, the people are to call on Yahweh for salvation as he regathers them from the nations (16:34-36). These words were applicable throughout Israel's history, but particularly so in a post-Babylonian world. What others failed to do must not be the same mistake for this generation of faithful Jews, or for believers today for that matter. Circumstances and heartbreak should never prevent us from looking to God as the only source of our salvation. As long as he is present in our lives, we have much to celebrate. The Lord's intervention to rescue us remains a means by which we give thanks to his name and offer him praise.

As the chapter concludes, the Chronicler includes arrangements for worship to continue before the ark (vv. 37-43). Now, with the ark forever lost, a postexilic community must persist with the praise of Yahweh in new ways, knowing their God remained present among them. Despite the construction of a second temple, New Testament Jews would later apply the same principle when they embraced Jesus as the fulfillment of the holy structure. Believers today should also resist exchanging the glory of Christ's presence for traditions surrounding religious symbols, no matter how cherished they might be. As members of God's household, we now celebrate that the Spirit of Jesus dwells within us everywhere we go (Eph 2:19-22). We worship knowing that God inhabits our praises (Ps 22:3) even as the Spirit bears witness that we are the children of God (Rom 8:16).

Reflect and Discuss

1. How would you articulate the difference between God's omnipresence and his manifest presence? How have you experienced the latter?
2. How do Christian symbols and traditions sometime become distractions to genuine worship and devotion?
3. How should God's holiness inform our expressions of worship? In what way is fearing God healthy?
4. Does Uzzah's sudden death seem unfair to you? What are practical ways we can revere the Lord?
5. How are David's increased notoriety and strength reflections of his growing maturity in the Lord?
6. In what practical ways can we seek God?
7. Why is worshiping God impossible apart from obedience? How does David's course correction model a healthy submission to Scripture?
8. Why was God's presence so important for the Jews? For Christians today? In what ways does God manifest his presence now?
9. What specific expressions of praise should we continue emulating today?
10. How does God's inclusion of Gentiles in his kingdom reveal an even deeper divine commitment to the Jews?

Grace upon Grace

1 CHRONICLES 17

Main Idea: The eternal nature of the Davidic covenant served as reminder that the harsh conditions of Israel's postexilic reality could not diminish God's unwavering commitment to his people. With Christ as the fulfillment of these assurances, believers today look back with humility and with gratitude for God's grace.

I. **God's Grace Is Revealed through David (17:1-15).**
II. **God's Grace Is Realized in Jesus (17:7-15).**
III. **God's Grace Is Redemptive for Us (17:16-27).**

The death of Victoria Ruvolo in 2019 made national headlines, not due to the way she died but because of how she lived. Most would not know her name were it not for the tragic events that took place in the fall of 2004. While driving her car in New York amid freezing rain conditions, she had no idea that a group of juvenile delinquents had just stolen a car and a credit card. Before taking a joyride, they drove to a video store and purchased $400 worth of DVDs and video games. For reasons no one can explain, they also bought a twenty-pound frozen turkey to go along with their refreshments.

By the time they got into the silver Nissan they swiped, Victoria was nearly home. At 12:30 a.m. the boys intersected her Hyundai on the highway. She has no recollection of their approach, or of the teenage thug hanging out of the car's window, hurling a bulky projectile toward her car. That frozen bird crashed through her windshield with such force that it bent the steering wheel before smashing her face, shattering every bone it touched. Three weeks later, after eight hours of surgery, Victoria woke up at Stony Brook University Hospital with no knowledge of why she was there. Titanium plates held her face together. Synthetic film steadied one eye. Wires held her jaw shut. A tracheotomy allowed her to breathe.

The media jumped all over the story, leading the world to cry for justice. Nearly one year after the incident, Victoria managed to walk into the courtroom on her own strength. Once there she met Ryan Cushing, the young man who heaved the turkey, face-to-reconstructed-face. Much to the dismay of spectators, the eighteen-year-old pleaded guilty to a lesser charge, putting him behind bars for just six months followed by five years of probation. The injustice was palpable. People were outraged. What fool would settle for a plea bargain in such a clear-cut case?

The answer still surprises me. It was Victoria. The victim requested leniency for her assailant. After the sentencing she embraced Ryan and whispered in his ear, "I forgive you. I want your life to be the best it can be." The tears began flowing. The world watched in awe. *The New York Times* dubbed it a moment of grace (Jeremiah, *Captured by Grace*, 9–11). It sounds completely outrageous. Grace goes against human nature and self-righteousness. Yet we immediately recognize it when we see it.

But where does it come from? And what will its end result be? If the world marvels when human beings are gracious, how much more should we stand in admiration when God shows grace? Remarkably, one of the Chronicler's goals is to demonstrate the divine *efforts* to display grace as well as his *expressions* of it. Though one could argue that our first glimpse of grace took place as far back as Genesis 3, this pericope lays a foundational stone to ensure its availability for future generations, Jew and Gentile alike.

With the military campaigns necessary to become king largely over, the ark resting safely in Jerusalem, and the construction of the monarchial palace complete, the ascent of David to Israel's throne reaches its culmination in what is appropriately called the Davidic covenant. This pericope may be the most important in 1 or 2 Chronicles because of its abiding implications not only for the postexilic faith community but also for all believers today. In its most immediate historical setting, this chapter assured a captivity-weary nation that the Lord initiated their original rise to prominence, bolstering their hope in a future with God as their strength and joy. Because the promises given to David outlived his earthly reign, there was reason to live by faith rather than sight despite their abysmal surroundings.

Today, these recollections lift our gaze to a new heaven and earth where the ultimate fulfillment of these same promises will unfold. Jewish and Gentile believers alike long for the day when a son of David once again reigns from Jerusalem's eternal throne. Additionally, sincere Christians enter this narrative to learn the futility of measuring God's promises against time. Our finite circumstances cannot measure, nor do they limit, God's infinite goodness. One of the greater tests of contemporary faith is possessing the contentment to delay reception of many of God's greatest blessings until after we die. In fact, after mentioning King David specifically, the writer of Hebrews celebrates the heroes of the faith as being "approved through their faith," even though, he elaborates, "they did not receive what was promised, since God had provided something better for us, so that they would not be made perfect without us" (Heb 11:39-40). Remarkably, the breadth of God's promises to David includes contemporary Christians. Likewise, the full scope of all that God accomplishes for his children will not be fully realized until eternity.

God's Grace Is Revealed through David
1 CHRONICLES 17:1-15

King David's desire to build a house for the Lord was rooted in the humility of comparison. After settling into his opulent palace, the meager accommodations for the ark of the covenant in a tent was both counterintuitive and alarming to the king (v. 1). Sensing the purity of his motive, Nathan the prophet blessed David's holy ambition with a green light to proceed (v. 2). Unexpectedly, however, the Lord intervened with a different plan.

In addition to God's historical contentment to dwell among Israel in a simple tent that moved from place to place, the Lord reminded Nathan that at no point had he requested a grand temple to house his presence (vv. 3-6). The issue was not that the concept of a temple was bad *per se* but that a greater promise was coming. After all, Deuteronomy 12:5-7 clearly indicated that the Lord would ultimately choose a permanent place for his dwelling among the people. Likewise, in short order the Chronicler revealed that Solomon was the chosen vessel to construct the temple, and the remainder of his account in 1 Chronicles records strategic efforts to make the necessary preparations. At this moment, though, the emphasis shifts to God's intention to build a "house" for David, not vice versa.

The theme of God's abundant grace emerges as the eternal covenant through David takes shape. The divine initiative in these verses illuminates the determination of the Lord to bless his people apart from their works of goodness. Fourteen appearances of the personal pronoun "I" leave no doubt concerning the unilateral nature of the Davidic promise.

- I took you from the pasture (v. 7).
- I have been with you wherever you have gone (v. 8).
- I have destroyed all your enemies (v. 8).
- I will make a name for you (v. 8).
- I will designate a place for my people Israel (v. 9).
- I ordered judges to be over my people Israel (v. 10).
- I will also subdue all your enemies (v. 10).
- I declare to you that the LORD himself will build a house for you (v. 10).
- I will raise up after you your descendant (v. 11).
- I will establish his kingdom (v. 11).
- I will establish his throne forever (v. 12).
- I will be his father (v. 13).
- I will not remove my faithful love from him (v. 13).
- I will appoint him over my house (v. 14).

These words reminded David, as well as us, that a relationship with God is born out of his work on our behalf, not the other way around. Though we rightly applaud the sacrificial work of Jesus on the cross, the monarchial runway laid down in this chronicle equally highlights God's determination to save sinners. The Davidic covenant leaves no room for boasting and is the Old Testament reminder that we are saved by grace through faith.

For postexilic Jews, this recollection also reaffirmed God's role in their previous success as a nation. By implication, the key to their rebirth after Babylon was not their personal strength or ingenuity, precisely because the impetus behind their initial rise rested solely in the Lord. In fact, the assurances given to David were not unique but a continuation of God's resolve to bless Abraham through the covenantal promises that gave birth to Israel in the first place. In this sense, the Davidic hope is the fulfillment of Abrahamic promises, not a substitute for them.

Consider, for example, how the ingredients of the Abrahamic covenant found in Genesis spring forth as the landmarks that shape the inheritance of David.

> *The LORD said to Abram:*
> *Go from your land,*
> *your relatives,*
> *and your father's house*

to the land that I will show you.
I will make you into a great nation,
I will bless you,
I will make your name great,
and you will be a blessing.
I will bless those who bless you,
I will curse anyone who treats you with contempt,
and all the peoples on earth
will be blessed through you. (Gen 12:1-3)

Land, seed, and blessing form the substance of the patriarchal legacy. Note how these three focal points repeat themselves in the following verses. The Lord assures David of land by declaring, "I will designate a place for my people Israel and plant them, so that they may live there and not be disturbed again" (v. 9). He guarantees the perpetual seed of David not only by promising to build his house (v. 10) but also by vowing, "I will raise up after you your descendant, who is one of your own sons, and I will establish his kingdom" (v. 11). Finally, we encounter a reaffirmation of divine blessing with the insistence that God will destroy all of David's enemies and make his name like the greatest on the earth (vv. 8,10).

Imagine how reassuring the reminder of these promises would have been to the feeble nation desperate to regain their identity and eager for any reason to believe they had a future. Though their surroundings appeared bleak, the Lord would have had to turn his back on David—and on Abraham for that matter—to forsake his commitment to his chosen people. Surely, they, like we, feared that the consequence of their sins was too great to overcome, leaving reconciliation with God impossible.

Yet as Israel grappled with the legacy of their historic king, the Chronicler bore witness that God's commitment to David was unshakeable. Did the man after God's own heart commit egregious transgressions? Without a doubt. But to renege on assurances given to David would have been an insult to Abraham who received them first. Was Israel's first patriarch perfect? Not even close. But violating his oath to provide land, seed, and blessing would have marred God's character irreparably. The Lord was, and is, intent on honoring his word whether his children deserve it or not. In Psalm 89, God explicitly says of David,

But I will not withdraw
my faithful love from him
or betray my faithfulness.
I will not violate my covenant
or change what my lips have said.
Once and for all
I have sworn an oath by my holiness;
I will not lie to David.
His offspring will continue forever,
his throne like the sun before me,
like the moon, established forever,
a faithful witness in the sky. (Ps 89:33-37)

God's Grace Is Realized in Jesus
1 CHRONICLES 17:7-15

The pressing question in front of this pericope is simply, How is this covenant fulfilled? Both the historical setting and the biblical record point to already-not yet realities surrounding the Davidic kingdom. Most immediately, it appears that David assumed Solomon and his completion of the temple marked the beginning of God's unfolding vows. Twice in the chronicle David speaks directly to his son by framing exhortations around these promises (see 22:11-13 and 28:9-10).

Not only did these applications make sense immediately after Nathan delivered God's covenantal pledge, but also in the early days of Solomon's reign there were partial fulfillments specific to the Lord's intentions to bless through the house of David. For example, Solomon's name spread due to his unrivaled wisdom (v. 8; cf. 1 Kgs 4:29-34). Likewise, peace on every side during Solomon's reign seemed to correlate directly to the kingdom reality foretold here (v. 9; cf. 1 Kgs 4:24). Furthermore, the house of the Lord and the throne of David's son were understood not as two subjects but one, signaling the consummation of the kingdom foretold (v. 12). Obviously, David did not see these developments through to their completion, but without question he saw them materializing through his most immediate heir to the throne. And indeed, for a moment, the serpent's head appeared to be crushed (Gen 3:15), and God was once again with his people (Gen 3:8).

Tragically, however, Israel's foretaste of the kingdom was short-lived. Despite the blessings surrounding his throne, Solomon's sexual immorality and idolatry resulted in his death rather than the perpetual reign anticipated. Worse still, the demise and split of the Israelite kingdom under the poor leadership of Rehoboam made plain to everyone that, though they were looking for *a* son of David, they had yet to encounter *the* son of David. By the time of the exile, these hope-filled prophecies were not only distant memories of better days gone by, but they seemed just as unlikely as they were unpredictable.

Realizing these hurdles, the Chronicler recalls the Davidic covenant in order to reassert its certain fulfillment as well as its encompassing hope. Unlike Solomon, the one whom God foretold would rule eternally from David's throne (v. 12). Both the house and the kingdom of the promised son will be perpetual (v. 14). The "descendant" celebrated by the historian (v. 11) is a singular "seed," reminding us that the succession of David's hope is not in the multitude who failed but in the one who suffered for the sins of others rather than his own (2 Sam 7:14).

Also of note is the aim of the chosen son who stands in the line of David's offspring. Just as David knew that the Lord established and exalted him for the sake of his people (14:2), the goal of God's messianic ruler is to bless his chosen people. Doing so will serve as the ultimate consummation of both the Davidic and Abrahamic emphases on land, seed, and blessing. For those who endured the hardships of Babylon, the implication of these restated hopes is that they should keep looking for the one who will bring these objectives to fruition.

Believers today read these verses with the fuller realization that Jesus Christ is the Messiah our Jewish brothers and sisters longed for. The New Testament not only makes the connection clear but also ties it directly to the covenant bound up in David. The angel Gabriel's announcement to Mary was more than a declaration that the chosen one had come; it was a celebration that the son of David had finally arrived. Thus, the nativity assures us, "He will be great and will be called the Son of the Most High, and the Lord God will give him *the throne of his father David. He will reign over the house of Jacob forever,* and *his kingdom will have no end*" (Luke 1:32-33; emphasis added).

Though contemporary Christians look back on this progression with joy *now*, we realize the fullest expressions of the Davidic reign are *not yet* reality. But like our Jewish ancestors, we enthusiastically anticipate the threefold inheritance of the eternal kingdom we will call home. In fact, our inclusion in the Davidic family is the fullest expression of their greatest longings for eternal glory (Heb 11:40).

Land Inheritance

Together, in Jesus Christ, believers from every age join both David and Abraham in anticipating the covenantal promise of land (vv. 9,14). Like a fulcrum looking back to the location and fellowship that were lost in the garden of Eden while also looking forward to the full restoration of that relationship with God in his designated place, the Chronicler broadens our expectations beyond the realities of the temporal to the realm of the eternal. Because Eden functioned like a cosmic temple (see chs. 13–16), the construction of Solomon's building served as a hint that God was working to reclaim what was forfeited in the curse. For ancient Jews discouraged by the temple's demise, reemphasizing the Davidic dynasty garnered attention for the reality the shrine pointed to rather than the mere shadow within the structure itself.

Just as the Lord claimed Jerusalem as the land of inheritance for his people previously, through Christ a new Jerusalem will descend from heaven to inhabit a new heaven and new earth (Rev 21:1-2). And just as God's presence fell on the ark in the holy city previously, the Lord will dwell among his people again as Jesus Christ reigns from the throne of his father David. The apostle John explained,

> Then I heard a loud voice from the throne: Look, God's dwelling is with humanity, and he will live with them. They will be his peoples, and God himself will be with them and will be their God. (Rev 21:3)

Christ will live among his people again, and because the kingdom in that place knows no end, we will be with our God forever and ever (1 Chr 17:14). Until that time, we should confess that we are strangers and exiles on the earth because we desire a better country prepared by God himself (Heb 11:13-16).

Seed Inheritance

Because the doorway to the great nation promised to Abraham is through the singular seed in David's line, we should recognize Jews and Gentiles alike as the spiritual sons and daughters of the patriarch. The kingdom promised to David is secured during the messianic age. Interestingly, after Paul and Barnabas relayed their evangelistic harvest among the Gentiles to the Jerusalem Council, James interpreted the conversion of those outside of Israel as a direct realization of the Davidic covenant. Acts 15:13-18 reads,

*After they stopped speaking, James responded, "Brothers, listen to me.
Simeon has reported how God first intervened to take from the Gentiles
a people for his name. And the words of the prophets agree with this, as
it is written:*

*After these things I will return
and rebuild David's fallen tent.
I will rebuild its ruins
and set it up again,
so that the rest of humanity
may seek the Lord—
even all the Gentiles
who are called by my name—
declares the Lord
who makes these things known from long ago."*

By quoting the prophet Amos's reference to the Davidic promise
(Amos 9:11), James emphasizes God's perennial objective for Israel to
be a means to reach the nations for the kingdom rather than exclude
them from it. Rather than view this as a new covenant reinterpretation
of the Lord's covenantal plan, we rightly acknowledge that this was
always part of the divine plan.

The prophet Isaiah envisioned this implication long before Jesus.
Isaiah 55:1-5 affirms,

*Come, everyone who is thirsty,
come to the water;
and you without silver,
come, buy, and eat!
Come, buy wine and milk
without silver and without cost!
Why do you spend silver on what is not food,
and your wages on what does not satisfy?
Listen carefully to me, and eat what is good,
and you will enjoy the choicest of foods.
Pay attention and come to me;
listen, so that you will live.
I will make a permanent covenant with you
on the basis of the faithful kindnesses of David.
Since I have made him a witness to the peoples,*

> *a leader and commander for the peoples,*
> *so you will summon a nation you do not know,*
> *and nations who do not know you will run to you.*
> *For the LORD your God,*
> *even the Holy One of Israel,*
> *has glorified you.*

Likewise, Daniel prophesied about the universal dominion the Ancient of Days would have over all people and nations,

> *He was given dominion*
> *and glory and a kingdom,*
> *so that those of every people,*
> *nation, and language*
> *should serve him.*
> *His dominion is an everlasting dominion*
> *that will not pass away,*
> *and his kingdom is one*
> *that will not be destroyed.* (Dan 7:14)

Later, the apostle John affirms the breadth of the seed fulfillment by extolling the Lamb who was slain for "every tribe and language and people and nation" (Rev 5:9). Their multitude, far more numerous than the stars in the heavens or the sand of the seashore (Gen 22:17), will stand before the throne celebrating, "Salvation belongs to our God" (Rev 7:10). These prophecies correlate directly to the seed promise of Abraham and David.

Blessing/Cursing

The assured blessings reflected in the dynastic reality of the covenantal kingdom can be seen through existing continuity between the reigns of David and Solomon. Olley wisely notes that the Chronicler intentionally omits the record of Solomon's shortcomings in order to focus on the favor that accompanies his obedient efforts to build the temple and thus perpetuate the divine agenda (*1–2 Chronicles*, 1014). The eternal nature of this throne should be understood as a contrast to the kingdom previously stripped from Saul (v. 13). Instead, Yahweh vows to be a father who offers the blessing of *faithful love* and an *eternal kingdom* (v. 14).

The Lord's commitment to subdue the enemies of Israel (v. 10) further reflects his prerogative to curse those who come against his people.

As previously stated, the peace of Solomon's reign offers a glimpse of these fixed assurances, yet only the messianic age can bring the full expectation of God's pledge to pass. Indeed, in Christ Jesus our greatest enemies will finally be defeated forever. The great enemy of the kingdom will be cast into the lake of fire and brimstone, never to plague the saints again (Rev 20:10). Then, death itself will be swallowed up in victory. The apostle Paul explains, "For he must reign until he puts all his enemies under his feet. The last enemy to be abolished is death" (1 Cor 15:25-26).

God's Grace Is Redemptive for Us
1 CHRONICLES 17:16-27

In the world of the text, the redemptive scope of these words was meant to admonish Jewish believers still recovering from the devastation of Persian captivity. Looking back at their plight reassured them, and us, that God's goodness toward his people is not limited by circumstances, nor are his promises threatened by the discomforts wrought from the consequences of our personal fallenness. King David's prayer of thanksgiving is worthy of our emulation based on these realities alone. When modern readers consider, however, the forward implications of this pericope, our understanding of and appreciation for the grandeur of redemption grows astronomically.

Overcome with gratitude to God for the grace shown to him, David humbles himself before the ark within its temporary shrine (v. 16). As with any accurate assessment of grace, the king cannot fathom God's goodness toward him. Despite realizing the implication of his distinction, David recognizes there is no room for boasting (v. 17). Perhaps even more remarkable is that God chose and blessed him with full awareness of his frailty and shortcomings (v. 18). Indeed, David is nearly left speechless. The nature of redemptive history functions entirely on God's initiative and his will (v. 19), making it obvious that there is no one like our God (v. 20). As the earliest beneficiaries of his promises, Israel, too, bears a uniqueness among the peoples of the earth (vv. 21-22). Perhaps these hopes seemed too good to be true, compelling David to repeat them back to the Lord with great courage in the effectual nature of God's word (vv. 23-27).

Modern believers can easily appreciate not only the gratitude that overwhelmed David but also the fuller unfolding of this redemptive plan. Knowing that the son of David predicted here became flesh and dwelt among us (John 1:14) as one greater than the temple (Matt 12:6) compels us to treasure the gifts that are ours in Christ Jesus. Because he made peace through the blood of his cross (Col 1:20), we not only receive the full benefits of redemption but also function as the greater fulfillment of David's hope. Just as God regarded David as a man of distinction, in Christ we become the righteousness of God (2 Cor 5:21).

These reminders humble believers even as they elicit our worship. John Newton, while preparing a sermon on David's prayer of thanksgiving, penned the words to the immortal hymn "Amazing Grace," thirty-one years after his conversion. Just as the king looked back over his life and felt unworthy of God's grace (v. 16), Newton captured the same essence with the phrase, "a wretch like me." Similarly, "through many dangers, toils, and snares" communicated the provision and care that comes from walking with the Lord. Finally, as he considered the distant favor of the Lord promised to David (v. 17), the former slave trader wrote in his journal, "The Lord has promised good to me, his word my hope secures; he will my shield and portion be, as long as life endures" ("Amazing Grace: The Scripture Texts").

Through Christ, God the Father lavishes his grace on us according to the good pleasure of his will (Eph 1:5-6). Truly,

> *In him we have redemption through his blood, the forgiveness of our trespasses, according to the riches of his grace that he richly poured out on us with all wisdom and understanding. He made known to us the mystery of his will, according to his good pleasure that he purposed in Christ as a plan for the right time—to bring everything together in Christ, both things in heaven and things on earth in him.* (Eph 1:7-10)

The concluding resolution of the chapter is the opposite of David's initial desire to build a house for the Lord. Though it seems counterintuitive, nothing about our relationship with God is based on our efforts for him. Instead, the whole of redemption rests in his efforts to reclaim us solely by grace through faith. With Christ as the living cornerstone, God the Father continues to build David's house with each believer representing a living stone in the kingdom that will know no end (1 Pet 2:4-5).

Reflect and Discuss

1. How is the encouragement the Davidic covenant provides believers today similar to that felt by those in the postexilic community?
2. How do our present circumstances sometimes overshadow the eternal promises of God?
3. Why was it preferable for God to build a house for David rather than vice versa?
4. What does God's initiative in David's life teach us about God's grace?
5. What does the reemergence of the Abrahamic promises appearing in God's assurances to someone like David teach us about the Lord?
6. In what ways is the Davidic hope yet to be fulfilled?
7. Where do you see evidence of God's kingdom already at work in the present?
8. What do Solomon's eventual failures teach us about God's promises?
9. How does David's grateful prayer in response to God's grace inspire you to worship the Lord?
10. How should Christians celebrate the Davidic covenant today?

Back to the Future

1 CHRONICLES 18–20

Main Idea: By looking back over the covenantal victories of David's kingdom, the Chronicler enables the postexilic community to imagine a future where their land is once again secured and their enemies are overcome. By remembering these ancient scenes, contemporary Christians enjoy a foretaste of the coming new heaven and earth where Jesus Christ, the son of David, assumes his throne.

I.   The Scope of the Kingdom Is Expansive (18:1-17).
II. The Strength of the Kingdom Is Eternal (19:1–20:8).

As the highest grossing film of 1985, the sci-fi thriller *Back to the Future* illustrates the unbreakable correlation between the past and the future. After Doc Brown transforms his DeLorean automobile into a time-travel machine, he accidently transports seventeen-year-old Marty McFly back to 1955. Once there, the teenage boy discovers the past causes of his mother's alcoholism, his father's timidity, and his siblings' social awkwardness. Through a number of twists and turns, Marty is able to correct many of the transgressions against his parents in order to improve the life of his family back in the future. Examining the past was the key to understanding and appreciating all that was ahead.

The same principle applies to the emphases of this particular pericope. Prerequisite to grasping the significance of these wartime recollections is to place yourself in the shoes of the original hearers as they looked out over the devastation of Jerusalem. By now, they all knew that David, though he prefigured their coming Messiah, was not the one who would reign eternally over them. Likewise, despite Solomon's wealth of wisdom and influence, he, too, had long been in the grave, having failed to meet their messianic expectations. Even worse, the kings who followed them, with a few exceptions, were tangibly wicked, leaving no question that the promised seed had not yet come to Judah.

With the temple destroyed and the Davidic throne empty, the Chronicler strategically points back to better days in order to admonish his brethren to keep looking for the kingdom. Remembering the conquests of David provided a glimpse of what to expect when the covenantal promises finally became a reality. Certainly, this afforded immediate encouragement to the struggling remnant too weary to rebuild, but the greater goal was to instill messianic hope within them. Therefore, after accounting for the divine initiative behind David's rise to the throne (1 Chr 11–12), the Chronicler submits the king's early validation and the initial unfolding of his dynasty as evidence for what is ahead. Stated simply, this is an argument from the lesser to the greater.

David's accomplishments on the battlefield (11:4-9; 18:1-13) as well as the lists of heroes who accompanied him (11:10–12:40; 18:14-17) serve as a chiastic structure around his rise to power, his placement of the ark, the covenant he received, and the confirmation of his dynasty (see Merrill, *A Commentary*, 229). Because the scope of his kingdom reflected God's previous commitment to Abraham, David's administration of justice also paints a picture of the messianic age and all the promises therein. These records were the Chronicler's way of admonishing the Jewish community to keep looking for the covenantal realities even after the exile. Neither the structural ruins of Jerusalem nor the appearance of an abdicated throne was a threat to God's determination to raise up a son of David to reign eternally over his people. Though these kingly conquests were intended to be an encouragement for the historical dilemma in Israel, they also serve as a redemptive shadow of Christ's coming kingdom for believers today.

The Scope of the Kingdom Is Expansive
1 CHRONICLES 18:1-17

Subduing the enemies of Israel was a precursor to the peace that followed during the reign of Solomon. In fact, David's exclusion from building the temple for being a man of war (22:8; 28:3) was no insult to the heroic king but the primary means for preparing the shrine's construction. The key thought that governs these military campaigns is the declaration, "The LORD made David victorious wherever he went" (18:6,13). Thus, these wars were signs of the kingdom's birth initially and became reminders of its existence after the exile. The regional peace known to Israel previously was but a foretaste of the coming rest and stability brought by a future son of David. Both the background and particulars of these victories are deleted to preserve the focus on their theological implication rather their historical contribution.

First, the downfall of the Philistines secured the western region for the kingdom (v. 1). Next, defeating the Moabites led not only to their servitude but also to a wealth of tribute coming from the east (v. 2). The demise of Hadadezer settled the northeast as far as the Euphrates River for Israel's dynasty (v. 3) while also increasing the size of David's army (v. 4). Defeating the Arameans who sought to aid the Zobahites (v. 5) resulted in additional resources and labor, not the least of which were gold and bronze that Solomon used for the basin, pillars, and utensils of the temple (vv. 6-8; 26:27-28). Geographical expansion was evidence of an Israelite empire.

In addition to Israel's offensive victories, Tou, king of Hamath, sought a peace treaty with David by voluntarily bringing tribute of his own (vv. 9-11). Like the plunder taken by force, these volunteered gifts were a primary source for funding the temple's construction. The gift serves as evidence that the kingdom of Israel was a blessing to neighboring Gentiles who recognized the strength of Yahweh. Israel's God had, in fact, accomplished for Tou what he could not achieve for himself, namely the defeat of this enemy, Hadadezer.

Here we see the firstfruits of the Abrahamic assurance that "all the peoples on earth will be blessed through you" (Gen 12:3). Prioritizing the Jewishness of the kingdom was never to the exclusion of Gentiles (Rom 1:16). Looking forward, the fuller reality of the Abrahamic hope unfolds in the new heaven and earth when "the nations will walk by its light, and the kings of the earth will bring their glory into it" (Rev 21:24). Through one man, Abraham, God raised up one nation, Israel, in order to bring forth one Savior, Jesus, so that all the nations of the earth could enjoy the blessings of God's favor.

In concert with David's efforts, his nephew Abishai put down the Edomites in the southeast region. A triumph of this magnitude was yet another testimony of the Lord's determination that David would succeed in his kingdom efforts. Consequently, the reputation of the king continued to grow (2 Sam 8:13). His reign was a time of unrivaled justice and righteousness in the land (1 Chr 18:14). These victories are not only the first signs of God's eagerness to plant his people in their divinely chosen location, but they are also evidence of God's commitment to overthrow their enemies systematically in order to exalt his chosen leader (17:8-10). Both expressions serve as a validation and celebration of the Davidic covenant revealed one chapter earlier.

Why was the overthrow of these enemies pivotal for the postexilic community after so many years? This record was not a lament about the lost glory days of Israel but a call to believe that the kingdom would rise again with even greater force and joy than before. With the Persian dictatorship looming over the shoulder of the Jews anxious to rebuild Jerusalem, the Chronicler reminds them that the seeds sown in the days and years immediately after the Davidic kingdom cast a much larger shadow over the direction of history. The previous downfall of Israel's enemies was evidence that God was still capable of securing a new generation in light of the same promises handed down to David. These events foreshadow both the stability and the peace that will always characterize the messianic dynasty.

But what is the significance of these ancient battles today? Why should we care about the expansion of David's empire? The pattern of success observed here guides twenty-first-century disciples of Christ as we continue looking for the final consummation of the kingdom promised and demonstrated through the seminal years of David's reign. The peace he enjoyed in every direction serves as a powerful reminder that the jurisdiction and influence of the Messiah's kingdom will spread to the four corners of the earth as our greatest enemies are defeated. Moreover, after all these years without an heir of Judah on Israel's throne, the possibility of eternal succession has long since passed. Now, as a matter of covenantal achievement, the only means left for God to honor his pledge is by means of an eternal Son who will rule from David's seat forever and ever.

The angel Gabriel tied this prophetic hope directly to Christ at the announcement of his birth by declaring,

> *He will be great and will be called the Son of the Most High, and* the Lord God will give him the throne of his father David. *He will reign over the house of Jacob forever, and* his kingdom will have no end. (Luke 1:32-33; emphasis added)

Much like our Jewish counterparts, by looking back at this announcement we see just enough kingdom momentum to keep us looking forward to the final consummation of Christ's work. And what are the similarities in the coming kingdom with those of David's prophetic empire?

When the prophet Isaiah spoke of the Christ child, he hinted at his ability to secure the kingdom by revealing that "the government will rest on his shoulders" (Isa 9:6). Even more important, though, was his explicit recognition that the Messiah will unleash the fullest potential of the Davidic throne. Unlike those before him, when the son of David assumes his rightful place as Israel's anticipated heir, he will overthrow our most threatening enemies once and for all. The prophet explained,

> *The dominion will be vast,*
> *and its prosperity will never end.*
> *He will reign on the throne of David*
> *and over his kingdom,*
> *to establish and sustain it*
> *with justice and righteousness from now on and forever.*
> *The zeal of the LORD of Armies will accomplish this.* (Isa 9:7)

By this point, the Jews understood far too well that neither David's nor Solomon's kingdom lived up to these lofty expectations. To them, the message of the Chronicler is: keep looking; the Messiah will finish what David started. The former glory of David's house does not even begin to compare to the latter glory (Hag 2:9). If the lesser was appealing (David's efforts to expand the kingdom), wait until the greater unfolds (the reign of Christ in the new heaven and earth). Though what was beforehand points to the kingdom of Christ, it cannot compare to what God has in store for those who love him (1 Cor 2:9). These recollections were not intended to incite another aggressive military campaign but to inspire confidence that God's kingdom of peace will expand again once the Messiah reigns (Knoppers, *1 Chronicles 10–29,* 701).

The scale of the coming messianic empire will dwarf even the greatest achievements of the Davidic rule. Zechariah 9:10 proclaims, "His dominion will extend from sea to sea, from the Euphrates River to the ends of the earth." The Messiah will lift the curse of sin and crush the head of the serpent, defeating forever any threats to his people (Gen 3:14-19). The great enemy, death, has been swallowed up in victory because of the atoning work of the cross (1 Cor 15:54). With the sting of sin removed, the architect behind humanity's rebellion will also be cast into the lake of fire and brimstone (Rev 20:10) along with death and hades (Rev 20:14). Likewise, all other enemies whose names are not written in the Book of Life will also face the second death (Rev 21:8).

The Strength of the Kingdom Is Eternal
1 CHRONICLES 19:1–20:8

Next, the opposing reality takes center stage when the curses associated with Abrahamic and Davidic covenants emerge in David's exchange with the Ammonites. Chapter 19 records the unusual—and avoidable—incident between King David and the Ammonites. The scene is nearly impossible to place chronologically, but it seems likely "David had taken care of Moab and Edom before this so as to obviate any attacks on his southern flank" (Thompson, *1, 2 Chronicles*, 154). After the death King Nahash, his son Hanun became the leader of the Aramean nation. In order to preserve the peace between the two nations as well as to return the goodwill he received from the previous king, David sent messengers to console the new monarch (19:1-2). Though there is no biblical record of Nahash's earlier kindness to David, it was significant enough for him to go above and beyond with this gracious gesture.

Unfortunately, the measure achieved the opposite of David's pure intention, causing suspicion of espionage. Rather than receive the Israelite messengers favorably, Hanun shamed them by cutting their beards and disrobing them from the waist down (19:4). The resulting humiliation flipped the narrative so that the comforters were now the mourners. Because both hair and clothing were indicators of male glory, stripping these symbols was an affront to David's empire and strength (see Leithart, *1 & 2 Chronicles*, 68). The Chronicler positions the whole scenario to demonstrate the full validity of the Davidic covenant despite opposition. The Israelite Empire is a force to be reckoned with because of God's commitment to his king.

Realizing that David was not one to take ignominious insults lightly, Hanun doubled down by hiring Mesopotamian charioteers and horsemen to join drafted Ammonites in battle against Israel (19:6-7). While David was willing to give his shamed soldiers a leave of absence from the fighting (19:5), he unleashed Joab and his elite troops to handle the unnecessary conflict (19:8). Efforts to assail Israel from two directions failed miserably, not primarily because of Israel's strength or craftiness but due to their commitment to defend the cities of God birthed out of Yahweh's covenantal commitment. Again, the Lord was making David victorious wherever he went as a declaration of the divine will (19:13).

With Joab and Abishai fighting back-to-back against enemies that surrounded them, each reinforced the other as necessary (19:9-12). Consequently, both the Ammonites and the Arameans fled out of fear the moment Israel engaged in battle (19:14-15). Sensing their defeat, the Arameans called for backup from Shophach's troops beyond the Euphrates River (9:16-17). When David swiftly pursued them, combat finally ensued, albeit briefly. In addition to Shophach's demise, thousands of soldiers fell to the sword of David that day before the Arameans finally surrendered, becoming vassals in the kingdom (19:16-19). Again, the Lord proved to be with David, further establishing the greatness of his kingdom and signaling the early momentum toward building the house of his king (17:8).

After fully subjecting the Arameans to the Israelite dynasty, the attention turned back to the overthrow of the Ammonite threat. The glaring omission in this account is David's affair with Bathsheba and its ensuing consequences. Between 20:1a and 2b, this record deletes nearly two chapters from the Deuteronomistic history (2 Sam 11:2–12:25), while nine chapters (2 Sam 13:1–21:17) disappear between verses 3 and 4 (Wilcox, *The Message of Chronicles*, 80). Selman correctly challenges our modern instinct for suspicion:

> At first glance, this is a somewhat artificial record of David's
> military successes, which has been produced by leaving out
> the more interesting narratives and those less favourable to
> David. This view is rather inaccurate, however, since positive
> elements such as the birth of Solomon, David's magnanimity
> to Saul's family, and David's psalms are also omitted. (Selman,
> *1 Chronicles*, 192)

Simply understanding the Chronicler's reason for writing should alleviate any concern modern readers might have about the trustworthiness of his record. Framing this portion of the narrative with the phrase, "in the spring when kings march out to war," ought to eliminate our contemporary concerns about a coverup because this language corresponds exactly with Samuel's account (2 Sam 11:1). For those with an inkling of Israel's history, hearing these words would have immediately brought to mind the salacious details documented elsewhere (2 Sam 11:2-27).

And that is precisely the point. Samuel's history effectively demonstrated that David was not the messianic king who would usher in the eternal kingdom. The Chronicler's audience was painfully aware that their beloved king was not the instrument by which they would experience the breadth of God's covenant. In addition to painful awareness of David's lifeless, entombed body in Jerusalem, God's chosen people had suffered for years as subjects in a foreign land due to their own sinfulness. The Jews were not just aware of David's shortcomings; they had repeated them many times over themselves. They needed no convincing whatsoever that David fell short of their messianic dreams.

What the Jews did need to know, however, and what the Chronicler diligently sought to convey, was that God's promises did not die with David. Furthermore, his message aimed to prove that the duress of the kingdom would not result in the defeat of the kingdom. The value here is not the legacy of David as an individual but the Lord's abiding commitment to keep his word. Even the well-known secret about the king's troubled personal life could not shake God's resolve to work through Israel to bless the world. Connecting David's wars to his covenant and temple preparation provided a hopeful perspective likely lost in the weeds of Babylon. Emphases on these past victories were the vehicles through which the recovering exiles could move beyond their present burdens in order to chase their eternal aspirations for the covenantal community.

So, with gracious focus the narrative expeditiously winks at the ordeal without gazing, moving from the defeat of the Arameans straight to the overthrow of the Ammonite threat. Another redaction, often overlooked but just as significant, is the removal of Joab's ability to secure the capital city of Rabbah without David's help (20:1; cf. 2 Sam 12:27-29). The Chronicles' account does not deny or distort Joab's contribution, but since the focus is on the kingdom that bears David's name, stressing his ineptitude here seems counterproductive for postexilic readers (Pratt, *1 & 2 Chronicles*, 224). Again, the Deuteronomistic historian's details are helpful elsewhere but not in this instance.

Instead, David claims the crown of his enemy and plunders the city for resources that will fund Solomon's temple (20:2-3). Additional subjects also signal the increasing strength of the empire God created. As David's fame spread, the confidence in the lasting impact of his covenant grew. These verses were intended to be a healthy reminder that God will finish what he started despite the Babylonian interruption and that the whole earth will eventually be under the rule of a Davidic king.

Even the means by which David earns victory over the Ammonites positions him as a type of Christ. On the surface, his actions do not appear heroic or decisive. Yet his willingness to reciprocate Nahash's kindness is a chief characteristic of God's determination to bless those who are a blessing to the kingdom (Gen 12:3). David's refusal to overreact when Hanun shamed his men is a subtle reminder that God's king did not take the kingdom by force; it was handed to him. Leithart explains,

> One would think that David's unheroic conduct would make him a loser, but David is a political winner. Somebody is defending David's honor, but it is not David. The whole affair is suffused with the irony of Yahweh. (*1 & 2 Chronicles*, 69)

Christ walked a similar path, refusing his own will in order to submit to the prescriptions of his heavenly Father. Doing so required resisting the human craving for revenge while also trusting God the Father to vindicate him in due time. Despite coming to his own and being rejected, Jesus endured the suffering and shame hurled at him from others (Heb 12:2). As result, God the Father has given the Son a name that is above all other names, commanding from friends and enemies alike the collective bow and confession that he is Lord (Phil 2:9-11).

Three episodes (paralleled in 2 Sam 21:18-22) with the Philistines offer a fitting conclusion to the pericope while also foreshadowing the Messiah. These enemies from the south were not just an ever-present thorn in the side of Israel; their defeat was also a symbol of David's ability to conquer all enemies outside of the covenant (thus fulfilling the prophetic word of Abner in 2 Sam 3:18). The shepherd boy who initially rose to fame by defeating Goliath was now instrumental in propelling Israel to prominence by defeating the giant descendants of his old nemesis. Stated differently, God's plans for a dynasty preceded David's kingship, bolstering confidence that the same intentions would outlive his rule as well.

The death of Sippai at the hand of Sibbecai was the first act of Philistine subjugation (20:4). Next, Elhanan slayed Goliath's brother Lahmi despite his great size (20:5). In the final incident, Jonathan, the son of Shimei, killed yet another giant in Gath, one with twenty-four fingers and toes (20:6-8). Eliminating these giants paved the way for the full possession of the land. Unlike Samson, who fell short during the period of the judges, this savior succeeds in driving the enemy out. In doing so, David again reminds us of the kind of champion we need while epitomizing a description of the Savior who is coming. The Lord promised to designate a place for his people (17:9-10), and one day, just like David, Jesus Christ will occupy Jerusalem's throne over a kingdom that is free from all her enemies (Rev 21:27).

Reflect and Discuss

1. What does the correlation between the Abrahamic and Davidic covenants teach you about God?
2. What do David's past victories teach us about the messianic age?
3. How does your understanding of David's expanding kingdom change your views about eternity?
4. How does David's willingness to resist his desire for revenge against the Ammonites motivate you to be more like Jesus?
5. What do the omissions concerning David's flaws teach us about our role in God's kingdom?
6. How does David's collection of treasures to construct the temple change your understanding of God's refusal to let David build his house?
7. How do God's dealings with the enemies of Israel encourage you? Frighten you?
8. How does looking forward toward the kingdom of Christ change your perception about the relevance of a passage like this?
9. How should we deal with our enemies until the final consummation of Christ's kingdom?
10. What is your most practical takeaway from this text? How will you implement it in your life?

The Gospel according to David

1 CHRONICLES 21

Main Idea: David's census and its resolution highlight the great payment necessary for the forgiveness of sin. By remembering this sordid occasion, the Chronicler inspired his audience to rebuild the place of sacrifice even as he pointed them, and us, to God's final atonement for sin.

I.   **The Reality of Sin Is Universal (21:1-6)**
II. **God's Reckoning for Sin Is Unavoidable (21:7-14)**
III. **Our Redemption from Sin Is Undeserved (21:15-30)**

> Amazing Grace! how sweet the sound
> that saved a wretch like me!
> I once was lost but now am found,
> Was blind, but now I see.

Though many people remember that John Newton wrote those immortal words, fewer realize that they are a fitting description of his life. Working as a slave trader for nearly ten years, he was indeed a wretch of a man. Describing himself, Newton said that his "delight and habitual practice was wickedness," and he "neither feared God nor regarded men."

Then, in March 1748 while on a slave voyage, Newton awoke to a storm rocking his ship. When he went up on deck, he heard his captain shouting, "Bring me a knife!" As soon as John went below to get it, a large wave washed the crewman standing beside him overboard. Knowing that God spared his life, Newton began to pray, and after the storm subsided, he buried himself in Scripture for the next three weeks of the journey until the ship anchored in Ireland. Once there, he called out to Christ for grace and forgiveness. For most of his latter years he served as a pastor.

Despite our attempts to romanticize his dramatic conversion, we often dismiss the painful details of John's sanctification. Our expectation is that he never boarded another slave ship and that he immediately wrote the words of the favorite hymn we cherish. As is often the case, his growth was much messier than we imagine. Would it surprise you to learn that Newton signed up for another slave mission soon after God saved him? And that he frequently read his Bible with hundreds of slaves beneath him? Or that it took him six years to completely abandon his wicked profession? He would not write "Amazing Grace" for another twenty-five years.

How is that possible, you ask? How could a Christian man continue in such blatant sin? Better still, how do we? Why do we continue in sin after coming to Christ? Why do our old habits linger? Why do we continually struggle as we do? Though our salvation occurs in an instant, the sanctification that follows is often a gradual process. We need continual grace to become the men and women God wants us to be. Over time, though, the changes are inevitable.

John Newton finally realized how egregious slave trading was. He even wrote a confessional titled *Thoughts on the African Slave Trade*, in which he admitted his past transgressions as well as his present inability to undo the pain he caused. Said Newton, "I hope it will always be a subject of humiliating reflection to me that I was once an active instrument in a business at which my heart now shudders" (Jeremiah, *Captured by Grace*, 66–67, 101–4).

Through God's continual grace, we can get there, too. God's grace is the remedy for every struggle with temptation, every attitude contrary to Scripture, and every indulgence to sin. John Newton's struggles were not unique, and neither are ours. All believers from every generation face the same struggle in our efforts to live out the gospel. Even King David repeatedly battled the weakness of his flesh.

Like a thorn rising from the perfect rose, this pericope emerges as a striking contrast to all the successes of the Davidic kingdom thus far. The Chronicler forces readers to wrestle not only with the identity of the *Satan* figure in the opening verse (v. 1) but also with the purpose for including such a damning error on the part of David after omitting his many other transgressions. This is not, however, the first failure listed by the historian as he seeks to encourage Jews weary from their seventy-year captivity.

David's previously highlighted misstep, even with less encompassing damage, resulted in a Hebrew casualty as he failed in his efforts to return the ark to Jerusalem (1 Chr 13). This account exposes an even more consequential blunder where the king's deadly census led to thousands of fatalities. In both instances, David's shortcomings as the priestly leader of Israel require intercession and sacrifice. Boda astutely observes,

> [B]oth times these failures are key to the development of Jerusalem as Israel's central place of worship, and in both cases David emerges as royal priest who intercedes on behalf of the people. (*1–2 Chronicles*, 173)

Each unsavory incident uncovers David's crucial role in preparing for the temple's construction (the primary reason for their inclusion), with the former focused more on the *priority* of worship within the nation and the latter giving attention to the *place* where Israel would assemble.

The Reality of Sin Is Universal
1 CHRONICLES 21:1-6

The opening verse is one of three Old Testament references using the title *Satan* for the devil (Job 1:6–2:7; Zech 3:1-2), and as one would expect, there is no shortage of controversy surrounding its usage. The Hebrew noun literally means "adversary," and it frequently refers to Israel's military or legal opponents (1 Sam 29:4; 2 Sam 19:23; 1 Kgs 5:4; 11:9-14,23,25; see Sailhamer, *First and Second Chronicles*, 53). Yet the absence of the definite article here likely means the word is a proper name in this instance. As in the early chapters of Job and Zechariah, the best understanding of the Chronicler's intent is to recognize the glory-stealing serpent from the garden of Eden as the referent.

Balancing this view with the Samuel record requires a brief explanation of how God carries out his divine purposes. The Deuteronomistic historian leaves the sinister intention of the Lord's archenemy out of his history, simply saying, "The LORD's anger burned against Israel again, and he stirred up David against them to say, 'Go, count the people of Israel and Judah'" (2 Sam 24:1). So, who was responsible, God or Satan? Is this a contradiction? How should contemporary readers reconcile the two accounts? Despite critical claims of inspirational incongruity, answers to questions like these surface when we maintain the tension of each author's purpose for writing. Thomas and Greear rightly insist,

> The author of Chronicles looks at the scene from the ground level, so to speak, and rightly says that Satan was the one prodding David. The author of Samuel looks at the

same scene from a different perspective and acknowledges
that God had a sovereign purpose even in Satan's acts.
(*1 & 2 Samuel*, 261)

The Lord, in his sovereignty, works through the free choices of fallen
creatures. Satan's temptation of David did not diminish the king's moral
responsibility, nor did it threaten the eternal agenda of God. Much like
in the scenario of Job 1, Satan was the one who incited David to sin, but
only with the permission of the Lord. What God allows always reflects
his greater purpose and design. Though they are baffling to the human
mind, God does not accept responsibility for these actions, nor does he
relinquish control over them. No wonder the apostle Paul declared with
contemplative praise, "Oh, the depth of the riches and the wisdom and
the knowledge of God! How unsearchable his judgments and untrace-
able his ways!" (Rom 11:33).

Apparently, the devil's enticement resonated with David's
fallen desires. Despite the pleading of Joab to the contrary, the king
quickly agreed to dishonor the Lord by numbering his army (vv. 2-6).
Admittedly, the wickedness behind this action is not readily apparent.
A census, in and of itself, was not sinful. Many lists in the Bible were
the result of similar efforts and were ordered by the Lord (Num 1:2-45;
3:40-43; 26:2-51). Moses went so far as to offer instructions about how
to count the people.

> *When you take a census of the Israelites to register them, each of the men
> must pay a ransom for his life to the LORD as they are registered. Then
> no plague will come on them as they are registered.* (Exod 30:12)

Nonetheless, the rebuke of Joab (v. 3) seemingly indicates that
counting in this way is a kingly affront to Yahweh, indicating David's
greater dependence on his army rather than on the Lord (Merrill, *A
Commentary*, 245). Indeed, totaling the number of armed men ready to
draw the sword reveals, at the very least, a prideful security stemming
from the strength of his military (v. 5).

The greater probability, though, is that David's priestly failure, the
second of its kind (cf. 1 Chr 13), was the most egregious transgression,
which angered the Lord. Just as David carelessly ignored the clear directives of the law regarding the ark's transportation, so, too, David will-
fully chose to act contrary to Scripture when executing the census. His
negligence in not receiving the necessary half shekel contribution to

the Lord from each person numbered made every Israelite registered vulnerable to the Lord's anger (Exod 30:13).

Our tendency to glorify war might lead us to interpret the Lord's response as an overreaction, and thus we would minimize the importance of a paid ransom prescribed by Moses. The nature of David's offense was both a personal and a legal slight against Yahweh. Much like his salacious episode with Bathsheba, here the king assumes the place of God as if the kingdom were his own.

> The census is as great a sin as adultery and murder, because it is a direct and flagrant trespass onto Yahweh's rights. It is a variation of David's sin with Bathsheba, but on a national scale: in 2 Samuel, David seizes the wife of a single warrior; in 1 Chronicles, David seizes the house of Yahweh and treats it as if it were his own. (Leithart, *1 & 2 Chronicles*, 73)

In addition, Johnstone explains how scandalous David's oversight was legally and why God required the payment.

> Killing on the field of battle is an inevitable consequence of war: but taking the life of another human being immediately warrants the payment of life for life. . . . The legislation in Exodus is concerned precisely with atonement, the maintenance of oneness between community and God, which will otherwise be broken even by acts of necessary bloodshed. (*1 and 2 Chronicles, Vol. 1*, 228)

Consequently, David transferred his guilt to all of Israel (v. 3), resulting in the entire nation's affliction (v. 7). The text positions these Israelites as willing participants in David's spiritual aberration, though, rather than unsuspecting followers deserving of pity. The resulting plague was the prescribed outcome for this kind of disobedience. By ignoring the parameters of Exodus 30, the Israelites bore just as much responsibility as David in the matter. The whole scene is a vivid reminder that no sin occurs in a vacuum. Individual rebellion, especially for those in authority, often leads to widespread corruption and trespasses, as is the case here.

Throughout their history, Israel vacillated between the blessings of their collective obedience and the curses of their wickedness. From top to bottom, no citizen of the kingdom was immune from the curse wrought by Eden's rebellion (Gen 3:1-7). Even David, the recipient of

God's eternal covenant, failed to live in light of who he was or who he pointed to. The shepherd boy from Judah was *a king*, but he was not *THE KING*.

Unfortunately, this incident was not unique to David's reign in Israel. The entire history of the kingdom is littered with one failure after another, as the people returned to their unfaithfulness even as a dog returns to its vomit (Prov 26:11). From the birth of the monarchy until its demise, each generation fell short of God's glory (Rom 3:23). Just before the exile, the Chronicler explained,

> *All the leaders of the priests and the people multiplied their unfaithful deeds, imitating all the detestable practices of the nations, and they defiled the LORD's temple that he had consecrated in Jerusalem.* (2 Chr 36:14)

Even after the exile, prophet after prophet warned the covenantal community about the dangers of remaining in their sins. Zechariah the prophet, before urging the postexilic community to rebuild the temple, said,

> *This is what the LORD of Armies says: Return to me—this is the declaration of the LORD of Armies—and I will return to you, says the LORD of Armies. Do not be like your ancestors; the earlier prophets proclaimed to them: This is what the LORD of Armies says: Turn from your evil ways and your evil deeds. But they did not listen or pay attention to me—this is the LORD's declaration.* (Zech 1:3-4)

Ezra, likewise, confronted the waywardness of the exiles who made their way back to Jerusalem, and he sought the Lord on their behalf (Ezra 9:1-15). The universal reality of sin throughout Israel was precisely why they fell to Babylon and precisely why they needed to return in order to keep looking for the promised Son of David who would one day reign in complete righteousness over his eternal kingdom (17:14).

Lest we look on stoically, completely divorced from the universal impact of *their* sin, we would do well to understand that *our* sin is just as far-reaching. Charles Spurgeon aptly noted,

> As the salt flavours every drop of the Atlantic, so does sin affect every atom of our nature. It is so sadly there, so abundantly there, that if you cannot detect it you are deceived. ("Honest Dealing with God")

Jew and Gentile alike have gone astray, turning to our own ways rather than the Lord's Word (Isa 53:6). Solomon lamented, "There is certainly no one righteous on the earth who does good and never sins" (Eccl 7:20). The apostle Paul even traced our plight back to the first man, pointing to Adam as the means by which sin entered the world and universally corrupted all people (Rom 5:12). The reality of sin in our lives today is just as evident as it was when Israel's most famous king failed the Lord.

God's Reckoning for Sin Is Unavoidable
1 CHRONICLES 21:7-14

Even worse than David's actions being detestable to Joab (v. 6) was their being offensive to the Lord. Almost instantly, God countered the king's carelessness with holy outrage, showering the whole empire with affliction (v. 7). Again, note the national focus of God's anger. David, in his sin, led others to follow in disobedience. Perhaps the immediate backlash from the Lord jolted him into reality, but whatever the means, David quickly realized both the gravity and recklessness of his conduct (v. 8). What unfolds in the remainder of the passage reminds us that consequences for sin are unavoidable, even if redirected.

The essential ingredients of repentance also surface in these verses as David casts himself upon the mercy of God. Notice, he makes no excuse for his wickedness ("I have sinned greatly"), and he identifies the census specifically ("I have done this thing") (v. 8). Next, he pleads for grace and forgiveness, realizing he is no position to take his guilt away. Perhaps the greatest indicator of all, though, is David's humility in submitting to whatever the Lord chooses next for him (v. 13). His example offers helpful criteria as we seek to gauge the sincerity and legitimacy of our own repentance. (1) Do I justify my sin or own it? (2) Am I willing to name it and turn from it? (3) Am I willing to forfeit my right to determine the consequences for my behavior?

Gad functioned as a lesser-known prophet who spoke the word of the Lord to David much as Nathan had previously (vv. 9-10). The Lord, through his servant, offered the king three options for the coming retribution: three years of famine, three months of defeat at the hands of enemies, or three days of plague wrought by the angel of the Lord (vv. 11-12). Again, the fruit of David's repentance is obvious as he lays down his agenda and yields to the Lord's holiness. Still, in an act of unavoidable reckoning, Israel lost 70,000 men in one day (v. 14). The effort to boast in the strength of his military left David weeping over his weakness and the most severe loss his army ever endured.

Moreover, in an even greater twist of irony, the king who often points readers to Christ is more reminiscent of an Egyptian pharaoh in this instance. During the exodus, God's death angel slaughtered Egypt's firstborn sons due to the hardness of Pharaoh's heart. Now this grisly messenger of the Lord is back, this time slaughtering the Israelites instead. By assuming the role of Pharaoh, David has turned Israel into Egypt, a place where a national leader exploits God's people for his own purposes (Leithart, *1 & 2 Chronicles*, 73). Thankfully, David will turn away from this typology before the incident concludes, even pointing us to Christ again, but only offering a sacrifice as propitiation for his sin.

Regardless of the redemptive narrative in front of the text, the most immediate lesson here magnifies both the universal presence and the consequence of sin. To modern observers, God's chastening hand after David's clear repentance seems harsh and excessive. Unfortunately, we often equate the remission of sins with the removal of consequence, failing to realize that forgiveness always comes at a great price. As new covenant believers, we realize that Jesus fully absorbed our punishment on the cross, making justification fully available by grace through faith. Yet, lest we forget that our atonement is costly, the Lord often allows us to face the earthly consequences for our sins, even when he mitigates them slightly, lest we trample the Son of God underfoot (Heb 10:26-30). God will not be mocked, choosing instead to let humanity, even his own people, reap what they sow (Gal 6:7).

Numerous accounts illustrate that, while God forgives, the damage caused by sinful choices often remains. Though the Lord forgave David for his adultery with Bathsheba, the child she carried still died because of the king's open contempt for the Lord (2 Sam 12:14). After the Israelites refused to enter the promised land in fear of the giants they encountered there, the Lord pardoned their iniquity, but he also refused to allow them into the land he pledged to Abraham (Num 14:20-23). Even Moses, despite his designation as the humblest man to walk the earth (Num 12:3), was not allowed to cross the Jordan River with Israel because he hit rather than spoke to the rock at Meribah (Num 20:12-13).

Our assurance in facing the unavoidable burdens our sins create is that God is always working for the benefit of our sharing in his holiness, knowing that his discipline produces the peaceful fruit of righteousness (Heb 12:10-11). Like David, even in our forgiveness we should be content to allow the Lord to choose the necessary results of our actions.

Our Redemption from Sin Is Undeserved
1 CHRONICLES 21:15-30

The scene transitions in verse 15, offering a proleptic view of the dramatic events about to unfold. With a breathtaking image of the terror of the Lord, an angel sent by God stands between heaven and earth with his sword drawn, ready to destroy Jerusalem (v. 16). Overcome with fear and agony over the sins that led to this moment of judgment, David and the elders of the city fall on their faces before God, pleading for mercy. Then, in a moment of messianic foreshadowing, David flips the script and once again separates himself from the failures of Saul and the wickedness of Pharaoh.

Accepting the breadth of his destruction, the king intercedes on behalf of his people, offering himself as a sacrifice for God's wrath against them (v. 17). Granted, David was in no position to die for the sins of others when he was guilty of his own transgressions. Yet his efforts point us to another who would indeed substitute himself as an acceptable sacrifice for sin, having no sin of his own (see 2 Cor 5:21). Even the three days of wrath poured out on Israel here (v. 12) offered the postexilic community a glimpse of what would be required for God to deal with their sins once and for all. For them, remembering the past gave them a clue for what was ahead. For us, looking back on the death of Christ provides the fullest expression of the intercession David sought and needed long ago. Our salvation is settled because for three days God the Son, David's seed, paid the full debt of our rebellion.

Understanding the relenting of the Lord concerning the destruction he intended to inflict on Jerusalem through this lens prevents our reading unbiblical theology into the text (v. 15). The course change does not reflect any change in the moral character of God, nor does it reveal his unawareness of future events—in this case David's forthcoming repentance. On the contrary, Scripture plainly states what God will do when certain conditions regarding his holiness are met (Jer 18:7-10). And David, knowing of the Lord's great mercy, "confessed his sins and followed through on the divinely prescribed obligations of repentance" (Klein, "David: Sinner and Saint," 13). Rather than an example of God's changing his mind, this episode is reminder of God's eagerness, even determination, to forgive and restore when his people repent.

With the king's lament on full display, the need for sacrifice cannot be left unattended. God's death angel will only pass over Jerusalem when the shedding of blood secures atonement for the people (cf. Exod 12). Through the prophet Gad we learn that the threshing floor of Ornan was the chosen site for constructing the altar for sacrifice. Despite Ornan's eagerness to offer the property as a gift to the king, David insisted that he would not give to the Lord what cost him nothing (vv. 22-25).

As the angel of destruction hovered over David's new altar, the king offered up sacrifices suitable to cover his sin, even if temporarily (v. 26). As the fire from heaven fell, the wrath of God subsided and the angel's sword was placed back in his sheath (v. 27). Again, we see David casting the shadow of Christ as he functions as a king and priest who saves his sheep from judgment (v. 17). Overwhelmed by the Lord's grace and forgiveness, and realizing the need for continual sacrifice on behalf of the people, David identifies this location as the chosen site for the temple Solomon would build (22:1).

Despite David's nefarious trespasses against the Lord, God continues to unroll his covenantal commitment to him by using him to prepare the house that will eternally bear his name. For a weary community recovering from exile, these words and examples would have been a healing balm. The passage illustrates that the Chronicler had no interest in covering the misdeeds of the king. Yet neither did he seek to shock his audience by rehashing well-known stories of failure. Instead, his carefully crafted record bore the single goal of reminding the covenant community of Yahweh's unfailing faithfulness. Including this royal malefaction serves his inspired end by highlighting the good God brought out of David's dereliction. Wilcock notes,

> Practically everything is now ready for the building of the temple—the initial idea, the confirmation from God, the restored ark, the beginnings of a store of materials, and now the site. . . . Construction will not start until David's warlike reign gives way to Solomon's peaceful one. (*1 and 2 Chronicles*, 398)

As a result, just as David found forgiveness by means of sacrifice, future generations would do the same through every offering they brought to the house of God. Jews looking back at this incident would recall their need for atonement through blood sacrifice. David's forgiveness became a prototype of their continued need as well as a personal motivation to rebuild the temple after the exile.

> The David of the census story is a person of confession and supplication *par excellence*, a human sinner who repents, seeks forgiveness, intercedes on behalf of his people, and ultimately secures the site of the future temple. Precisely because David is a pivotal figure, David's repentance and intercession are paradigmatic. (Knoppers, *1 Chronicles 10–29*, 764)

Likewise, New Testament believers rest knowing that Christ has died for our sins once and for all, fulfilling the hope that Old Testament sacrifices pointed to (Heb 10:1-12). Only by the blood of God's Son can the wrath of God be averted. Romans 3:25 even declares,

> *God presented him as the mercy seat by his blood, through faith, to demonstrate his righteousness, because in his restraint God passed over the sins previously committed.*

The Israelites spared during the reign of David were saved by the blood of Christ, along with those charged to rebuild the temple after returning to Jerusalem. All previous sacrifices ensured the Lord's patience until the spotless Lamb of God could offer himself for sin.

Later, in 2 Chronicles 3:1, we learn that the dedicated plot for Solomon's temple was on Mount Moriah, the same place where Abraham made atonement for Isaac by trusting that God would provide a lamb (Gen 22). David's sacrifice here was for an entire nation through a similar offering. Then, generation after generation of Hebrew families would come to the temple on the Day of Atonement as their sins were transferred to a male goat in this exact spot. And all of them pointed to the single sacrifice of God's only begotten Son, who was obedient to the point of death on our behalf (Phil 2:7-8). This is the gospel according to David.

Reflect and Discuss

1. How are we sometimes guilty of treating sin flippantly because we misunderstand the grace of God?
2. How does pride make us vulnerable to Satan's temptations?

3. What does the perpetual sinfulness of Israel teach us about our need for God's grace?
4. How should we reconcile God's love for us with his discipline in our lives?
5. If Jesus paid our entire sin debt, what are other reasons God sometimes chooses to allow us to experience the full consequences of our transgressions?
6. In what ways could your sinful choices cause others to disobey God as well?
7. How does David contradict and epitomize the life of Christ in this pericope?
8. What does God's ability to use sinful acts in order to accomplish good purposes teach us about his sovereignty?
9. Why is the Chronicler so careful to teach us David's role in preparing for the temple's location and construction?
10. What is the gospel according to David?

Christianity in the Shadows

1 CHRONICLES 22–29

Main Idea: As a picture of God's determination to dwell among his people again, King David's preparation for the temple has much to teach us about our role in the kingdom of God and the priorities that reflect a sincere commitment to the Lord.

I. The Sacredness of the Temple Reenergizes Our Passion (22:2-19).

II. The Servants in the Temple Refocus Our Perspective (23:1–27:34).
   A. Organizing the Levites (23:6-23)
   B. Organizing the priesthood (24:1-31)
   C. Organizing the musicians (25:1-31)
   D. Organizing the gatekeepers (26:1-32)
   E. Organizing the army and administrative leaders (27:1-34)

III. The Stewardship of the Temple Requires Our Purity (28:1-21).

IV. The Sacrifices for the Temple Reorder Our Priorities (29:1-30).

Raising sons and daughters is not for the faint of heart. Whether we have one or several, kids have a way of pushing us to the limit of our sanity. The humorous story of a mother at her wits' end over the behavior of her two sons has always resonated with me. From her perspective, the boys were not children; they were uncontrollable forces of nature. One day while sharing her struggles with a neighbor, her friend said, "I took my son to the pastor, and he hasn't given me a problem since."

Though the single mother of two could not imagine what difference her pastor could make, she was all out of ideas and didn't have anything to lose. After school she loaded both of her sons in the car and drove to the church for them to meet with their pastor. Once there, the clergyman worked like a masterful police detective who was interrogating two suspects. He separated the boys, choosing to deal with the older one first while the younger son waited nervously. Without even introducing himself, the robed minister shut the door behind him and immediately questioned the boy with a somber tone, "Where is God?"

No answer.

The pastor repeated, "Where is God?"

The lad looked at the floor, up to the ceiling, and all around the room, but still no answer. Before the silence could linger any longer the pastor thundered a third time, "Where is God?"

This time the brother leapt to his feet and ran out of the office, into the waiting room, and straight for the exit. On the way out he grabbed his brother and shouted, "Let's get out of here! They've lost God and they're trying to pin it on us!" (David Jeremiah, *Life Wide Open*, 150).

Obviously, God cannot be lost, but there are times in our lives when he seems noticeably absent. His silence can, at times, be deafening, and his distance sometimes seems unbearable. Though it is theologically impossible, it feels like God is missing. I imagine that is how the Jews must have felt during the postexilic period. As they regathered in Jerusalem with no temple, Yahweh seemed to be a million miles away with no intention of dwelling among them again. Thus, recalling David's preparation for the temple's construction became the Chronicler's method for reassuring the Jews of God's intention to be among them again.

Overstating the importance of the temple for Jewish faith and practice is nearly impossible. Here, its construction takes center stage as a demonstration of God's unfolding commitment to his people. While David's instructions for and Solomon's building of the structure are substantial contributions of this pericope, the greater emphasis is on the encompassing work of God among his people as a direct fulfillment of his covenantal goals. The blending together of the reigns of David and Solomon clarifies the agenda of the Lord as the focal point of the narrative rather than the achievements of any one king. One throne gives way to the other because both are part of God's design to establish the eternal seat of the Messiah. These chapters reveal more about the character and competency of God than of his chosen instruments.

To identify David as "a man of war" (28:3) and Solomon as "a man of rest" (22:9) is not to insult the former while praising the latter. On the contrary, the Chronicler is celebrating the contributions of both leaders in response to the Lord's direction. These chapters are about

> the passing of a nation from war to peace. More correctly and fully, it is a movement away from the circumstances and necessities of the one and towards the circumstances and possibilities of the other. It has been David's function to win

> the wars: it will be Solomon's task to establish the peace. The
> first reign sees the clearing of the ground, the second sees the
> work of construction. One king quells opposition, the other
> gains admiration. (Wilcock, *Message of Chronicles*, 99)

Together, these earliest leaders of the Davidic dynasty paint a picture of both the scope and the impact of God's redemptive ambitions dating all the way back to the garden of Eden. The temple's rise is a vivid indicator that God will ultimately crush the head of the serpent (Gen 3:15).

Understanding Eden as a cosmic temple that houses God's presence magnifies the significance of the historic progress recorded here (see comments in chs. 13–16). Because Adam and Eve's sin broke mankind's fellowship with God, believers continue to look forward to a new heaven and earth where that relationship is fully restored. Along the way, God offered clues of his resolve to dwell among his people again. First the tabernacle and then the temple signaled that God was working to reestablish the connection that was lost after Eden's curse.

Just as God sanctified the earth with his presence by resting on the seventh day of creation (which was akin to his enthronement), so he also sanctified Israel by being enthroned in the temple Solomon built over seven years (2 Chr 6:42). Both Levenson and Walton successfully argue that the creation narrative and the tabernacle/temple records mirror each other (Levenson, "The Temple and the World," 275–98; Walton, *Genesis 1 as Ancient Cosmology*, 187). Though not the final solution, the construction of the temple is a nod back to the paradise Adam and Eve lost, as well as a preview of the coming reign of God when we will freely enjoy his presence once more.

King David's three speeches govern the development of the pericope (22:2-19; 28:1-21; 29:1-9), with the physical and organizational provisions in between (chs. 23–27). These chapters are unique to Chronicles, containing details found nowhere else in Scripture. Numerous allusions to Moses's transfer of leadership to Joshua served as another implicit reminder to the floundering nation that God was still in control. After the turmoil of leaving Egypt and wandering in the desert under the leadership of Moses, God gave his people rest through the guidance of Joshua. Likewise, following the bloody ascension of David, God prospered his people under the peaceful reign of Solomon (Wilcock, *1 and 2 Chronicles*, 399). The subtle implication for the postexilic community, and even for us, is that God was still capable of advancing his agenda *for* them and *through* them.

The Sacredness of the Temple Reenergizes Our Passion
1 CHRONICLES 22:2-19

While the details of David's temple preparation can, at times, be cumbersome, the world of the text offers modern readers a unique glimpse of what God has prepared for his saints when the promised Son of David reigns in Zion. Appreciating these shadows of future kingdom realities reenergizes our passion for the Lord's work, both in the present and in the future. The temple was a sacred structure not only because it was a temporary means for God to dwell among his people but also because it pointed to the eschatological reality of Jesus walking among and reigning over his saints in the new heaven and new earth.

Realizing that the youth and inexperience of Solomon did not match the enormity of the task (v. 5), David planned virtually every detail of the temple's construction and maintenance. He began by appointing stonecutters (v. 2) and supplying resources like iron, bronze, and cedar logs (vv. 3-4). Next, the king turned to Solomon in his first speech to cast a vision for what was ahead (vv. 6-16). His remarkable words characterize the hope and peace of the messianic age.

The first order of David's speech is to offer his recollection of God's refusal to allow him to build the temple despite what was in his heart (vv. 7-8). As stated previously, this admission is no indictment against Israel's covenant king. The blood David shed was the means of ushering in the peace of God's presence. Solomon's name literally means "man of peace" and was a sign of the kind of reign he would enjoy (vv. 9-10) With the shadow of Persian rule looming in the Jews' not-so-distant past, the postexilic community certainly viewed these contrasting thrones as complements to each other rather than a dichotomy. David leveraged the progression to motivate his son to pick up the work of building God's house.

With the gift of hindsight, from both our contemporary perspective as well as the Jewish recollection after the exile, we know just as Israel did that Solomon's peace was merely temporary, only pointing to the peace the Son of David will one day bring. Like David, the Messiah will cast down the enemies of the kingdom by smiting the nations

(Rev 19:15-16). And like Solomon, he will bring healing to the nations that results in eternal, not temporary, peace (Rev 22:2-3). In other words, the emphasis of the text is not either-or but both-and. The choice is not *either* David *or* Solomon, as if the former falls short due to bloodshed while the latter typifies Christ through peace. On the contrary, the Chronicler celebrates *both* David *and* Solomon, realizing that the father provides the foundation on which his son stands. Each, in his own way, points us to the Promised One who will defeat all our enemies in order to preside over a peaceful dynasty.

David's prayer for Solomon underscores the profound importance of passing this torch successfully (vv. 11-13). Overhearing these paternal blessings fans our passion to do God's work in God's way. The king prays for his son's success in building the temple as well as for insight and understanding that will enable him to keep God's law. No detail of Solomon's throne was untouched by David's preparation. Even the wisdom that so marked the man of peace was admonished and prayed for before he assumed the throne.

Next, David inventories his numerous provisions, including resources and workers, in order to admonish, "Now begin the work" (vv. 14-16). Leaving no stone unturned, he then challenges his leaders to join in the work not only for the sake of Solomon but also for the glory of the Lord (vv. 17-19). Though Solomon will soon enjoy the accolades of completing this defining work, it is no exaggeration to say that the project is turnkey thanks to the preliminary efforts of David.

Contextually, the whole scene is replete with affirmations of God's relentless desire to be among his people again as he was in Eden. With the temple as a step toward the ultimate goal of cosmological redemption, David assures Solomon that this effort is the will of God, fully reflective of the promise of God (vv. 9-10). He also magnifies God's faithfulness with language reminiscent of Moses's installation of Joshua (Boda, *1–2 Chronicles*, 182–83). The call to be strong and courageous is a reminder that God brought the people into the promised land for this purpose, and he will bring it to pass as Solomon remains close to him.

Contemporary Christians can also take great comfort in these words as a descriptive acknowledgment of the Lord's steadfast commitment to redeem us eternally. The glory of God's presence in the temple points to but does not rival the glory of God that indwells every Christ follower (1 Cor 3:16). Furthermore, we look forward to entering the heavenly Jerusalem, where God will make his dwelling among his people, being with us in human flesh forever and ever (Rev 21:3).

The Servants in the Temple Refocus Our Perspective
1 CHRONICLES 23:1–27:34

The Chronicler does not record the controversy surrounding David's choice of Solomon to succeed him (1 Kgs 1–2), largely because the matter had been settled for generations and his goal is to interpret Israel's history rather than merely record it. Though Solomon did not officially replace his father as king over Israel until 29:22-25, his initial installation occurred much earlier due to David's determination to transition well (23:1), resulting in significant overlap between the two. Solomon's gradual rise was key to his success because it allowed ample time for the necessary preparations to be made.

In contrast to David's reckless efforts to number his military (1 Chr 21), the census of Levi's tribe followed the prescribed pattern of Numbers 1:17-46 (23:2-5). Though the king's earliest expectation was that only Levite heads of household age thirty and above would serve in the temple (23:3), he later lowered the birthdate to include those twenty and older, likely due to need (23:24,27). Such a move was not without precedent (compare Num 4:3 and Num 8:24). After counting, 38,000 men were available to serve in the temple (23:3). These were divided into four groups with specific assignments (23:4-5).

Reestablishing these divisions signaled to Jews returning to Jerusalem that their bleak circumstances were not an indicator of their heavenly position in God's kingdom. Seeking God's presence again through their rebuilding and organizational efforts shifted their focus away from the burdens of the present, freeing the chosen people to live for the blessings of eternity instead. Likewise, these verses paint a vivid picture of the coming kingdom for new covenant saints.

Organizing the Levites (23:6-23)

David's arrangement of the Levites to serve within the temple was just as important as his planning and preparing the materials necessary for construction. Worshiping in the Lord's designated place was the first fruit of enjoying God's dwelling again. Thus, the Lord instructed,

> *Instead, turn to the place the LORD your God chooses from all your tribes to put his name for his dwelling and go there. You are to bring there your burnt offerings and sacrifices, your tenths and personal contributions, your vow offerings and freewill offerings, and the firstborn of your herds and flocks.* (Deut 12:5-6)

Initially, God's chosen location was Gilgal, then Shechem, then Shiloh, and then Solomon's temple in Jerusalem (*CSB Study Bible*, 283). For Jews anxious to rebuild the temple, the reminder of Yahweh's commitment to be among them would have been encouraging. Christians today understand that after Christ's resurrection and ascension, the eschatological opportunity to meet with God will be the throne of David from which the Messiah will reign in the new heaven and earth. The apostle John frames our expectation:

> *Then he showed me the river of the water of life, clear as crystal, flowing from the throne of God and of the Lamb down the middle of the city's main street. The tree of life was on each side of the river, bearing twelve kinds of fruit, producing its fruit every month. The leaves of the tree are for healing the nations, and there will no longer be any curse. The throne of God and of the Lamb will be in the city, and his servants will worship him. They will see his face, and his name will be on their foreheads. Night will be no more; people will not need the light of a lamp or the light of the sun, because the Lord God will give them light, and they will reign forever and ever.* (Rev 22:1-5)

These "divisions" (1 Chr 23:6) correspond to the number of Levi's sons and the families under each (vv. 6-23). Three clans emerge: the Gershonites (vv. 7-11), the Kohathites (vv. 12-20), and the Merarites (vv. 21-23). Each name demonstrates the historicity of the Bible. Though three more specific roles will soon be named for particular families of Levi, this entire tribe was responsible for the general welfare and service of the temple.

Anticipating the peace ahead is tied to the previous Davidic promise as well as the eschatological reality (vv. 24-25). In this sense, the text positions David as a new Moses who delivers his people into the peace of his successor. Like the deliverer in the desert, David will not enter the new promised land or experience its covenantal realities. And like the humblest man to live to that point (Num 12:3), Israel's king would not only interpret God's law for the people but also expand the Levitical duties laid out in Numbers 4 (1 Chr 23:25-32).

By doing so, David also foreshadowed the future son of David who will expand these Levitical roles again. His temple will rise from living stones, forming an expanded priesthood that will do the work of ministry within the church as he gifts each one for service (1 Pet 2:4-5). The apostle Paul explains,

> *And he himself gave some to be apostles, some prophets, some evangelists, some pastors and teachers, to equip the saints for the work of ministry, to build up the body of Christ, until we all reach unity in the faith and in the knowledge of God's Son, growing into maturity with a stature measured by Christ's fullness.* (Eph 4:11-13)

Two New Testament lists, though not comprehensive, identify various spiritual gifts within the body of Christ (Rom 12:6-8; 1 Cor 12:4-11,28). Additionally, Scripture celebrates the unique contribution of every member of the church as essential (1 Cor 12:12-26).

Organizing the Priesthood (24:1-31)

Next, David organizes the priesthood within the temple. The aim here is to trace the familial records of the priesthood back to Aaron (vv. 1-2). Though no mention is made of Nadab's and Abihu's sin due to the interpretive agenda of the Chronicler (Lev 10:1-2), clearly all lines tie back to Eleazar and Ithamar. The result is twenty-four ancestral families, sixteen from the former and eight from latter (vv. 3-5). The head of each household served at the temple in rotation after receiving assignments designated by lot (Prov 16:33).

To modern readers, the distinction between the priesthood and the tribe of Levi is less obvious, but it is significant nonetheless. Stated simply, all priests were Levites, but not all Levites were priests. Those lines blur again, though, when the Chronicler cites an additional Levitical generation traced back to the Korathites and Merarites (vv. 20-31) after detailing the four thousand designated descendants of Aaron for the priestly function (vv. 6-19). Olley wisely suggests that, rather than view this as a latter revision, we should view the structure as an intentional chiastic arrangement meant to affirm the parity between the two groups (*1–2 Chronicles*, 1055).

The presence of the Old Testament priesthood was a reminder to the faith community of the need for sacrifice in order to approach the Lord. For contemporary believers, these verses anticipate the coming son of David who functions as our eternal high priest, making one sacrifice on our behalf. The writer of Hebrews magnifies his work:

> For this is the kind of high priest we need: holy, innocent, undefiled, separated from sinners, and exalted above the heavens. He doesn't need to offer sacrifices every day, as high priests do—first for their own sins, then for those of the people. He did this once for all time when he offered himself. For the law appoints as high priests men who are weak, but the promise of the oath, which came after the law, appoints a Son, who has been perfected forever. (Heb 7:26-28)

Organizing the Musicians (25:1-31)

David chose Asaph, Heman, and Jeduthun to lead the music ministry of the temple through their descendants (v. 1). With 24 total sons among them, the entire pool of musicians to choose from totaled 288, which were divided into twenty-four groups of twelve (vv. 2-31). Apart from blowing trumpets (Num 10), there is no mention of music's role within Israelite worship before this. As a gifted musician and writer of psalms himself, David seems most responsible for incorporating these expressions into the temple liturgy, including choirs as well as musical instruments (Wiersbe, *The Wiersbe Bible Commentary*, 607).

The charge to prophesy underscored both the opportunity and responsibility for all music to proclaim divine truth through its lyrics (v. 1). Clearly, these trained and skillful leaders would have performed with excellence (vv. 6-7), yet the prophetic emphasis, however defined, elevates the content of their music above its quality, though there need not be any dichotomy between the two. Certainly, the Chronicler holds forth this standard as the freed exiles regathered and resumed their efforts for corporate worship as a faith community. These priorities also hold as a helpful guide for the encouragement of New Testament churches as well. Note the attention to substance:

> Let the word of Christ dwell richly among you, in all wisdom teaching and admonishing one another through psalms, hymns, and spiritual songs, singing to God with gratitude in your hearts. (Col 3:16; cf. Eph 5:19)

If believers exercised this much care to share prophetic music while looking for the promised son of David, imagine the scene around the eternal throne of the Messiah as saints and angels join in the heavenly chorus. The apostle John anticipates,

> *When he took the scroll, the four living creatures and the twenty-four elders fell down before the Lamb. Each one had a harp and golden bowls filled with incense, which are the prayers of the saints. And they sang a new song: You are worthy to take the scroll and to open its seals, because you were slaughtered, and you purchased people for God by your blood from every tribe and language and people and nation. You made them a kingdom and priests to our God, and they will reign on the earth. Then I looked and heard the voice of many angels around the throne, and also of the living creatures and of the elders. Their number was countless thousands, plus thousands of thousands.* (Rev 5:8-11)

Organizing the Gatekeepers (26:1-32)

The primary charge assigned to the gatekeepers was the security and daily operation of the temple (vv. 12-19) and its storehouses (vv. 20-28). These descendants of Korah and Merari watched over the shrine's physical structure as well as its internal treasures. In addition, these servants functioned as officers and judges who adjudicated spiritual matters outside the temple complex and throughout Israel (vv. 29-32). A more specific list of additional gatekeeper duties appears in 9:17-27.

The inclusion of Obed-edom is curious, primarily because the Chronicler previously identified his homeland as Gath (13:13). Did this mean he was an honorary Levite? Or was he an Israelite who was born in Gittite territory? Some surmise that Obed-edom did not hail from Philistine territory but from the Levitical city of Gath-rimmon within the tribe of Ephraim (Boda, *1–2 Chronicles*, 199). Regardless, he clearly ranks among the clans of Korah as a legitimate gatekeeper in Israel. Previously, God blessed this man greatly because he secured the ark of the covenant in his home for three months (13:13-14). Here, the text ties the substance of the divine blessing to the size of his family, totaling sixty-two children and grandchildren, while also enumerating the strengths and capabilities of the same (26:4-7).

The presence of the gatekeepers powerfully conveys the abiding consequence and devastation of Eden's curse. These guards functioned much like the cherubim God stationed at the east of the garden to prevent access to the tree of life (Gen 3:24). Even though God was present among his people again within the innermost sanctuary of the temple, only the priests by means of sacrifice could gain entry before Yahweh. Similarly, no sinful person will enjoy the presence of God in the new heaven and earth (Rev 21:27). The gatekeepers remind us that sin brings death by breaking our fellowship with God. Even while rebuilding the temple, the need to reinstall security measures like these reassured the Jews that God would continue to be among them but also showed that the postexilic world was not the ultimate resolution.

The fundamental difference between the image here and our eternal paradise will be the absence of these servants. Rather than a temple that veils the presence of God among his people, "the Lord God the Almighty and the Lamb" are the temple within the heavenly Jerusalem (Rev 21:22). Forever freed from the curse, the gates of the eternal city will never close because all who gather there will know life with God in our midst (Rev 21:25).

Organizing the Army and Administrative Leaders (27:1-34)

If we need further evidence that Israel's return from Babylon did not commence the final messianic age, chapter 27 catalogs twelve divisions of twenty-four thousand soldiers each within David's army (vv. 1-15). The leaders of each allotment also appear in the previous record of David's mighty men (11:11-47). These individuals operated as liaisons between the field of battle and the king. During times of peace, each unit served one month out of every year.

In addition to a standing military, David also organized personnel who functioned like governors over each tribe (27:16-24). Though representatives for Gad and Asher are absent from the list, leaders for the two halves of Manasseh both appear (vv. 20-21), along with two distinct envoys for the tribe of Levi (v. 17). The Chronicler concedes that his numbers are incomplete due to the interruption of David's sinful census (vv. 23-24). Yet a nod back to the innumerable descendants of Abraham reassures readers that the absence of these figures in no way threatens the eternal agenda of the Lord.

Finally, a team or royal cabinet attended to the kingdom properties and served as counselors to the king (vv. 25-34). Storehouses (v. 25), land with its produce (vv. 26-28), and livestock (vv. 29-31) were among the primary treasures they oversaw. David's benefit from their collective wisdom (vv. 32-34) likewise indicated a strong dynasty prepared to be handed over to Solomon. Both the wealth behind the temple preparation and the comprehensive scope of it give us the perspective of eternity as we look for a city whose maker and builder is God (Heb 11:8-10).

The Stewardship of the Temple Requires Our Purity
1 CHRONICLES 28:1-21

After charging Solomon privately (22:7-13), David then addressed him publicly in an effort to ready the nation's acceptance of him. This chapter also serves as the beginning of David's farewell, which the Chronicler then used to remind returning exiles of their responsibility to steward the temple's significance well. Certainly, God used his anointed king to plant the seeds of an eternal covenant and to initiate the construction of the Lord's house. With both David and Solomon now completely off the scene, the Chronicler's history lesson subtly yet strategically portrays Yahweh's ability to raise the nation out of the ashes of their rebellion and sin. Despite years of heartache and shame, the Lord's throne was not in jeopardy, nor were his promises uncertain. The faces and names would change, but Yahweh was still leading his chosen nation. With the temple in ruins, these memories were a reminder that their most valuable spiritual treasures were untouchable.

And why should we concern ourselves with Israel's temptation to idolize their leaders, and even the temple, above the Lord himself? Similar pitfalls in a local church are not difficult to imagine. Leaders come and go, but the God we worship and the kingdom he is building will last forever. Personnel changes, while seldom easy, should never derail our commitment to God's work. To use the language of the apostle Paul,

> *For whenever someone says, "I belong to Paul," and another, "I belong to Apollos," are you not acting like mere humans? What then is Apollos? What is Paul? They are servants through whom you believed, and each has the role the Lord has given. I planted, Apollos watered, but God gave the growth. So, then, neither the one who plants nor the one who waters is anything, but only God who gives the growth.*
> (1 Cor 3:4-7)

Likewise, church traditions evolve over time, and little, if anything, stays the same. Our focus should be on God rather than on the ways we worship him or on who leads us.

As part of his commission, David recalls his desire to build God a house and the Lord's refusal (vv. 1-3). Before all the leaders of Israel, the king reminisces over God's covenant with him followed by affirming his choice of Solomon to assume the throne and lead the temple project (vv. 4-6). Anticipating potential rivals, David equates his full endorsement of Solomon with his unwavering intention to obey God. Note the emphasis on both the new king's and the nation's obedience to Mosaic law as the key to their preservation. Though God's Davidic promise was unilateral, Israel's stewardship of the royal dynasty required purity and obedience (v. 7). Therefore, David appealed to his son along with the entire nation to follow the Lord's commands in order to avoid his judgment (vv. 8-10). Merrill explains, "The promise of retaining the kingdom and passing it on was conditioned by being faithful to Yahweh's commands" (*A Commentary*, 299).

Surely, these words resonated at a visceral level for a nation still reeling after seventy years of captivity. The destruction of the temple and Jerusalem was a direct consequence of Israel's failure to obey God. The Chronicler will eventually confess as much by admitting, "They kept ridiculing God's messengers, despising his words, and scoffing at his prophets, until the LORD's wrath was so stirred up against his people that there was no remedy" (2 Chr 36:16). For us, the lesson is one of moral clarity. No one is exempt from God's standards of purity and righteousness. Stewarding God's presence in our lives cultivates personal holiness so as not to quench the Spirit within us (1 Thess 5:19). Even with our salvation secure in Christ, enjoying the blessings of his presence is impossible apart from taking his commands seriously.

The plans David handed over to Solomon, along with their specificity, reinforce the divine initiative behind the undertaking (vv. 11-19). The level of detail here is astounding and even more so when we realize the Lord actively directed even the miniscule nuances of the work. "By the LORD's hand on me," David admitted, "he enabled me to understand everything in writing, all the details of the plan" (v. 19). Again, we are but minor players within the redemptive movement of history. God's presence and the work he empowers are privileges to steward with faithfulness and purity. We can trust the Lord to do his work through us, but we must remain steadfast in our commitment to him (vv. 20-21).

The threefold instruction to "be strong," to be "courageous," and to "do the work," coupled with assurance to resist fear and discouragement in light of the Lord's presence (v. 20), follows the pattern of Moses's words to Joshua almost precisely (Deut 31:6-8; Josh 1:5-9). The commonality is significant because, like the temple, the promised land Joshua claimed was a step of renewal toward recapturing a designated place for God's presence similar to the garden of Eden. Now, the Chronicler reminds us that building the temple narrowed the focus even more by establishing a particular place for God to reside.

Interestingly, the same language appears in Hebrews:

> *Keep your life free from the love of money. Be satisfied with what you have, for he himself has said, I will never leave you or abandon you. Therefore, we may boldly say, The Lord is my helper; I will not be afraid; What can man do to me?* (Heb 13:5-6)

Why is this reference significant? How does avoiding material temptations within the new covenant relate to the temple narrative of Chronicles? The theme of Hebrews 13 is the common denominator because it, too, prioritizes the redemptive goal of returning to the realities of Eden. Hebrews 13:14 reads, "For we do not have an enduring city here; instead, we seek the one to come." In other words, the great goal behind the temple is the eternal city of God. Like Solomon, we should continue to be strong and courageous until the fullest expression of God's presence in Eden is fully restored.

The Sacrifices for the Temple Reorder Our Priorities
1 CHRONICLES 29:1-30

Having charged the people of Israel to accept Solomon, David then challenged them to sacrifice in order to fund the work of constructing the shrine. By doing so, he challenges postexilic Jews to step forward in faith again in order to fund the work of God. Far more than an ancient capital campaign, this section of the pericope inspires believers today in matters of giving and sacrifice. The basic reset that leaps off these pages is that our lives and possessions are to be spent building God's kingdom rather than our own.

The purpose behind the temple's construction, namely the glory of God rather than man, is also the motive behind all earthly generosity (v. 1). As with every good leader, David sought to be an example to the kingdom not only by preparing the treasury of Israel for the work but also by giving out of his personal abundance (vv. 2-5). All of these measures drive to a moment of decision and commitment with the question, "Now who will volunteer to consecrate himself to the LORD today?" It is worth noting that the king equated sacrificial offerings toward the temple with consecration before the Lord.

What God sought here was not the resources necessary to be successful but the heart of every Israelite citizen. One of the greater misunderstandings about financial stewardship is that those who receive benefit more than those who give. Without a doubt, the generosity of God's people is a means the Lord uses to bless others and build his kingdom. Even more significant though, is the profound pull of our possessions on our hearts. Jesus instructed,

> Don't store up for yourselves treasures on earth, where moth and
> rust destroy and where thieves break in and steal. But store up for
> yourselves treasures in heaven, where neither moth nor rust destroys,
> and where thieves don't break in and steal. For where your treasure is,
> there your heart will be also. (Matt 6:19-21)

Remarkably, Christ insists that our wealth does not follow our hearts. Quite the opposite—our hearts follow our money! Do you desire to be more kingdom minded? Do you want to be more passionate about God's work? The solution lies in your giving patterns.

Imagine how motivating the history lesson was to ancient Jews anxious to see God work among them as he had before. Similarly, God invites his children today to join him in expanding his kingdom. Reducing these verses to a model for a successful building campaign in a local church is a narrow mistake. For one thing, the closest equivalent to constructing the temple in our context is building the people of God. Scripture plainly says that those in Christ are now the temple of the living God (1 Cor 6:19-20). Sacrificial offerings aimed toward spreading the gospel and discipling the saints is the closer application of this text.

In addition, keeping your heart anchored to the kingdom is just as important when there are no buildings to build as it is when the church has a specific material need. Efforts to direct our hearts is not limited to a particular campaign. The example here is a model for reordering our priorities around becoming more like Christ. And what kind of example was Jesus to us regarding giving? While motivating the Corinthian church to give an offering that would relieve the poverty of the Jerusalem church, Paul appealed specifically to the sacrifice of God's Son:

> *For you know the grace of our Lord Jesus Christ: Though he was rich, for your sake he became poor, so that by his poverty you might become rich.* (2 Cor 8:9)

Even in their giving to erect a house for God, these early Israelites were pointing us to the ultimate Giver, who made himself a ransom for many (Mark 10:45). Their wholehearted sacrifice not only funded the work (1 Chr 29:6-9) but also captured the spirit of cheerful sacrifice that God desired (2 Cor 9:7). Despite our frequent resistance, sacrificial giving really is an act of worship.

As David rejoices with his people, it is interesting to observe that his praise is directed toward God rather than his citizenry (vv. 10-19). He acknowledges that all earthly treasures belong to the Lord (v. 11) and that he distributes them as he wills (v. 12). The whole exercise was, and is, humbling for all who are in a position to give back to God what is already his (v. 14). To think our sacrifices can bear eternal consequences despite our brief time on this earth is astounding (vv. 15-16). Optimism for the future abounded because the people's commitment did not stop short of their material possessions (vv. 18-21). The joyful pattern is just as instructive today as it was immediately after the exile.

Solomon's official coronation and the summary of David's life conclude the pericope (vv. 22-30). The new king's purpose will become clearer in the Chronicler's coming chapters, but as the recipient of God's eternal covenant faded off the scene, Babylon-weary believers must have felt more grateful than nostalgic. For those facing incredible challenges of their own, the record was a reminder that no matter what changed, how their circumstances evolved, or who led them, the kingdom work continued. Why? Because David, like all of us, was a minor character in God's redemptive story. And that is why we have hope for the future.

Sensing this, the apostle Peter declared,

> *Brothers and sisters, I can confidently speak to you about the patriarch David: He is both dead and buried, and his tomb is with us to this day. Since he was a prophet, he knew that God had sworn an oath to him to seat one of his descendants on his throne. Seeing what was to come, he spoke concerning the resurrection of the Messiah: He was not abandoned in Hades, and his flesh did not experience decay.*

> *God has raised this Jesus; we are all witnesses of this. Therefore, since he has been exalted to the right hand of God and has received from the Father the promised Holy Spirit, he has poured out what you both see and hear. For it was not David who ascended into the heavens, but he himself says:*
> *The Lord declared to my Lord, "Sit at my right hand until I make your enemies your footstool." Therefore let all the house of Israel know with certainty that God has made this Jesus, whom you crucified, both Lord and Messiah.* (Acts 2:29-36)

Through the temple we learn that God is determined to be among us again. Jesus became a temple of human flesh in order to restore the fellowship that was lost due to sin. And David served his purpose of pointing us to him, but David was *NOT him* (Acts 13:35-36).

Reflect and Discuss

1. Why was the temple a sacred structure for the Jews? What does it teach us about God's intentions for us?

2. How do the reigns of David and Solomon complement each other? How do they each point us to the work of Jesus on our behalf?

3. How does the emphasis on the Old Testament temple enhance and endear your appreciation for being the temple of the Holy Spirit under the new covenant?

4. What does the organization of the temple teach us about the new heaven and earth?

5. What does worship in the temple teach us about the quality, content, and focus of our worship in the church?

6. How does the concept of stewarding God's kingdom work for a generation motivate you to serve the Lord? Or how does it humble you as you serve?

7. What particular assignments or contributions do you believe God has called you to make in your faith community?

8. If our hearts follow our resources, how does that change your plan for generosity in the future?

9. How does David point us to Jesus through sacrificing his personal resources for the building of the temple?

10. What purpose do you believe God wants you to fulfill before you die?

The Path of Restoration

2 CHRONICLES 1–9

Main Idea: Using the reign of Solomon as his backdrop, the Chronicler seeks to inspire his audience with the glory of their past as they renewed their efforts to walk with God again. Today, these images compel Christians to greater faithfulness by painting a clear picture of Christ's future kingdom as well as a clear path of restoration to God when we stray.

I. **Our Greatest Struggle Is Pride (1:1-17).**
II. **Our Greatest Need Is God (2:1–5:14).**
III. **Our Greatest Hope Is God's Promise (6:1–7:11).**
IV. **Our Greatest Test Is Repentance (7:12-22).**
V. **Our Greatest Joy Is God's Kingdom (8:1–9:31).**

Robert Robinson lost his father when he was just a boy. Life in England was tough during the eighteenth century, and his mother realized she could not support her son by herself. The now single mother's solution was to send Robert to London for training to be a barber. While he was there, Robinson became a Christian through the ministry of George Whitefield and dedicated himself to gospel ministry. At the age of twenty-five, he became the pastor of a prestigious church in Cambridge. As his fame spread, his future seemed unlimited.

According to some sources, at the peak of his success, Robinson disqualified himself from ministry due to immorality. His fire of influence burned out just as quickly as it had been set aflame. Years later, while traveling by stagecoach, the former minister found himself seated by a woman reading intently from a book. Soon, she turned to him and asked his opinion on the passage she was reading. His eyes focused on the first few lines,

> Come, Thou Fount of every blessing
> Tune my heart to sing Thy grace;
> Streams of mercy, never ceasing,
> Call for songs of loudest praise.

After reading the words, Robinson looked away and changed the subject. After the woman pressed him for a response, tears welled up in his eyes as he said, "Madam, I am the poor unhappy man who wrote that hymn years ago, and I would give a thousand worlds if I had them to enjoy the feelings I had then." Ironically, the same hymn seemed to capture the conundrum of Robinson's soul with the words,

> Prone to wander, Lord, I feel it,
> Prone to leave the God I love;
> Here's my heart, O take and seal it,
> Seal it for Thy courts above. (Charles Swindoll, *Simple Faith*,
>   166–67)

Most of us can relate to the tragedy of leaving the God we love. Finding our way back to God requires a new vision for who he is and what he desires to do in our lives. As the postexilic community prepared to reinhabit the land of promise, the Chronicler unveils some of the obstacles that could hinder their complete restoration. These matters of the heart still guide believers today when we stray from the Lord.

Like David's before him, most of Solomon's fallibilities disappear from the Chronicler's history, not because of an effort to conceal them but in order to reveal a vision for the future messianic age. In fact, his resume here is flawless, with no mention of the lingering effect caused by his foreign wives and their idolatry. Neither do we find admission that the nation split during the subsequent reign of Rehoboam as a direct result of God's determination to pry most of the kingdom away from Solomon's hand due to his wayward heart (1 Kgs 11:9-13).

Rather than assume the Chronicler had sinister motives, however, we should read 2 Chronicles with the full realization that Jews emerging underneath the thumb of Persian oppression were not only familiar with these scandals, but they had likely recounted them repeatedly, along with others, as they tried to make sense of God's heavy hand against them. What they were searching for, instead, were reasons to believe that God still had a future for them. As we often do, they needed reassurance that their sin did not exceed God's grace. Thus, Israel's biographer sought to rekindle their hope around the Davidic covenant and all of its promised inevitabilities.

By painting with a broad brush, the opening chapters of 2 Chronicles present Solomon as a messianic figure whose kingdom is a foretaste of the new heaven and earth. Magnifying the best ingredients of his rule was a means to inspire the rebirth of the Jewish nation. Longman and Dillard explain:

> This idealization of the reigns of David and Solomon could be dismissed as a kind of glorification of the "good old days." Yet, when coupled with the Chronicler's emphasis on God's promise to David of an enduring dynasty (1 Chr 17:11-14; 2 Chr 13:5,8; 21:7; 23:3), the Chronicler's treatment of David and Solomon reflects a "messianic historiography." David and Solomon in Chronicles are not just the David and Solomon who were, but the David and Solomon of the Chronicler's eschatological hope. At a time when Israel was subject to the Persians, the Chronicler still cherished hopes of a restoration of Davidic rule, and he describes the glorious rule of David and Solomon in the past in terms of his hope for the future. (*Introduction*, 197)

It might be best, therefore, to see Solomon's throne in its immediate context as a model of what to reach for. Yet for believers in the present age, his kingdom is an archetype of what is to come during the messianic age.

Even Solomon seemed to grasp the foreshadowing potential of the Davidic dynasty. In Psalm 72, even as he prayed for himself, Solomon's aim was to depict what was ahead. God's justice and righteousness were certainly characteristic for much of his time at the helm of Israel but not for its entirety (Ps 72:1-4). Knowing that eternality is a central marker of God's promised kingdom, Solomon petitioned for an eternal ruler who would far exceed his decades on the throne (Ps 72:5-7). The vastness of his kingdom is well documented in this pericope, but Solomon seems to recognize the universal reign of the Messiah's kingdom (Ps 72:8-11) along with the compassion, abundance, and glory it will bring (Ps 72:12-20) (Hunter and Wellum, *Christ from Beginning to End*, 163–68).

One subtle difference between the records of 1 Chronicles and 2 Chronicles seems to be a shift from bolstering Jewish confidence in God's covenantal commitment to helping the nation avoid similar heartache and consequences for rebellion in the future. Though the two books were a single account historically, the progression of the Chronicler's message seems to shift from a consoling tone to one that is more instructive. What lessons did the Jews need to learn after seventy years of captivity? How could they find their way back to God? Better still, what realizations will lead us back to the Lord after backsliding?

Our Greatest Struggle Is Pride
2 CHRONICLES 1:1-17

Just as we saw the complementary nature of David's preparation and Solomon's ascension to the throne previously, the link between the two unfolds further in this pericope as the logical progression of the Davidic hope (v. 1). Apart from Solomon, David's work would have been left undone. And without David, Solomon's rise and success most assuredly would not have happened. The two function together as a declaration that God is winning the war against the serpent as they firmly establish the throne that the Messiah will one day occupy. Ironically, the Chronicler's history devotes more time and space to the reigns of David and Solomon than to any other kings in Judah, yet the congruence between their leadership subtly indicates that both are but minor characters in the divine drama that is unfolding.

With the tabernacle and bronze altar still in Gibeon, Solomon convened a gathering of Israel's commanders and judges, along with each family head (vv. 2-3). The ark's presence in Jerusalem further clarified the need for the temple as means to unify the cultic experience of the nation (vv. 4-5). Solomon's eagerness to inquire of the Lord and sacrifice burnt offerings (as many as a thousand) was a strong indicator of his resolute commitment to seek the Lord on behalf of the nation (v. 6). Again, we see continuity as the new king follows the pattern set forth by his father David (1 Chr 29:21).

For Jews anxious to begin again in a city plundered and ravaged as a casualty of exile, this lesson in humility was essential for their restoration and healing. Recounting their illustrious past was not a call to pull themselves up by the bootstraps but to humble themselves before God in a way that gave rise to their previous success. Israel did not need another David or another Solomon. Instead, the call to rebuild demanded an increased dependence on God's wisdom and leadership over them.

Perhaps the greatest turning point in the young king's life came during his encounter with the Lord through a dream while at Gibeon (vv. 7-12). When given the opportunity to ask anything of the Lord, Solomon anchored his future to the plan of God rather than his own impulses or desires. His acknowledgment of God's faithful love to David (v. 8) demonstrates his grasp of the Davidic kingdom concept (1 Chr 17:11-14). Likewise, his reference to a people more numerous than the dust of the earth harks back to the Abrahamic promise

(Gen 13:16) while inextricably linking the two covenants (2 Chr 1:9). Solomon not only had a mental grasp of these assurances but also saw his reign as a divine mandate fulfilling them.

As is the case with every young believer, owning the faith inherited from his father was key for Solomon. Most surprising, by far, was his overwhelming humility. Sensing his need for wisdom in order to lead a multitude of God's people (v. 10), Solomon forgoes the typical ambitions of youth in exchange for a selfless request. The Lord responds by answering his humility with exaltation, as evidenced by granting both wisdom and knowledge, but also adding the benefit of riches, wealth, and glory like none who came before him (vv. 11-12). Here we have the first inkling that Solomon's kingdom will have a messianic flair primarily because he anticipates Jesus's measure of true greatness as well as because of his rise to David's throne.

The apostle Paul explains that though Christ was

> *existing in the form of God,*
> *did not consider equality with God*
> *as something to be exploited.*
> *Instead he emptied himself*
> *by assuming the form of a servant,*
> *taking on the likeness of humanity.*
> *And when he had come as a man,*
> *he humbled himself by becoming obedient*
> *to the point of death—*
> *even to death on a cross.*
> *For this reason God highly exalted him*
> *and gave him the name*
> *that is above every name,*
> *so that at the name of Jesus*
> *every knee will bow—*
> *in heaven and on earth*
> *and under the earth—*
> *and every tongue will confess*
> *that Jesus Christ is Lord,*
> *to the glory of God the Father.* (Phil 2:6-11)

Sometimes we falsely assume that Jesus's exaltation was a guaranteed gift because of *who* he was, but Scripture emphasizes it was *what* he did that lifted his name above all others. He, like Solomon, yielded to the wisdom of the heavenly Father by resigning himself to a plan and agenda that were not his own.

Need further proof? Consider the last of Jesus's three temptations in the wilderness. Scripture says that after taking the Savior to a high mountain and showing him the kingdoms of this world, the devil hissed, "I will give you all these things if you will fall down and worship me" (Matt 4:8-9). No correction follows the serpent's proposition because he is indeed "the god of this age" (2 Cor 4:4) and "the ruler of the power of the air" (Eph 2:2). The apostle John later admitted, "[T]he whole world is under the sway of the evil one" (1 John 5:19). Those kingdoms were truly Satan's to give, and he was willing to lose them as long as Jesus did not sacrifice himself for sinners. Yet rather than pursue immediate glory for the sake of his name, Christ humbled himself even to the point of dying on a cross. And that is precisely why God the Father exalted him as the forever King over the new heaven and earth.

Likewise, Solomon's humility and the significant reign that followed were thoroughly connected to each other. Consequently, the rulership of Solomon typifies the kingdom of Christ because he came into the kingdom through the doorway of humility as Jesus would also. Because of God's raising him in honor, Solomon left Gibeon and reigned over Israel with a glory that will not be known again until Christ assumes the same seat in Zion. A list of his great wealth helps us grasp the breadth of Solomon's success and influence as king (vv. 14-17). With gold and silver as common as stones in Jerusalem, it's not difficult to envision how his kingdom foreshadows a place where we will walk on streets of gold (Rev 21:18-21).

And what was the lesson for the postexilic community here? Better still, what does this text communicate to contemporary saints? After years of, quite literally, being held captive by their sins, the Chronicler paints a vision for the future rooted in the posture of their past rather than its personalities. Even before rebuilding the temple, he makes plain that receiving the provisions of the Lord is no substitute for submitting to his plan. God was eager to give grace to the humble after the exile but more determined than ever to resist the proud (Jas 4:6). In contrast to their rebellious past, the beginning of Solomon's reign was a vivid portrayal to returning exiles of how God can and will meet all of their needs if they will set their hearts on seeking his kingdom first (Matt 6:33).

The same is true for us. Receiving all that God has for us requires living with open hands so God can place in or take out as he sees fit.

When we seek exaltation, God will humble us. But when we yield ourselves to his agenda, the Lord is sure to lift us up (Matt 23:12). Our entrance into the kingdom of God is through the doorway of trusting God's wisdom rather than our own. Salvation is impossible apart from walking the narrow road of humility.

> *Where is the one who is wise? Where is the teacher of the law? Where is the debater of this age? Hasn't God made the world's wisdom foolish? For since, in God's wisdom, the world did not know God through wisdom, God was pleased to save those who believe through the foolishness of what is preached. For the Jews ask for signs and the Greeks seek wisdom, but we preach Christ crucified, a stumbling block to the Jews and foolishness to the Gentiles. Yet to those who are called, both Jews and Greeks, Christ is the power of God and the wisdom of God, because God's foolishness is wiser than human wisdom, and God's weakness is stronger than human strength.* (1 Cor 1:20-25)

Likewise, after we come to know Christ, God calls us to die daily to ourselves as we yield in humility to God's wisdom for our path. We are to wear our humility like a garment (Col 3:12) and to walk in our humility with full dependence on our Savior (Eph 4:1-2). Stated simply, we should humbly crave divine wisdom like a young king desperate before God due to his acknowledged inadequacies.

Our Greatest Need Is God
2 CHRONICLES 2:1–5:14

With God's wisdom leading him, Solomon begins construction on the temple (2:1-2). For the Israelites, the temple was a physical sign of Yahweh's presence among them, though the Lord's dwelling was not without holy responsibilities. In fact, a defining measurement of each king in Israel was God's inhabitation of the temple or lack thereof (Thompson, *1, 2 Chronicles*, 202). The sin of idolatry is a major emphasis throughout the book. During the time of restoration, it's almost as if the single aim of the record were to prevent another catastrophic judgment like the exile. The Chronicler is subtly admonishing the staggering nation not to repeat the sins of the past. Whereas 1 Chronicles seeks to reassure the struggling nation that God is not finished with them, 2 Chronicles is a historical lesson about how to avoid the transgressions that led to their downfall. Having God in their midst again was by far the greatest need for the stumbling nation anxious to steady themselves.

Also of note is Solomon's building, like his father David, a royal palace for himself while constructing the temple complex. With both of these structures in Jerusalem, the dynasty of David and God's rule intertwined to the point of being indistinguishable. The Chronicler's subtle point seems to be that the renewal of the Davidic hope was still possible even as the capital city of the kingdom lay in ruins (Boda, *1–2 Chronicles*, 239).

Panning out even further, the marriage between the divine and human leadership of Israel during Solomon's reign was never repeated after the Persian period. In fact, much the opposite, the human leadership of the chosen nation seemed to be more at odds with their God than in cooperation with him, so much so that when Jesus entered the temple court, he overturned tables as he chastised the money changers (Matt 21:12-13). What God intended as a house of prayer had become nothing more than a den of thieves! Yet the second coming of Christ will mark a union that Israel has not known since the days of Solomon, for, through his incarnation, the promised Son of David took on human flesh eternally. Finally, the divine and human leadership of the kingdom will function in intricate harmony once again, indistinguishable for ages to come.

Key to our understanding of the temple's significance is grasping the profound role it played in reflecting who God is to the people of Israel. Solomon's ambition to build a magnificent structure was born out of his deep appreciation for the superiority and glory of Yahweh. Stated simply, the temple had to be great because God is great (2:5-10). The skill of the workers (vv. 7,13-14), the tremendous resources set aside (vv. 8-9), and the location of the shrine (3:1; 1 Chr 21:28–22:1) were indicative of the glory Yahweh deserved, the wealth he possessed, and the holiness he exuded. Even the inclusion of the Gentiles (2:3), a theme Solomon will come back to (9:1-12), underscores the scope of God's redemptive plan to bring salvation to Jew and Gentile alike.

Ultimately, King Hiram of Tyre was not only drawn to the work of the temple (2:13-16) but also to the Lord of the temple (v. 12). The same phenomenon occurred when Jesus was born in Bethlehem. In the Gospel of Matthew we read,

> *After Jesus was born in Bethlehem of Judea in the days of King Herod, wise men from the east arrived in Jerusalem, saying, "Where is he who*

has been born king of the Jews? For we saw his star at its rising and have come to worship him. " (Matt 2:1-2)

Because Jesus replaced the temple as the place to meet God, Gentiles from the east were drawn to him at his birth in a way that was similar to Hiram's compulsion to assist with the delivery of the first temple. When Jesus tabernacles with humanity in the new heaven and earth, those outside Israel will once again long to walk in the presence of Zion's true King (Rev 21:24). The image is in keeping with Abraham's ambition to bless all the families of the earth (Gen 12:3) and the apostles' ministry to those not born of Jewish descent (Gal 3:8). The emergence of the temple advanced the divine agenda significantly. The Lord is preparing the way for all people to enjoy his presence.

Before understanding more of the broader significance of the holy sanctuary, we should do the hard work of appreciating the finer details of its construction. Placing the house on Mount Moriah establishes meeting God on the basis of blood sacrifice (3:1). The level of specificity here was undoubtedly meant as a guide for the postexilic community as they rebuilt the temple, in particular the dimensions of the main hall, the portico, and the most holy place (vv. 2-3,8). True to the need of starting over and realizing how few people had actually seen the inner parts of the temple, the Chronicler is more specific than the Kings record by stating that the ceiling beams, doorframes, walls, doors, and carved cherubim were covered with gold (v. 7) (Pratt, *1 & 2 Chronicles*, 309).

Two gold overlaid cherubim spanned the entire length of the most holy place, symbolically protecting the ark of God (3:10-13). Likewise, the veil separating the holy place also pictured these angelic servants keeping watch over the presence of God (v. 14). Solomon named the two pillars that bore the weight of the porch Jachin and Boaz, the former meaning "he is the one who establishes" and the latter "in him is strength" (Thompson, *1, 2 Chronicles*, 219).

The bronze altar was for sacrificing burnt offerings (4:1). The metal basin was for the priests to wash themselves before performing their duties (vv. 2-5). Solomon placed ten smaller water basins reserved for washing sacrificial animals (v. 6). Ten golden menorahs provided light in the temple (v. 7), ten tables to the right and left held one hundred bowls containing coals used to burn incense (vv. 7-8). Smaller, practical utensils were also necessary before Hiram completed his work (v. 11). A detailed inventory lauded the contribution of the friendly Gentile to the north (vv. 12-18). They included pails to hold ashes off the altar, shovels, and bowls to receive blood sacrifices. Verses 19-22 also outline previously mentioned items, with the addition of a few new ones. A list like this would have been invaluable for the Jews as they resumed temple life after their Babylonian captivity.

Finally, Solomon completed the temple, doing so with so much abundance that many of the treasures David prepared were stored within the treasury of the shrine (5:1). Next, he consolidated the ministries of the ark and the tent of meeting by bringing the former out of its temporary Jerusalem tent and the latter up from Gibeon (vv. 2-5). Having learned from David's fatal blunder (1 Chr 13:9-10), the poles carrying the ark were so long they protruded from beneath the curtain of the most holy place (5:9) once it was situated (vv. 6-8). All that remained in the ark at this point were the tablets on which Moses wrote the Ten Commandments (v. 10).

As the people began to praise God with instruments and singing, a cloud filled the temple as the glory of the Lord fell on the place (5:11-14). This, too, was reminiscent of Sinai, where God's presence hovered over the mountain within a thick cloud (Exod 20:21). Likewise, the scene anticipates the glory of the incarnation as revealed at the transfiguration. When the full glory of Jesus came bursting forth, soon a bright cloud covered Peter, James, and John as the voice of God thundered, "This is my beloved Son, with whom I am well pleased. Listen to him!" (Matt 17:5; Luke 9:34-35). What are we to make of all these connecting images?

For Jews eager to rebuild their covenant relationship with God, the glory of God in the temple had long since departed due to their exile in a foreign land (Ezek 10:18-19; 11:22-23). Through the Chronicler's efforts the text looks back at what was in the past in order to inspire the people in the present. At the same time, the glory of the second temple could not rival what the people had previously known. Therefore, the history lesson also foreshadows what was in the future when the Word becomes flesh in order to reveal the glory of God (John 1:14). Someone greater than Solomon was coming (Matt 12:42), and the temple was a mere temporary means to point to him.

Because the presence of God is also what made the garden of Eden an earthly paradise, we should also see Solomon's temple as significant progress in the ongoing effort to restore humanity once and for all. While the temple blueprints found in chapters 4 and 5 are not the most inspirational reading, the details therein reveal moving realities that signal a reconstruction of the Edenic existence. Though a temporary solution, the rise of the temple edifice demarcates significant movement in Israel's history indicating the fuller aim of God's plans for his people. The corresponding details between the garden of Eden and the temple structure are both heartening and breathtaking.

Gordon Wenham's work is extremely helpful when elucidating these textual allusions ("Sanctuary Symbolism"). Consider, for example, that the temple was like the garden because it was a designated place that housed the presence of God (2 Chr 3:3-4,8; 5:7; Gen 3:8). The cherubim functioned as guards over the floor plan, much as they did at the east of the garden (2 Chr 3:7,10-14; Gen 3:24). Also, the abundance of gold overlaying the portico, the inner temple, and the most holy place (3:5-10), along with its adornment of precious stones (3:6), harked back to the wealth of God's initial cosmic temple (Gen 2:11-12). Ten menorahs on each side of the sanctuary indicated that God would one day again provide access to the tree of life (4:7-8; Gen 2:9). Finally, the bronze altar positioned in front of the temple (4:1) served as reminder of the need for a sacrificial covering much like Adam and Eve received when the Lord covered them with coats of skins long ago (Gen 3:20).

The images of Eden remind us of what was lost—namely, humanity's freedom to enjoy God's presence. Though God banished Adam and Eve from the garden so that, in their sins, they could not eat from the tree of life (Gen 3:22-23), the temple suggested that their exile, along with ours, would not last forever. The view from the portico of God's house also casts our eyes forward to the full restoration of eternal life in the presence of God. When Christ sits on the throne of his father David, we will once again have access to the tree of life without the afflictions of the curse (Rev 22:2-3a). Most importantly, though, the Lamb will be with us, even as he walked in the garden with the first man and woman, and we will see his face (Rev 22:3b-4).

The lesson for us today is that Christ is our greatest reward. What we need, more than any blessing God gives, is God himself. The goal of our existence is to count all things as loss so that we might gain him and be found in him, being resurrected to walk in newness of life (Phil 3:7-11). This is why we crave an encounter with the Almighty. This is why we are drawn to the light of his goodness. And this is why the cry of every human heart is to be unashamed in his presence. God has made us in his image not only so that we will reflect his glory but also so that we will rest in his presence.

Our Greatest Hope Is God's Promise
2 CHRONICLES 6:1–7:11

The theme of God's faithfulness to his people emerges as Solomon dedicates the temple by tying its completion back to the Davidic covenant. Because of the tabernacle, God was in the midst of his people throughout their wanderings in the desert by means of a dark cloud (6:1; cf. Exod 20:21; Deut 4:11; 5:22). Now, because of the Lord's directive, Solomon built an exalted complex for Yahweh's inhabitation (6:2; 1 Chr 17:12). The realization of the temple was a fulfilment of God's promise to build the house of David (6:3). Despite his previous resistance to a particular place or person, the Lord chose Jerusalem and David as the means to deliver his eternal throne (vv. 4-11). These verses reminded the postexilic community that God had done all that he promised despite their generational rebellion. These words were like a healing balm for every Jew who feared that God's mercy had run out.

Likewise, today we do well to realize that God's faithfulness to us is not diminished by our sinfulness either. The chosen son of David will preside over God's eternal kingdom, keeping every promise he has made to his own. No one, including ourselves, can prevent the eternal life he bestows; no one can snatch us from the hand of our faithful God (John 10:28-29). And though we often stumble in our walk, reassurances like these remind us that God is anxious to blot out our sins and remember them no more (Isa 43:25). Even if we doubt God's commitment to us, we should rest knowing of his steadfast determination to accomplish all that he promised King David.

Through Solomon's dedicatory prayer, we learn much about the nation's activities at the temple beyond offering sacrifices. Again, this recollection was the Chronicler's effort to take the people back to where their covenantal reality was born in order to demonstrate the faithfulness of God and the way back to him after years of chastening. The prayer Solomon offers on behalf of the people is the longest petition in all of Scripture. With arms outstretched, he stood on a temporary platform calling out to God. Note that he comes before the Lord in the context of Israel's covenantal relationship. Solomon fully acknowledges God's faithfulness to keep his promises even as he pleads with the Lord to continue doing so (6:14-17).

Next, Israel's wise king acknowledges the omnipresence of Yahweh, expressing both his immanence and transcendence (6:18). The notion

that God would live on earth among human beings is nearly unimagi-
nable yet true nonetheless. The Lord's willingness to be present in no
way diminishes the reality that the vastness of creation cannot contain
the God who is outside of time and space (Acts 7:47-50; 17:24-25). Lest
we think the totality of the prayer is petition only, sprinkled throughout
Solomon's words are numerous other expressions of God's attributes,
including his uniqueness (6:14), transcendence (v. 18), infinity (v. 18),
justice (v. 23), forgiveness (vv. 25,27), omniscience (v. 30), grace (v. 33),
and mercy (vv. 38-39) (MacDonald, *Believer's Bible Commentary*, 408).

The thrust of the entire prayer is a plea for God to hear and respond
to his people when they seek him at the temple (6:19-21). What follows
are the various petitions that were common and would have been especially applicable to those previously exiled. The centrality of God's house
is easy to appreciate due to the breadth of these guidelines, which con-
solidate practices that previously took place at the tabernacle and other
holy places to one central location. Intended to be a house of prayer,
the temple was a place to call out to God when offering oaths (6:24-25),
preparing to go out to battle their enemies (vv. 34-35), and seeking forgiveness of sin that results in various consequences, including military
defeat (vv. 24-25), drought (vv. 26-27), famine, and pestilence (vv. 28-
31). Again, Gentile inclusion emerges as a substantive theme, primarily
so that the fame of Yahweh will spread (vv. 32-33).

Perhaps most gripping is the detailed description of prayer and
repentance in the event the nation is exiled to a foreign land due to
their sin (6:36-39). In what could have been a headline story in the
Jerusalem Gazette, the Chronicler reminds them of Solomon's prayer for
the Lord to be so gracious as to hear his people despite their worst-case
scenario, a possibility that had played out in full after 586 BC. Can you
imagine how encouraging this reminder would have been to a citizenry
jaded by their own transgressions? This testimony was a clear call to trust
the Lord to answer Solomon's prayer from long ago. The king, perhaps
anticipating the nation's frailty, essentially pleaded for God's gracious
forgiveness no matter what was ahead. Now was the time to lean into
God's faithfulness.

Believers today must walk a similar path. Despite the grief our sins
cause or the consequences we must endure, we should rest knowing
that God "is faithful and righteous to forgive us our sins and to cleanse
us from all unrighteousness" (1 John 1:9). The gospel reminds us that
we have a Savior who delights in showing mercy by pardoning sins and

forgiving iniquities, even to the point of casting them into the depths of the sea (Mic 7:18-19). God is faithful to us though we often stray from him.

One fundamental difference, however, is that disciples of Christ do not need to pray at or toward the temple, or even the church for that matter, in order to be heard by the Lord. Indeed, Jesus desires for his house to be a place of prayer (Matt 21:13), but within the progression of redemptive history, we know that, because Christ is the new temple of God (John 2:19-21), we should direct our prayers to him rather than toward a geographical location. Stated differently, we pray to the Father through the Son (1 Tim 2:5). Furthermore, in Christ the church is being knit together as a spiritual house that functions as the true sanctuary of God (1 Pet 2:4-5). With the Spirit of Christ within us, every born-again believer is the house of God. Thus, becoming a house of prayer is not determined by what we do at church but how we communicate with God each day.

Finally, Solomon concludes by asking God to hear his prayer, to assume his resting place, and to cover his priests with grace and joy (6:40-42). As argued previously (see 1 Chr 13–16), the image of God's resting place should be understood as a throne. The prophet Isaiah foresaw the Messiah's enthronement: "The nations will look to him for guidance, and his resting place will be glorious" (Isa 11:10). Thus, Solomon petitions Yahweh to begin his active reign over the nation. We, too, can join in on this appeal, longing for the Lord to faithfully lead us in light of who he is and what he promised his servant David.

As chapter 7 unfolds, the Lord finally responds to Solomon's prayer by consuming the sacrifices offered and saturating the temple with his glory (7:1), so much so that the priests could not enter the building (v. 2). The pattern here follows the dedication of the tabernacle years before it. For the second time we read of the peoples' awareness of and deep awe over the goodness of God (7:3; cf. 5:13-14). Their response teaches us a subtle, often neglected indicator of genuine worship—namely, a deep sense of who God is and how great he is. Sadly, the modern church often jettisons God-centered worship in order to promote the consumerism of felt needs and self-love.

The celebratory scene that follows is an expression of sincere thanksgiving marked by elaborate sacrifices and praise (7:4-7). The people came for the Festival of Shelters, a time to commemorate God's provision during the forty-year wilderness wandering, only to see God supply their greatest need, his presence, in a more permanent way. From the entrance of Hamath in the north to the Brook of Egypt in the far south (7:8-10), or stated plainly, from top to bottom, the entire nation was abuzz over the temple's completion. Much as in the messianic age he foreshadowed, Solomon accomplished all God put in his heart for the kingdom (7:11). The Lord was, and is, faithful to bless the work we do for him.

Our Greatest Test Is Repentance
2 CHRONICLES 7:12-22

Indicating God's previous acceptance of the temple was a persuasive move to build consensus for rebuilding the temple as the people returned from Babylon (v. 12). With Yahweh's support clear, there was little room for the people to resist such a divine initiative (Pratt, *1 & 2 Chronicles*, 341). By recalling God's response to Solomon's prayer, this history lesson offered the Jews returning to Jerusalem much more than a simple assurance that God would answer them if they called out to him in humility and faith. These words offered both an explanation for the exile and a road map to rise from its ashes. The clarity with which God lays out the cause-and-effect reality of Israel's use of the temple is intended as a gentle admonition not to repeat the mistakes of the past due to their certain consequences.

Through three hypotheticals ("If I shut the sky"; "if I command the grasshopper"; "if I send pestilence") the Chronicler voices God's determination to deal with the sins of his people by any means he deems necessary (v. 13). The solution offered to these extreme measures constitutes what is without question the most recognizable verse in the entire chronicle (v. 14). Because of its popularity, the commands for Israel to humble themselves, pray, seek God's face, and turn from their wicked ways are often quoted out of context, usually as a formula for any nation to experience national revival. And while it would be just like the Lord to bring healing to the people of any country who collectively seek him and turn from their transgressions (Ps 33:12), the closer application is for the people of God ("my people") who turn back to him. The church, not a geopolitical government, holds this sacred promise in trust.

We should also recognize that this is a specific answer to a particular prayer offered by Israel's king. At its heart, this pledge is about maintaining God's presence in the temple for generations to come. For the returning exiles, it was a commentary on their past failure as well as an invitation to renewal. If only they had repented sooner, the devastation of their sin could have been avoided. But then, with refreshing simplicity, they were reminded to stay humble, to keep praying and seeking God's face, and to continue turning away from their wickedness because of the surety that the Lord would remain attentive to them (v. 15) at all times (v. 16).

The opposite was also true. If they resolved to be stiff-necked and idolatrous (v. 19), God would undertake to uproot them, remove his presence (v. 20), and defame the temple (v. 21) in such a way that the surrounding nations would know of Israel's idolatry (v. 22). For the Jews, these guarantees and warnings were like headlines from their local news outlets. The record described with painful accuracy what had been even as it inspired for what could be. The greatest test that lay before them was not the numerous construction projects required to rebuild their beloved city but the responsibility to own their wrongdoing in order to turn away from it.

Believers today should receive the admonitions of the pericope as both positive and negative. Williamson captures the immediacy of these promises in both directions:

> It can hardly be doubted that the intention behind this is fully kerygmatic; that is to say, there is an appeal here to the Chronicler's own readers to respond in like manner, for much of what follows is then designed to illustrate that no circumstances are too formidable to prevent God's immediate, direct and, if necessary, miraculous move to fulfil his promise. (*1 and 2 Chronicles*, 225)

God is eager to hear, forgive, and heal, but we must not fail to repent when we stray. Yet the Lord likewise uproots our hedonistic comforts, often by withdrawing his presence from us and unleashing the full consequences of our actions. Christians should be quick to repent lest the disciplinary hand of our heavenly Father come against us (Heb 12:5-11). Affirming salvation by grace through faith does not negate or dichotomize the importance of holy living. The severe outcomes of waywardness are not contrary to the grace of God but expressions of it. Even to the point of death, God loves his children too much to leave them unscathed in their carnality (1 John 5:16-17).

Corporately, calling the church back to her first love ought to be a regular occurrence. The healing God promised the Jews manifests today as the bride of Christ avoids the trappings of legalism on the one hand and antinomianism on the other, serving instead with humility and holiness. Healthy churches are the surest sign God's people take repentance seriously. While we pray that the fear of the Lord would reverberate through the halls of government, the awakening a nation needs must begin in the pulpits and pews of churches, not in the capital. Only then will the light of Christianity shine brightly into the darkness of broken political systems.

Our Greatest Joy Is God's Kingdom
2 CHRONICLES 8:1–9:31

The remaining chapters devoted to Solomon's reign recall his continued success and prosperity. With unrivaled power and wealth, the king's sustained commitment to worship and his continual use of wisdom paint a picture of the life God is preparing for his people. In the world of the text, the Chronicler is calling the people back to the life God intended for them to enjoy. For us, these glimpses are powerful shadows of the coming kingdom Christ will enjoy after claiming the seat of his father David. These details offer an appendix to the temple narrative in order to solidify the breadth and strength of Solomon's territory, revealing the comprehensiveness of our future when we rule over the earth on behalf of our Savior (Rev 22:5).

Possessing Hiram's gifted cities within the land of Galilee is but the end of a longer story in light of 1 Kings 9:10-14 (2 Chr 8:1-2). Apparently, Solomon awarded this territory to the king of Tyre in light of his generous supplies for building the temple and royal palace, but, perceiving them to have no value, his Gentile friend returned them. Rather than receive them back as an insult, Solomon built something out of what others perceived to be nothing.

As the only record of Solomon's conquests, 8:3-6 further establishes the continued prosperity of the nation. With Hamath-zobah nearly three hundred miles north of Jerusalem, Tadmor 150 miles northeast of Damascus, the region of Beth-horon ten miles northwest of Jerusalem, and Baalath to the west in the territory of Dan (Merrill, *2 Chronicles,* 626), Israel's king secured a major trade route for commercial success as well as fortified cities that guaranteed a strong defense. Though not mentioned here, his boundary also extended to Hazor, Megiddo, and Gezer (1 Kgs 9:15).

Furthermore, Solomon's friendly partnership with Hiram resulted in Israel's expanded wealth again (8:17-18). With access to the Red Sea, all the wise king needed was ships for commerce. Owning cargo vessels with no harbor meant that Hiram was eager to share his fleet in order to gain access to the Arabian Peninsula. In whatever he desired to build or accomplish, Solomon's kingdom flourished. Forced Gentile labor, while not part of God's design, indicated the abundance and vigor of Israel during the early days of their existence (vv. 7-10).

Even in Solomon's mistakes we discover God's provision for him. Having already understood the reasons the Chronicler does not dwell on the shortcomings of Judah's leadership, here we learn of his diplomatic marriage to a daughter of Pharaoh (8:11). The point, however, is less about the king's apparent contradictions and more about his great respect for the presence of God. Fearful that his unbelieving wife would defile the temple area, Solomon builds her a house of her own that is farther away. Furthermore, the arrangement denotes that Israel's rise in status placed Solomon on equal footing with the world's strongest leaders of the day.

Moving beyond the strength of the kingdom to the joy of the same, 8:12-15 illustrates this son of David's strict observance of Israel's ceremonial laws (cf. Lev 23; Num 28–29). While maintaining the Levitical divisions laid down by his father, Solomon offered sacrifices commemorating the Hebrews' hasty exit from Egypt (Festival of Unleavened Bread), God's provision for the people (Festival of Weeks), and their years roaming in the wilderness (Festival of Shelters) (8:13). These cultic expressions portrayed the harmony between God and his people that postexilic Jews would have craved.

In all these accomplishments we realize that Solomon not only completed his work on the temple but also all that he set his heart to do (8:16). Again, the Chronicler sought to inspire his readers to reclaim what was lost in the devastation of captivity. Beyond the glory of rebuilding their sacred traditions, though, was the renewal of Israel's covenantal expectation that God would not fail to preserve the eternal dynasty associated with the house of David (7:17-18). Despite the interruption caused by Israel's unfaithfulness, the messianic fulfillment of God's promise was unshaken.

Modern believers also benefit from the vision cast through the eyes of Solomon's empire when we accept it as the firstfruits for what is ahead. Certainly, the fullest harvest of all that God has planned for his people will be greater than any achievement Solomon enjoyed, but it will not be any less than what Solomon attained. Jesus, while teaching us about the futility of worry, went so far as to say,

> *Observe how the wildflowers of the field grow: They don't labor or spin thread. Yet I tell you that not even Solomon in all his splendor was adorned like one of these.* (Matt 6:28-29)

If the glory of lilies God causes to grow in the countryside exceeds the regal wonder of Solomon's attire, can you imagine how magnificently the place he is preparing for us will surpass any accomplishment we have ever known?

In addition to his wealth and power, the fame of Solomon also spread as a shadow of the nations coming to Christ. By carefully weaving into the narrative the king's famous meeting with the queen of Sheba (9:1), the writer again typifies the coming messianic reign. Hearing the wisdom of God's king (v. 2) and observing the glory of his kingdom (v. 3) left the Gentile leader from modern-day Yemen breathless (vv. 3-4). The whole scene is an *a fortiori* argument as the text entices us to marvel over the grandeur of Israel at its peak, knowing that what is coming exceeds it in every way. For the postexilic community that did not live through the reign of Solomon, this remembrance was likely intended inspiration for the task of rebuilding. Believers today should marvel over our inability to grasp the depth, wisdom, and knowledge that drives God's unsearchable judgments, which include Jew and Gentile alike (Rom 11:33-36).

Overwhelmed by what she saw and experienced, the Queen of Sheba's unbelief gave way to praising Yahweh for his goodness (9:5-8). Despite her limited exposure, this woman celebrated the eternal reality of justice and righteousness due to the Davidic covenant (v. 8). As a result, she presented Solomon treasures he used to build walkways within the temple complex (vv. 9-11). For those living during a time when Israel's glory had long since departed, the Chronicler's memory of this queen was a reminder that Jerusalem would not only rise again but also be a blessing to the Gentiles. Specifically, the text says that despite the gifts she brought, Solomon gave more in return to the Queen of Sheba than she ever sacrificed for him (v. 12). Christians today experience similar provision by seeking first the kingdom of God (Matt 6:28-33).

During this season, Solomon's wealth was unrivaled (9:13-21), his wisdom unmatched (vv. 22-24), and his strength undeniable (vv. 25-28). God's willingness to bless beyond imagination before would have an inspiration for the current Jewish nation. Panning out even further, if Solomon's kingdom was truly but a microcosm of the messianic age, the Queen of Sheba's presence, along with other world leaders who sought Solomon's counsel, was a dramatic portrayal of the nations coming to Christ when he reigns in Jerusalem. One day, God's light will rest on his chosen city as the Messiah assumes the throne established by David and formerly occupied by Solomon. The prophet Isaiah predicted,

> *Raise your eyes and look around:*
> *they all gather and come to you;*
> *your sons will come from far away,*
> *and your daughters on the hips of nursing mothers.*
> *Then you will see and be radiant,*
> *and your heart will tremble and rejoice,*
> *because the riches of the sea will become yours*
> *and the wealth of the nations will come to you.*
> *Caravans of camels will cover your land—*
> *young camels of Midian and Ephah—*
> *all of them will come from Sheba.*
> *They will carry gold and frankincense*
> *and proclaim the praises of the LORD.* (Isa 60:4-6)

Immediately, images of magi from the east fill our minds as partial fulfillment of these words:

> *After Jesus was born in Bethlehem of Judea in the days of King Herod, wise men from the east arrived in Jerusalem, saying, "Where is he who has been born king of the Jews? For we saw his star at its rising and have come to worship him."* . . . *Entering the house, they saw the child with Mary his mother, and falling to their knees, they worshiped him. Then they opened their treasures and presented him with gifts: gold, frankincense, and myrrh.* (Matt 2:1-2,11)

In other words, another like Solomon, who will rule over an eternal kingdom, was born in Bethlehem. Because of his sacrifice for the sins of the whole world (1 John 2:2), multitudes from every nation, tribe, people, and language will gather around his eternal throne to worship (Rev 7:9). Scripture highlights not just the glory of Christ's future kingdom but also the presence of the nations there:

The city does not need the sun or the moon to shine on it, because the glory of God illuminates it, and its lamp is the Lamb. The nations will walk by its light, and the kings of the earth will bring their glory into it. Its gates will never close by day because it will never be night there. They will bring the glory and honor of the nations into it. (Rev 21:23-26)

In addition to the eschatological shadows of the pericope, it is also interesting to learn from Jesus's use of the incident as a rebuke of his scribal and Pharisaic critics who sought signs from him (Matt 12:38-42; Luke 11:29-32). By mentioning the Ninevites in the same context, Jesus highlights believing Gentiles who responded to the truth they had despite possessing much less revelation from God. Next, the Lord refers to himself as one who is "greater than Solomon" in order to sternly rebuke the Jewish leaders who rejected him while celebrating the glories of the past. Clearly, the application centers on our need to respond to God's Word with action rather than a passive critique. As stewards of a complete canon of Scripture, we are accountable for the breadth of what God has made known to us. And because the witness of the Bible points us to Christ, the Ninevites and the Queen of Sheba will stand over us in judgment if we reject him (John 5:39-40).

With Solomon in the grave (2 Chr 9:29-31) and his numerous shortcomings well documented by the Deuteronomistic historian (1 Kgs 11), it was clear to all that he was not the son who would usher in the fullness of the Davidic hope. The implication for Jews returning from captivity was to keep looking for their messianic king. Today, we celebrate that he has come even as we eagerly await his return and the final consummation of his kingdom.

Reflect and Discuss

1. What does Solomon's kingdom teach us about the coming kingdom of Christ?
2. How does our pride work against God's wisdom in our lives? What can we learn from the humility Solomon showed early in his life?
3. How are we sometimes guilty of celebrating the provisions of the Lord rather than his presence?
4. What does the centrality of God's presence in the temple teach us about our need for God today?

5. How does viewing the temple as a temporary movement toward the restoration of the Edenic existence enhance or change our understanding of the new heaven and earth?

6. What does Solomon's dedicatory temple prayer teach us about repentance?

7. What does Israel's worship during the temple dedication teach us about the nature of genuine worship today?

8. How do the positive and negative realities around repentance motivate us to walk closer to God?

9. What does the inclusion of the Gentiles in Solomon's kingdom teach us about God's love for people? Our evangelistic efforts?

10. How does the witness of the Queen of Sheba motivate us to respond to Scripture with action?

Never Too Late to Repent

2 CHRONICLES 10–12

Main Idea: The division of the kingdom presents the pattern of decline that will shape the rest of 2 Chronicles. By expanding his record to include King Rehoboam's previously unknown repentance, the Chronicler admonished the postexilic community, and us, to walk in humility and submission before the Lord.

I.   A Pattern We Should Resist (10:1-14; 11:1-23)
II. A Principle We Should Remember (10:15-19)
III. A Possibility We Should Receive (12:1-16)

Norman Borlaug may be the most important man you have never heard of. When he was honored by *ABC News* as the person of the week, most people were puzzled due to his obscurity. Those in the know, however, give him accolades for his role in saving an estimated two billion lives from the danger of famine. In the 1940s, Borlaug hybridized high-yield, disease-resistant corn and wheat for dry climates. Places like West Africa, South America, Siberia, and much of Asia benefitted the most from his work. He later won a Nobel Peace Prize and the Presidential Medal of Freedom for his efforts.

One could argue, though, that a man named Henry Wallace was primarily responsible for saving all those people instead of Norman Borlaug. Wallace was one of three vice presidents during the presidency of Franklin Roosevelt. Wallace leveraged his influence to build a station in Mexico for the purpose of producing hybridized corn and wheat. Borlaug was his choice to lead the effort, but Henry Wallace deserves the greater acclaim for making it all possible.

And yet, we might need to travel back in time even further to discover the real hero behind this major step toward ending world hunger. Perhaps George Washington Carver was the true inspiration behind the remarkable breakthrough. More of us will recognize this important name. Carver, as you might recall, promoted 266 products made from peanuts and 88 from sweet potatoes. His most important achievement, though, may have been his inspiring a six-year-old boy while teaching at Iowa State University. Because the instructor took the child along for his botanical experiments, his young pupil walked away with a love for plants. The boy's name was Henry Wallace, who later became vice president of the Unites States and built a station in Mexico to develop weatherproof crops for the region.

Or we might need to go back to Moses to identify the individual most responsible for feeding billions of people. I'm not referring to the Hebrew Moses who led God's people out of Egypt through the desert but a simple farmer in Diamond, Missouri. This modern Moses did not believe in American slavery, which made him the target of bandits determined to destroy his property. One tragic evening violent criminals burned his farm to the ground and dragged a woman named Mary away with her infant son. Moses and his wife Susan negotiated to exchange his only horse for the two victims. The outlaws deceived the good Samaritan by taking his horse and only returning the baby, half dead in a burlap bag. The godly couple nursed the child back to health and later gave him a quality education to honor his mother. That rescued son was George Washington Carver. Without him, there would have been no one to inspire Henry Wallace. And without Wallace, no one would have hired Norman Borlaug. And without Borlaug, the world would be without hybridized corn and wheat. And without all those crops in arid lands, two billion people might have died (Andy Andrews, *The Butterfly Effect*, 64–100).

I could keep going, but by now you get the point. Everything we do, whether good or bad, is consequential because our lives are inseparably intertwined with others. Like dominoes in a long line of people, our actions, and the momentum they cause, impact the lives of everyone around us in ways we can discern and in other ways we cannot. This pericope positions the life of Rehoboam as a key transition in the history of Israel. His mistakes began a trajectory of compromise that ultimately ended in divided kingdoms destined for exile. While we might be tempted to put all the negative outcomes from this point forward at the feet of Rehoboam, a closer look incriminates Solomon's carnality as well. The sins of these chapters left God's people reeling for generations to come.

If the reigns of David and Solomon offer a prototype of the kingdom God desired for his people as well as the coming new heaven and earth, 2 Chronicles 10 marks a significant departure in order to explain the devastating transgressions leading up to the Babylonian captivity. In fact, the verbal echoes from this point forward resemble the wayward period of the judges more than the vision of a Davidic dynasty (Leithart, *1 & 2 Chronicles*, 128).

We cannot emphasize enough that the Chronicler's goal for those coming out of exile was less historical and more interpretive. With the records of Samuel and Kings already available, the aim here is helping the postexilic community eliminate the sinful cycles that led to their demise in the first place. In order to abate the previous pattern of rebellion, Rehoboam's story as found here highlights the possibility of choosing a different course by modeling the impact of genuine repentance. In fact, the division of the kingdom was altogether avoidable, or at least reversible, had those most responsible continued in their contrition.

Toward that end, the Chronicler departs from the Kings account by introducing new, more positive remembrances of Rehoboam. As before, this was not an effort to conceal or rewrite the common tradition of the nation. On the contrary, it appears that the postexilic historian's intent is for their earlier sources to be read alongside his deduced implications from the past. With the concluding analysis of Rehoboam's life remaining unchanged (12:16-19), his situational repentance, despite its effectiveness, may actually be more damning than previous recollections. After learning firsthand the benefits and restoration of repentance, the new king chose to continue in his sin and resulting condemnation.

This carefully arranged history is the Chronicler's less than subtle way of inviting his audience to learn from the mistakes of the past by choosing repentance when they drift away. If God was anxious to restore wicked kings like Rehoboam, postexilic Jews and Christians today can be certain the heavenly Father is anxious to receive contemporary prodigals who come home. Truly, it is never too late to repent.

A Pattern We Should Resist
2 CHRONICLES 10:1-14; 11:1-23

After the death of Solomon, with no clear transition plan in place, Rehoboam sought the nation's approval to become their new king when the twelve tribes gathered in Shechem (10:1). Though we might expect these events to take place in Jerusalem, Shechem is more practical than a casual glance with modern eyes reveals. Because this was the location of Abraham's first altar (Gen 12:6-7), Jacob's altar (Gen 33:18-20), Joshua's covenantal renewal (Josh 24), and Abimelech's evil plot to become king (Judg 9:1-6), Israel saw the location as a place of spiritual and political significance (Merrill, *A Commentary*, 380–81). At forty-one years old and the only son of Solomon mentioned in the Old Testament, Rehoboam seems to be the undisputed heir to the Davidic throne.

The appearance of Jeroboam in the text initially feels abrupt, yet an appreciation of the broad responsibility for the downfall of the nation merits it. In other words, the Chronicler has no interest in laying the full blame of Israel's split kingdom at the feet of Rehoboam, regardless of his recklessness, when Solomon and Jeroboam share significant blame as well. This awareness does not diminish the foolishness of Rehoboam but instead strengthens the passage's focus on God's willingness to forgive and restore when his people repent of their sins. If the Lord was eager to pardon Solomon, Rehoboam, and Jeroboam for their complicity in the kingdom's division, Jews returning from Babylon could be confident God was equally prepared to do the same for them after the captivity. Likewise, believers today should find hope within this display of God's extravagant grace.

Though Jeroboam does not appear until now in the chronicle, Jewish readers were well aware that he previously rebelled against Solomon (1 Kgs 11:26). In addition, the prophet Ahijah tore his own cloak into twelve pieces, gave Jeroboam ten of those pieces, and prophesied that each represented one tribe Jeroboam would rule over in a kingdom of his own (1 Kgs 11:29-33). Furthermore, God promised to bless him as long as he did not depart from the faith (1 Kgs 11:37-38).

Within this framework, the pattern of rebellion seems much less inviting. Jeroboam confronted Rehoboam with a request for relief from the burdens imposed by Solomon (10:3-4). These were serious charges, equating the former king with oppression akin to Pharoah during Israel's Egyptian enslavement (Exod 5:9). Given that this history also compares Judah's final king, Zedekiah, to Pharoah in order to justify the exile (2 Chr 36:13), these descriptions intentionally baited the interest of the postexilic community by associating their rebellion with earlier patterns. Tragically, after taking time to deliberate (10:5) and seeking the counsel of both the old and young advisors within Israel (vv. 6-11), Rehoboam behaves more like Pharoah than a Davidic ruler (vv. 12-14).

The resulting collapse of the kingdom marks a second major historical turning point that was from the Lord (10:15). Previously, God had transferred the kingdom from Saul to David in order to establish his eternal covenant (1 Chr 10:14). Now, similar language indicates an act of divine judgment that will lead to the kingdom's immediate division followed by its inevitable collapse (Selman, *2 Chronicles*, 377). Rather than enjoy God's favor, Rehoboam's folly left him with jurisdiction over just two tribes, leading like a tyrant over subjects rather than a Davidic shepherd (10:16-19). These seminal steps ultimately led to exile.

Due to his compromised position and defensive posture, Rehoboam immediately organized for war (11:1). Thankfully, Yahweh intervened through his prophet Shemaiah, who prevented bloodshed being added to the separation (vv. 2-5). As is often the case when we disobey God, paranoia prevented Rehoboam from enjoying God's peace fully. He fortified the cities of Judah and Benjamin as a result (vv. 6-14). At this point one might ask why God responded with such severity to Rehoboam's stubbornness. According to the Chronicler, this was a fulfillment of Ahijah's prophetic judgment against Solomon's idolatries (10:15).

Proving that sin does not happen in a vacuum, Rehoboam also repeated the sins of his father by marrying eighteen wives and sixty concubines, including his half cousin and great aunt (11:18-21). His favorite wife, Maacah, reinforced the national movement toward idolatry. Judah's king sought multiple wives for his sons as well (vv. 22-23).

Was Rehoboam wicked? Clearly. But the passage reminds us that his behaviors were symptomatic of the example provided by his father. The Deuteronomistic historian explains,

> *King Solomon loved many foreign women in addition to Pharaoh's daughter: Moabite, Ammonite, Edomite, Sidonian, and Hittite women from the nations about which the* Lord *had told the Israelites, "You must not intermarry with them, and they must not intermarry with you, because they will turn your heart away to follow their gods." To these women Solomon was deeply attached in love. He had seven hundred wives who were princesses and three hundred who were concubines, and they turned his heart away.*
>
> *When Solomon was old, his wives turned his heart away to follow other gods. He was not wholeheartedly devoted to the* Lord *his God, as his father David had been. Solomon followed Ashtoreth, the goddess of the Sidonians, and Milcom, the abhorrent idol of the Ammonites. Solomon did what was evil in the* Lord*'s sight, and unlike his father David, he did not remain loyal to the* Lord*.*
>
> *At that time, Solomon built a high place for Chemosh, the abhorrent idol of Moab, and for Milcom, the abhorrent idol of the*

*Ammonites, on the hill across from Jerusalem. He did the same for all
his foreign wives, who were burning incense and offering sacrifices to
their gods.* (1 Kgs 11:1-8)

This is the context in which God speaks through his prophet, tearing
the kingdom away from Solomon by giving ten tribes to Jeroboam. You
can hear the lament in the Lord's words:

*For they have abandoned me; they have bowed down to Ashtoreth,
the goddess of the Sidonians, to Chemosh, the god of Moab, and to
Milcom, the god of the Ammonites. They have not walked in my ways
to do what is right in my sight and to carry out my statutes and my
judgments as his father David did.* (1 Kgs 11:33)

Until now, the flaws of Solomon were strategically diminished. Yet
his waywardness now obliterates the viability of his kingdom. The king
who had it all needlessly squandered the blessings and favor of God.
His demise was entirely avoidable but altogether predictable. While
Solomon dedicated the temple, Yahweh assured him,

*If you turn away and abandon my statutes and my commands that
I have set before you and if you go and serve other gods and bow in
worship to them, then I will uproot Israel from the soil that I gave
them, and this temple that I have sanctified for my name I will banish
from my presence; I will make it an object of scorn and ridicule among
all the peoples.* (2 Chr 7:19-20)

The Jews receiving this message would have simultaneously grieved over
Solomon's obstinance even as they remembered their own. The descent
toward exile began after just two generations of blessing when a trajectory of decline dominated the movement of the nation. If these two
examples were not enough, Jeroboam clearly emerges as a third example of disobedience's deadly pattern and the resulting consequences.

Due to the well-documented wickedness of the people and leaders throughout Samaria, readers might falsely assume that disobedience
was the northern kingdom's only choice. Yet God's message through
Ahijah was one of promise and opportunity for Jeroboam:

*After that, if you obey all I command you, walk in my ways, and
do what is right in my sight in order to keep my statutes and my
commands as my servant David did, I will be with you. I will
build you a lasting dynasty just as I built for David, and I will*

give you Israel. I will humble David's descendants, because of their
unfaithfulness, but not forever. (1 Kgs 11:38-39)

Yet with the temple in Jerusalem, Jeroboam's refusal to allow Levitical
priests to return there all but guaranteed their allegiance to Rehoboam's
southern kingdom (2 Chr 11:13-14). Remarkably, his solution was to
appoint his own priests and thereby sanction idol worship (v. 15). These
remarkable acts of blasphemy were an unnecessary forfeiture of divine
opportunity. The harshness of the Chronicler toward Jeroboam appears
later when he assesses,

> *Jeroboam son of Nebat, a servant of Solomon son of David, rose up*
> *and rebelled against his lord. Then worthless and wicked men gathered*
> *around him to resist Rehoboam son of Solomon when Rehoboam was*
> *young, inexperienced, and unable to assert himself against them.*
> (2 Chr 13:6-7)

Clearly, the text does not impose the blame on one person alone
but acknowledges the pernicious path of each. With all these kings in
all these scenarios, God's eagerness to bless was not persuasive enough
to break the enticement of sin. Their rebellion, like ours, was irrational and self-destructive. Not only did these verses enhance the Jewish
appreciation for the events that led to their seventy-year exile, but they
also aid Christ followers in our efforts to prevent similar heartache and
devastation. Though we are free to choose these egregious patterns,
they can, and should, be avoided.

A Principle We Should Remember
2 CHRONICLES 10:15-19

Having established the foolery of Rehoboam (10:13-14) and Jeroboam
(13:6-7) while also acknowledging Solomon's encompassing responsibility for Israel's downgrade (10:15), a holy, even mysterious principle
emerges in the text that requires our deliberation. Namely, the realization that these failures of leadership were "a turn of events from God
that the LORD might establish His word" (v. 15 NASB). Here we have
Yahweh presiding over events, even using them strategically, without
bearing any moral culpability for their insidiousness. Throughout the
ordeal, God remained in control of each king's wickedness, though he
was not responsible for it.

Though counterintuitive, the Lord used the selfish, sinful actions of his people to accomplish his desired goals. But why did the exilic generation need a lesson about God's sovereignty? And why do we? Because this was precisely how God intervened in order to repurpose their wickedness through the hands of Babylon. God planned the exile as an act of judgment against his own people while also holding the instruments of his plan fully accountable for their actions. Just as Rehoboam and Jeroboam were the tools used to tear the kingdom out of Solomon's hands (1 Kgs 10:31), so the Babylonian Empire was the divine resource used to humble the people of God. The Lord explained through Habakkuk,

> Look at the nations and observe—be utterly astounded!
> For I am doing something in your days
> that you will not believe when you hear about it.
> Look! I am raising up the Chaldeans, that bitter, impetuous nation
> that marches across the earth's open spaces to seize territories not its own.
> They are fierce and terrifying;
> their views of justice and sovereignty stem from themselves.
> Their horses are swifter than leopards and more fierce than wolves of
>   the night.
> Their horsemen charge ahead; their horsemen come from distant lands.
> They fly like eagles, swooping to devour.
> All of them come to do violence; their faces are set in determination.
> They gather prisoners like sand.
> They mock kings, and rulers are a joke to them.
> They laugh at every fortress and build siege ramps to capture it.
> Then they sweep by like the wind and pass through.
> They are guilty; their strength is their god. (Hab 1:5-11)

Note, the Lord fully acknowledged how evil these agents of judgment were. Yet God providentially and simultaneously unleashed their wickedness in order to accomplish his work while also holding the Chaldeans responsible for their deplorable acts. How are we to reconcile these mind-boggling realities? Habakkuk struggled, as we do:

> Are you not from eternity, LORD my God?
> My Holy One, you will not die.
> LORD, you appointed them to execute judgment;
> my Rock, you destined them to punish us.
> Your eyes are too pure to look on evil,

and you cannot tolerate wrongdoing.
So why do you tolerate those who are treacherous?
Why are you silent
while one who is wicked swallows up
one who is more righteous than himself? (Hab 1:12-13)

Why does God choose to work this way? Questions like these are natural to ask, but answering them requires a good dose of theological humility. In reality, no explanation will capture the full scope of the *why* behind God's *what*. A helpful parameter, though, is the admission that God cannot be tempted by evil, nor does he entice others with vile allurements (Jas 1:13). For the postexilic period, with the opportunities of blessing or judgment before God's people again, the Chronicler's revelation was meant to be motivational. In light of the Davidic promises, Yahweh would be Israel's greatest ally or their biggest threat. This lesson was invaluable for a nation anxious to rebuild.

In these instances, rather than viewing rebellious people as a *threat* to the divine plan, we humbly admit that they *were* the plan. This principle held true amid the darkest moment of history. The cross of Jesus was the single most heinous, villainous aggression ever committed. The hatred of Jewish religious leaders for their Messiah is a settled fact. Likewise, the brutality of the Roman executioners is seldom debated. Even more significant, the shenanigans of hell were on full display as the Savior hung between heaven and hell. These nefarious agents live in infamy because of their joyful participation in crucifying the Son of God. Yet Scripture is equally clear that the Lamb was slain before the foundation of the earth (Rev 13:8) and the eternal purpose of God was carried out through Christ the Son (Eph 3:11). At Pentecost, the apostle Peter declared, "Though he was delivered up according to God's determined plan and foreknowledge" (God's sovereignty), "you used lawless people to nail him to a cross and kill him" (human responsibility; Acts 2:23).

God punished those responsible for the cross even though he sovereignly imposed his redemptive agenda on their freedom to rebel. The same was true of Babylon. Habakkuk 2:2-20 assures the prophet that God would punish the Babylonians who facilitated Judah's consequence. Again, who can explain these improbable means? Perhaps we should emulate Habakkuk's submissive posture: "But the LORD is in His holy temple. Let all the earth be silent before Him" (Hab 2:20 NASB).

Christians today should take comfort in knowing that God is always in control. He is never alarmed or threatened by the evil of a fallen world. When the ungodly attack us, our first reaction is often to assign their hurtful course to the work of the devil. Yet more often than we realize, God is on the move to advance his kingdom work. Even in our sinfulness, the Lord advances his work in us and through us. Our most severe consequences fall under the purview of the Lord's agenda to discipline and sanctify his own (Heb 12:4-11).

A Possibility We Should Receive
2 CHRONICLES 12:1-16

The common denominator throughout the pericope is that every major character disobeyed God's direction and fell woefully short of his expectation. Yet within every exchange, the possibility of and the invitation to repentance remains. The progression of the narrative reinforces God's eagerness to restore us when we stray. The momentary repentance of Rehoboam and the blessings that followed are illustrative of the gracious possibilities that exist for those who humble themselves before God.

Under the leadership of Rehoboam, Judah drifted further and further away from the Lord. The king's heart hardened as his kingdom grew stronger and he forsook the law of God (12:1). As a result, God again raised up a Gentile enemy to oppress the Israelites (vv. 2-4). With the Egyptian threat looming large, the prophet Shemaiah delivers a word of rebuke and explanation from the Lord (v. 5). The revelatory initiative of Yahweh subtly reminds that he is anxious to forgive if only his people repent. Loving confrontation is a sign of God's commitment to his people, not the lack thereof.

Remarkably, both Rehoboam and his princes humble themselves and submit to the Lord's righteousness (v. 6). As a result, God forgives and withholds his full wrath, even as consequences remain (vv. 7-8). Shishak's plundering of the temple and the king's palace further humbled Rehoboam, and Yahweh's anger subsided (vv. 9-12). These positive additions to Rehoboam's record do not represent an effort to rehabilitate his image. On the contrary, including these positive remembrances paints a lavish picture of God's magnanimous grace and willingness to forgive the worst of sinners.

Sadly, every time Rehoboam became strong, he stopped seeking the Lord (vv. 13-16). As with Saul before him (1 Chr 10:13-14) and Uzziah after him (2 Chr 26:16), the son of Solomon's refusal to seek the Lord consistently is a sad commentary of the binding power of sin over our lives. For the exiles returning to Jerusalem, the account is a call to avoid a similar plight as God's blessings returned. Idolatry and rebellion would always be temptations. Knowing that God could not be deterred in his work and that he remained anxious to show compassion to his covenantal people were intentional motivators. If God responded to the repentance of Rehoboam, whose life fell far short of the Lord's expectation, how much more could he be trusted to heal and restore weary exiles desperate for a new beginning?

As for us, we should celebrate the God whose grace is always greater than our sin (Rom 5:20). We should be quick to repent and slow to sin. With confidence, we should confess our sins, knowing that through Christ God will cleanse and forgive us (1 John 1:9). We should learn from the mistakes of those blinded by the entrapments of evil. And when God blesses us, we should refuse to abuse his gifts by becoming proud and strong. We should recognize and avoid the danger of turning back to evil after having received the forgiveness of God.

Reflect and Discuss

1. What does the stubborn blindness of Solomon, Rehoboam, and Jeroboam teach us about our own propensities toward sin?
2. What do we learn from this text about the broad impact of our disobedience? About how our disobedience hurts others?
3. How does God's sovereignty over sin motivate us to resist temptation and walk in purity?
4. What does God's disciplinary hand teach us about God's willingness to forgive our sins?
5. What does the providential nature of the cross teach us about the character of God?
6. Why is theological humility so important when we study the Bible?
7. Does God's control over evil events comfort you? How does it challenge you?
8. How can the blessings of God become a deterrent to our obedience?
9. How do examples of God's forgiveness encourage you? What do they teach you about God's grace?
10. What do we learn from this text about the urgency of repentance?

Relying on the Lord More Fully

2 CHRONICLES 13–16

Main Idea: Relying on the Lord is a lifelong process of continual faith and dependence. God desires to show himself strong for a covenantal people who will seek him until the end.

I.   **The Lord Wants to Fight for Us (Whom You Belong To) (13:1-21).**
II. **The Lord Wants to Be Found by Us (What Is Available to You) (14:1–15:19).**
III. **The Lord Will Not Falter like Us (How Vulnerable You Are) (16:1-14).**

J. Wilbur Chapman, a popular Presbyterian evangelist at the turn of the twentieth century, once had the opportunity to meet Methodist preacher and founder of the Salvation Army, General William Booth, while in London. By this time, the old humanitarian was past eighty years of age and somewhat reflective. Chapman's most memorable inquiry during their exchange was direct but sincere: "What has been the secret of your tremendous success? How have you managed to make such impact and influence on this world?" The question moved the aged minister.

General Booth hesitated for a moment, and then, as tears came into his eyes and rolled down his cheeks, he answered, "I will tell you the secret. God has had all there is of me. There have been men with greater brains than me, men with greater opportunities, but from the day I got the poor of London on my heart, and a vision of what Jesus Christ could do with these men, I made up my mind that God would have all of William Booth there was. If there is anything of power in the Salvation Army today, it is because God has all the adoration of my heart, all the power of my will, and all the influence of my life."

Chapman left the meeting that day with a single truth burning in his heart: "*The greatness of a man's power is in the measure of his surrender*" (*King's Business*, 511; emphasis added). Indeed. Total surrender to God is more powerful than any human planning or scheming. The principle, while easy to understand, is just as difficult to live by today as it was in the years after the Babylonian oppression of Judah ended.

This portion of the chronicle celebrates seasons of renewal and blessing in order to inspire the postexilic generation as they return to Jerusalem. By recalling God's desire for sincere devotion and his eagerness to protect his covenantal people, the text provides a road map back to the Lord after years of heartache. Not surprisingly, these insights offer profound application for believers today as well.

As with each of the kings in Judah's history, the reigns of Abijah and Asa point us to Christ in both their godliness and their shortcomings. The faithfulness of David's sons magnifies the qualities of the Messiah each anticipated, while their transgressions underscore the need for a "Wonderful Counselor, Mighty God, Eternal Father, Prince of Peace" (Isa 9:6). In addition, these ancient rulers provide models to avoid or embrace as we live out our faith. We know that "whatever was written in the past was written for our instruction, so that we may have hope through endurance and through the encouragement from the Scriptures" (Rom 15:4).

To accomplish his exhortation, the Chronicler centers this pericope on the themes of seeking God and relying fully on him. Doing so requires tremendous faith and dependence—commitments alternately displayed and contradicted by the aforementioned leaders. By learning from their mistakes and adopting their virtues, Christians today can learn to lean more fully on Christ in their pursuit of righteous sanctification. To do so, three remembrances are necessary.

The Lord Wants to Fight for Us
2 CHRONICLES 13:1-21

After the death of Rehoboam, while King Jeroboam still ruled over the northern kingdom, his son Abijah assumed the throne of David in Judah (v. 1). Astute students of Scripture will note that the Deuteronomistic historian spells Abijah's name as "Abijam" in 1 Kings. While the difference could be nothing more than a spelling variation, it is more likely an intentional distinction that reflects the new material added by the Chronicler. Mabie correctly observes that the "jam" suffix (Hb *yam*) used in 1 Kings could reveal a loyalty to the Canaanite sea god Yam ("my father is Yam") while the "jah" suffix (Hb *yah*) points to the fatherhood of Yahweh ("1 and 2 Chronicles," 218). Certainly, this is in keeping

with the covenantal promise, where God assures David that he will be a
father to his descendants (2 Sam 7:14), as well as Abijah's boast of the
same in his speech to Jeroboam (2 Chr 13:5,8,10).

The greatest question behind the text is the competing perspectives
of Chronicles, which positions Abijah as a hero, and a Kings record that
portrays him as an evil leader. Outside of 1 Kings 15:1-2, the contents
of this pericope do not overlap at all. The challenge for interpreters is
not new material, for such is often helpful when filling historical gaps
left behind by previous writers. No, the issue here is not uniqueness but
apparent contradiction. Most shocking is the elimination of the condemnation found 1 Kings 15:3:

> Abijam walked in all the sins his father before him had committed,
> and he was not wholeheartedly devoted to the LORD his God as his
> ancestor David had been.

Can these competing visions of Abijah's contribution be reconciled?
And what does this controversial king have to teach modern readers?

The key to answering interpretive questions like these is to once
again yield to the Chronicler's distinctive motivation for writing. The
primary agenda of the text is less about the character of Judah's controversial king and more about his substantive covenantal reminder that
would prove helpful to the postexilic community. No effort is made to
hide Abijah's carnal resemblances to his father and grandfather or the
fuller record of his life found in the familiar writings of the prophet
Iddo (vv. 21-22). Thus, there is no denial of the broader deficiencies
that characterized Abijah generally.

The focus, however, is a specific demonstration that the lamp of
Judah burned brightly even after the kingdom of Israel divided. The
earlier history of Kings states in two verses what the Chronicler turns
into an entire illustrative narrative.

> But for the sake of David, the LORD his God gave him a lamp in
> Jerusalem by raising up his son after him and by preserving Jerusalem.
> For David did what was right in the LORD's sight, and he did not turn
> aside from anything he had commanded him all the days of his life,
> except in the matter of Uriah the Hethite. (1 Kgs 15:4-5)

Rather than view Abijah as a scoundrel turned exemplar, we should
receive this passage as tangible evidence that God kept his covenantal
responsibilities to his people. Namely, and most apropos for the

generation after the exile, providing a messianic throne and kingdom through David and a sanctioned cultic expression at the temple.

For Jews returning to Jerusalem from Babylon, Abijah's speech serves as a subtle warning not to fabricate a new kingship as Jeroboam had, even as it incentivized rebuilding the temple as an effort to resume the blessings of their covenantal relationship with Yahweh. As war unfolded between the northern and southern tribes of Israel (v. 2), Judah's king positioned his troops in battle formation (v. 3) but offered corrective words of rebuke aimed directly at Jeroboam before the battle ensued (v. 4).

First, Abijah insists that David received God's covenant; therefore, the only qualified kings are his descendants (v. 6). Because the king spoke in third person, it appears that his speech was aimed at northern tribes with hopes they might usurp their leader. He recounts Jeroboam's manipulative rise to power at Rehoboam's expense while insisting that his apparent success was still contrary to God's design (vv. 7-8a). Next, Abijah mocks Israel's idolatry as the only reason their faux priesthood can exist (vv. 8b-9). Finally, he offers a stark contrast by insisting that Judah has not abandoned the Lord, as evidenced by the appropriateness of his throne (v. 8) and the legitimacy of the priesthood serving in Jerusalem (vv. 10-11). Consequently, because the kingdom of Judah was the recipient of the messianic hope, to fight against them is to battle God himself (v. 12).

Again, these charges levied by Abijah were equally applicable as the Jewish captivity ended. Idolatrous Samaria forsook their heritage because of *who* they followed and *how* they worshiped. Ironically, these were the same issues that ultimately led to Judah's exile. Thus, the Chronicler highlights the same deadly pattern in the north in order to inspire returning Jews to avoid the same trap in the future.

Though our context is vastly different, Christians today face the ever-present temptations of deifying lesser "gods" and attempting to worship the true God on our own terms. Rather than live according to our former ignorance, God calls us to live with heartfelt obedience and holiness because of our redemption through the precious blood of Christ (1 Pet 1:14-19). *Who* we worship and *how* we live are just as important now as they ever have been.

To illustrate the blessings of resisting temptation and walking in covenantal faithfulness, 13:13-22 celebrates Yahweh's provisional protection in response to Judah's humility. Despite being ambushed by Jeroboam's troops (v. 13), Israelites to the south called out to God for help, and he answered (v. 14). With nothing more than blowing trumpets and sounding a battle cry, the Lord overcame Abijah's enemy, resulting in excessive causalities (vv. 14-17) and a greatly weakened northern kingdom (vv. 18-20). The whole scene is a powerful illustration of the Lord's eagerness to fight on behalf of his people.

The immediate benefit of Abijah's faith served as a strategic invitation for postexilic Jews to enjoy the blessings and favor of God again. Though the Davidic covenant is eternally irrevocable, the generational benefit varies according to obedience. The testimony of empowered dependence under the leadership of Abijah is a reminder of the conditional nature of the abundant life. Covenantal *security* was not then, nor is it now, a guarantee of covenantal *satisfaction*. The original hearers and contemporary believers alike benefit from the appropriate call to an active, obedient faith characterized by relying on the Lord at all times (v. 18). Refuse to turn back. Keep trusting Yahweh. Remember, strength does not come from our independence but from our dependence on our great God, who rewards the faith of imperfect people. These admonitions are just as true today as they ever were. God is still eager to honor the devotion of his people.

Tragically, Abijah failed to maintain the level of commitment we read about in this pericope. His short tenure as king (1 Kgs 15:2) likely indicates God's retribution against him that came just as quickly as the blessed intervention we read about here. The testimony of 1 Kings 15:3 further highlights Abijah's eternal failure, without the specificity the Chronicler offers (2 Chr 13:21-22). Once again, disgraceful polygamy turned the heart of David's son away from the Lord. Abijah was not the Promised One the Hebrew people needed.

The Lord Wants to Be Found by Us
2 CHRONICLES 14:1–15:19

If Abijah is an example of how beneficial humility and dependence on God can be, Asa becomes a model of what sustained commitment looks like. While the former typifies momentary survival in the heat of battle, the latter casts a vision for thriving as God's people for a generation. After succeeding his father, King Asa presided over a period of peace for much of his reign (14:1). The kingdom was largely undisturbed despite two military threats, primarily because of the righteousness of David's heir.

The themes of relying on God and seeking God dominate this portion of the pericope. With the verb translated *to rely, lean, depend* (Hb *sha'an*) occurring five times in chapters 13–16 (13:18; 14:11; 16:7,8) but nowhere else in Chronicles, and the verb translated *to seek* (Hb *darash*) appearing nine times (14:4,7; 15:2,4,12,13,15; 16:12), it is difficult to over-estimate the importance of these ideas (Selman, *2 Chronicles*, 402). Again, the conditional implication of the Davidic covenant (2 Chr 6:16-42) brought with it a theology of retribution. Seeking the Lord and relying on him fully were means to blessing and prosperity, while disobedience and independence were sure guarantees of devastating consequences.

With much of his life characterized by the reforms he brought to Judah, Asa foreshadows the reigns of Hezekiah and Josiah (14:2). Remarkably, these verses offer explicit evidence that the idolatry nor-mally associated with the northern kingdom made its way into Judah. Therefore, Asa removed pagan altars, high places, and statues that com-peted with worshiping Yahweh in Solomon's temple (vv. 3-5). The peace that followed was an obvious result of these reforms. Lest there be any question, the text plainly states it was the Lord who gave him rest (v. 6). In addition, Asa constructed fortified cities for future protection while insisting that the land they possessed and the peace they enjoyed were in direct correlation to their seeking the Lord (v. 7). Despite building a great army, the king's hope remained steadfastly in Yahweh (v. 8). The nation grew and prospered because of Asa's leadership.

Therefore, despite the size of Zerah's imposing army, the Ethiopian threat was no match for the strong hand of Yahweh (v. 9). Knowing this, Asa aligned his troops in battle formation (v. 10), and they cried out to the Lord (v. 11) with confidence according to the pattern established by Solomon (6:34-35). With full reliance on Yahweh as their only shield and the glory of their God at stake, the Israelites routed the Cushites in the most dramatic way possible, leaving no doubt for readers *who* fought on their behalf (14:12-15).

As with the previous applications, the lesson for postexilic Israel was one of dependence. As they rebuilt Jerusalem and the temple, their vested strength and protection into the future were necessarily from the Lord's hand. Human wealth, skill, and wisdom simply could not substi-tute for the blessing and provision of David's God. If they would seek Yahweh as Asa did, no enemy would be a real threat.

Followers of Christ today must also learn to trust the Lord as he fights our battles. This means resisting the urge to seek revenge, refusing to gos-sip in order to set the record straight, and letting go of the impulse to con-trol everything and everyone around you. Romans 12:17-19 reminds us,

> *Do not repay anyone evil for evil. Give careful thought to do what is honorable in everyone's eyes. If possible, as far as it depends on you, live at peace with everyone. Friends, do not avenge yourselves; instead, leave room for God's wrath, because it is written, Vengeance belongs to me; I will repay, says the Lord.*

Seek the Lord and depend on him. Draw near to God, trusting that he will draw near to you (Jas 4:8).

Next, we learn more of the assurance that trust in God brings as we encounter the preaching of Azariah (15:1). This godly messenger assured King Asa, and us, that the Lord wanted to be found if only they would seek him (v. 2). To contrast, Azariah recounted Judah's past burdens and missteps.

- There was religious anarchy (v. 3).
- There was social strife and division (v. 5).
- There was national and political insecurity (v. 6).

While we cannot be certain about the particulars of these descriptions, we know Solomon's life ended in severe waywardness that forfeited the kingdom, Rehoboam presided over the split to the kingdom, and Abijah promoted idolatry within the kingdom. The language here is more akin to the period of the judges than to the Davidic dynasty.

Not surprisingly, these were the debilitating realities felt by the exilic generation for more than seventy years! Thus, in the midst of illustrating the common rebellion that plagued Judah from the beginning, Azariah also assured his audience that it need not be this way (v. 4). God was, and is, anxious to be found by those who seek him with a pure heart. We should note, however, that God troubled his people when they turned away (v. 6). This recollection was both comforting and convicting because it functioned as a reassurance and a warning. When we refuse to seek the Lord who desires to be found, he is more than capable of finding us!

It is not difficult to see how powerfully this message would have resonated with Jews coming out from under Persian rule. The key to their rebirth was a renewed dependence on the Lord. Even today, Christians feel the devastation of turning away from our Savior. While no contemporary nation constitutes the people of God now, the church of the Lord Jesus often vacillates between biblical fidelity and egregious idolatry, following Israel's ancient tendency of turning away from God. Many mainstream denominations are more than willing to capitulate to the culture by redefining marriage and gender. Likewise, many who boast in the name of Christ are more than willing to sacrifice the sanctity of human life on the altar of personal autonomy and convenience. Loose morals and corruption seem pandemic in the modern church. In other words, God's people are just as willing to do what is right in our own eyes as our Hebrew counterparts from long ago (Judg 21:25).

Thankfully, it does not have to be this way. Despite our claims to the contrary, we can have as much of God as we are willing to seek. The problem is not that God doesn't want to be found but that we have little interest in pursuing him. Thus, Azariah admonished, "Be strong; don't give up, for your work has a reward" (15:7). Incredibly, Asa followed this wise counsel to the letter (vv. 8-15). Removing pagan idols throughout the land declared *who* deserves worship (v. 8). Renovating the altar in front of the temple's portico highlighted *how* the people should worship (v. 8). The king's gathering of defectors from the northern kingdom hints that the key to a unified nation is the proper worship of Yahweh (v. 9). His numerous sacrifices served as a tangible demonstration of what seeking God entails (vv. 10-11). Finally, Asa renewed God's covenant and sought the Lord with all his heart (v. 12) while also making it the clear expectation for everyone in Judah, resulting in rest in every direction (vv. 13-15).

In another exceptional move of allegiance, Asa also confronted the idolatry of his wicked grandmother, Maacah, by destroying her obscene Asherah pole (v. 16). Such personal sacrifice left no doubt concerning the king's wholehearted devotion to Yahweh (v. 17). Jesus later codified the same standard for those who follow him by stating, "If anyone comes to me and does not hate his own father and mother, wife and children, brothers and sisters—yes, and even his own life—he cannot be my disciple" (Luke 14:26).

The remaining high places were likely in northern territories that Asa captured because there is no textual condemnation for their presence (v. 17). Also, the king prioritized the centrality of Yahweh worship in the temple by refurbishing its silver, gold, and utensils (v. 18). God rewarded Asa's diligence and consistency with over thirty years of peace. Did Israel long for similar peace after the exile? Were they willing to seek the God who is anxious to be found? Thus far, the reign of Asa was an accurate road map for the wayward Israelites to find their way back to God. Our willingness to seek God's kingdom above all else will also be the key to our constant renewal (Matt 6:33).

The Lord Will Not Falter like Us
2 CHRONICLES 16:1-14

Tragically, the story of Asa does not end after chapter 15. Much like Solomon before him, the king turned away from the Lord in his later years. Breaking his pattern of being more complimentary than the Kings record, the Chronicler is more critical of Asa than the Deuteronomistic tradition. By faltering near the end of his reign, the king functions like a parable of Judah as a whole and a warning to contemporary believers. After thirty-five years of leading with integrity and enjoying peace, Asa stumbled near the finish during his last five years by depending more on his personal strength and wisdom than on Yahweh.

When Israel's northern king, Baasha, came against Judah to reclaim the territories gained by Rehoboam, he pushed the boundary back south to the city Ramah (16:1). Fortifying this area created a blockade that closed any trade routes to the north of Jerusalem. The move also levied a religious restriction that rivaled the resulting economic devastation of such a move. Rather than seek the Lord with full reliance as before, though, Asa chose to handle the threat by means of political treaty with Ben-hadad, king of Aram. Even worse, he emptied the temple treasury in order to fund his unholy alliance (vv. 2-3).

Unfortunately, the scheming worked initially (vv. 3-6). The fundamental flaw here was greater confidence in the flesh than in God's power and goodness. Contrary to his dealing with the Ethiopian crisis, Asa was now comfortable taking matters into his own hands. It seems the years of peace and prosperity increased the king's self-confidence while diminishing his desperation for divine intervention. Therefore, the prophet Hanani steps onto the scene with a strong rebuke for the Davidic heir (v. 7). Exposing the foolishness of Asa was as simple as recounting the Cushite rout from years ago (v. 8). Most convicting, however, is the messenger's precise articulation of what God most wanted from his people (v. 9). Woven into the Lord's desire to be strong for those devoted to him is the nature of the Davidic covenant. God repeatedly assessed the devotion of his people by measuring their obedience and dependence. In the end, Asa was more committed to himself than to Yahweh despite decades of divine faithfulness.

The implications are just as far-reaching for Christians today as they were for postexilic Jews long ago. After decades of Babylonian captivity due to their idolatrous independence, Jewish believers could not afford complacency as Jerusalem rose from the ashes. Likewise, modern followers of Christ must resist the arrogance of personal autonomy and self-sufficiency that often pulls our hearts away from God. All too often, professing Christians live like practical atheists, merely doing what seems right in their own eyes. Ignorance of Scripture, the absence of prayer, and the overconsumption of self are all indicators that Asa's independent streak lives on in each of us.

In another stunning turn, rather than repenting over his self-reliance, Asa responded with anger and hostility by mistreating Hanani and others (v. 10). This, too, is a dangerous sign that we are distant from and cold toward the Lord. A key marker of genuine repentance is responsive anger at our sin rather than at those who expose it. Our lament over offending God should always be greater than our frustration with the consequences sin brings. Blaming others and making excuses will only drive us further away from the Lord. Judah could not afford to point the finger at others if they wanted to thrive in their relationship with God again. Neither the prophets who warned them nor the Babylonians who exiled them were responsible for their falling away. The same is true when we're reeling from the outcomes our disobedience might bring.

The wars that plagued the remainder of Asa's reign (v. 9) and the severe disease in his feet (v. 12) only seemed to increase his bitterness and cynicism. The entire nation of Judah suffered due to the stubbornness of their leader. For years it appeared as though Asa might have been the chosen son of David, yet in the end, he was another sinner who dug his own grave (v. 14). In addition to his preparation of a personal burial site, Asa also readied his coffin with oils and spices. Even in death he attempted to maintain control! Sadly, even those who began with promise before the Babylonian captivity ended up rotting in the grave.

What Israel needed was a faithful heir to David's throne whose life was righteous from beginning to end. One who prepared for death not by embracing it but by overcoming it. One who would only borrow a tomb for three days before rising victoriously. One who was not there when his followers came to embalm him with burial spices. One who refused to live independently but who prayed, "Not my will, but yours, be done" (Luke 22:42). Psalm 20:6-7 described him this way:

Now I know that the Lord gives victory to his anointed;
he will answer him from his holy heaven

> *with mighty victories from his right hand.*
> *Some take pride in chariots, and others in horses,*
> *but we take pride in the name of the* LORD *our God.*

Asa's faltering at the end of his life signals our own need for a new covenant rooted in the obedience of another. We, like Israel, are incapable of walking in complete devotion to the Lord. Thus, while God's new covenant of grace maintains the divine expectation of obedience, through the giving of his Son, the Father meets his own standard of holiness. In Christ, the righteousness God requires from you is the righteousness God gives to you. In addition, through the indwelling of the Holy Spirit, the Father transforms and empowers his people to live according to his righteous demands (Jer 31:31-33).

Reflect and Discuss

1. What do the differing historical perspectives regarding Abijah found in 1 Kings and 2 Chronicles teach us about the conflicting realities of walking with God?
2. What does Abijah's speech teach us about the exclusivity of the gospel?
3. How does Abijah's tragic end motivate us to avoid the dangers of generational sin?
4. What does God's intervention during the reign of Abijah, who was largely wicked, teach us about his enduring commitment to his people.
5. What does the reign of Asa teach us about the importance of Scripture for our walk with God?
6. How does our commitment to Christ sometimes create tension with the people we love the most?
7. What are some practical threats to our sustained dependence on God?
8. What are practical ways we can seek the Lord and find him?
9. What does Asa's tragic end teach us about our own vulnerabilities as we serve Christ?
10. How does our increased dependence on God make us more like Christ?

Our Greatest Weapons

2 CHRONICLES 17–20

Main Idea: The prioritization of Scripture and the discipline of worship were chief characteristics of Jehoshaphat's reign as king of Judah. His life provides examples to follow as well as warnings about the subtleties of compromise, all while deepening our security in Christ.

Introduction (17:1-6)

I.   The Strength of the Word Is Prophetic (17:7-19).

II. The Subtleties of Weakness Are Problematic (18:1–19:11).

III. The Security of Worship Is Powerful (20:1-30).

    A.   Our praise should reflect God's previous works (20:5-9).

    B.   Our praise should be rooted in God's prophetic word (20:10-19).

    C.   Our praise should be regarded as God's powerful weapon (20:20-30).

Conclusion (20:31–21:1)

Nadin Khoury was only five feet two inches, maybe a hundred pounds, when he and his immigrant mother moved to Philadelphia. He never stood a chance when a group of neighborhood kids began to bully him daily. As their taunting escalated, it led to full-blown assault on a cold day in January. For thirty straight minutes, the ruthless thugs kicked and beat the thirteen-year-old boy. Next, they dragged his body through the snow and stuffed him into a tree. Finally, they suspended him from a seven-foot iron fence before a passerby chased them away.

The attackers were so arrogant, though, that they filmed the whole episode and posted it on YouTube. Soon, police got involved and the abusers found themselves in jail. Nadin, on the other hand, became a hometown celebrity. When producers of *The View* learned of the incident, they invited him to be on the show. Unbeknown to the boy, three members of the Philadelphia Eagles football team—wide receiver Desean Jackson and two linemen—were there to surprise him. They gave the boy signed jerseys, and then, on national television, Jackson handed Nadin his cell phone number and said, "Anytime you need us,

I got two linemen right here." From that day forward, would-be villains thought twice before harassing the kid with NFL linemen on speed dial (Max Lucado, *Begin Again*, 93–95).

Who wouldn't want that kind of protection? Amazingly, God offers much the same for us. Psalm 121:7-8 says, "The LORD will protect you from all harm; he will protect your life. The LORD will protect your coming and going both now and forever." The kingship of Jehoshaphat is a powerful testimony of the Lord's desire to take care of his people. By walking the path of Scripture and unleashing the power of praise, this son of David offers both an account from the past and an ambition for the future. Though far from perfect, his reign offers a glimpse of the messianic age while also challenging readers to greater faithfulness and devotion.

In what is a considerable break from the encompassing history of 1–2 Kings, the Chronicler continues to prioritize Judah in his efforts to inspire and instruct the postexilic community. The absence of Elijah from the chronicle is not a commentary on the prophet's significance but rather an expression of the writer's motivating purpose. Understanding the Babylonian captivity without the trappings of the northern kingdom's apostasy provided a better path forward for those charged to rebuild Jerusalem. The details surrounding Jehoshaphat's throne double previous records, making its prominence second only to Hezekiah within the post-Solomon period (Japhet, *I & II Chronicles*, 793).

The kingdom Jehoshaphat assumed during a time of turmoil enjoyed divine blessing and favor because of his obedience and devotion to Yahweh. As an active builder and protector of the nation, he shared many similarities with his father Asa (17:1-2). His refusal to worship false gods, his eagerness to seek after God as David had done, and his removal of pagan high places and Asherim were the greatest reflections of his character (17:3-6). And all of this took place while Ahab and Jezebel reigned in the northern kingdom. Jehoshaphat's faith served as a continual contrast to the wickedness of his neighbors in Israel, making his integrity all the more inspiring and his shortcomings all the more puzzling. Prophetically, the pericope presents the throne of David prospering despite the wickedness around it, as it will in the days of the Messiah. The lessons here for returning exiles and modern believers alike are threefold.

The Strength of the Word Is Prophetic
2 CHRONICLES 17:7-19

One of the more remarkable efforts during Jehoshaphat's reign was his attempt to teach the book of the Lord's instruction to the entire nation (vv. 7-9). Like his father before him, the king was serious about relying on the Lord in accordance with his revealed word. What is more explicit, though, is Jehoshaphat's desire for the citizens of Judah to do so as well. His sending out princes, Levites, and priests amounted to five officials and eleven religious personnel teaching the Pentateuch within his borders. Clearly, the Chronicler is holding the development up as an example for a new generation of Jews seeking to live in covenant with God.

The challenge is not lost on believers today either. With the fuller canon of Scripture now available, one key to our fellowship with God is a sustained commitment to knowing and living the Scriptures, which give us wisdom that leads to salvation through faith in Christ Jesus (2 Tim 3:15). Truly, "faith comes from what is heard, and what is heard comes through the message about Christ" (Rom 10:17). This is why Paul reasoned from the Scriptures each time he taught in the synagogue (Acts 17:2-3). Knowing that the whole Bible is inspired by God, we trust its profitability "for teaching, for rebuking, for correcting, for training in righteousness" (2 Tim 3:16). We simply cannot afford to be professing inerrantists who are practical errantists.

In addition to the obviously practical emphasis, the text also paints a vivid picture of a future son of David who also came teaching the Word of God city by city (Matt 9:35). Then, he sent his disciples out two by two to do the same (Mark 6:7). Finally, in what we would come to call his Great Commission, he sends all believers of all ages as far as the ends of the earth in order to teach others to observe all that he commanded (Matt 28:19-20).

For Jehoshaphat, fear fell on the surrounding nations as Judah prioritized the word of God (2 Chr 17:10). Past enemies, such as the Philistines and Arabians, even brought tribute in the form of gifts, silver, and animals in order to avoid war with Israel (v. 11). The magnitude of these peace offerings is often lost on us. Can you imagine Iran or Saudi Arabia bringing similar gifts to Israel today? All because they feared the God of the Hebrews? As Judah's king submitted to Scripture and obeyed

God, fear of Yahweh's power spread throughout neighboring pagan nations because he was so assuredly with Jehoshaphat.

Likewise, during the messianic age the entire world will fear Israel's King and will bow before him as a result. The nations will come before the Messiah due to their hunger for his word. The prophet Isaiah explains,

> *In the last days*
> *the mountain of the LORD's house will be established*
> *at the top of the mountains*
> *and will be raised above the hills.*
> *All nations will stream to it,*
> *and many peoples will come and say,*
> *"Come, let's go up to the mountain of the LORD,*
> *to the house of the God of Jacob.*
> *He will teach us about his ways*
> *so that we may walk in his paths."*
> *For instruction will go out of Zion*
> *and the word of the LORD from Jerusalem.* (Isa 2:2-3)

In addition to the vastness of his eternal kingdom, Isaiah also celebrated the coming tribute that kings and former adversaries will bring to the final son of David out of adoration and fear:

> *Then you will see and be radiant,*
> *and your heart will tremble and rejoice,*
> *because the riches of the sea will become yours*
> *and the wealth of the nations will come to you.*
> *Caravans of camels will cover your land—*
> *young camels of Midian and Ephah—*
> *all of them will come from Sheba.*
> *They will carry gold and frankincense*
> *and proclaim the praises of the LORD.*
> *All the flocks of Kedar will be gathered to you;*
> *the rams of Nebaioth will serve you*
> *and go up on my altar as an acceptable sacrifice.*
> *I will glorify my beautiful house.* (Isa 60:5-7)

Solomon predicted the same outcome in Psalm 72:

> *May he rule from sea to sea*
> *and from the Euphrates*

to the ends of the earth.
May desert tribes kneel before him
and his enemies lick the dust.
May the kings of Tarshish
and the coasts and islands bring tribute,
the kings of Sheba and Seba offer gifts.
Let all kings bow in homage to him,
all nations serve him! (Ps 72:8-11)

Those who refuse to serve the Messiah will perish, and those nations that choose to ignore him will be laid to utter waste (Isa 60:12). His greatest oppressors will bow low before him out of fear (Isa 60:14). The strength and impact of God's Word in Judah is a prophetic reminder of what is ahead when the promised Son reigns from the throne of David.

As Jehoshaphat continued to obey the Lord's Word, the resulting divine favor and prosperity were in keeping with the Davidic promise and reminiscent of Solomon's best days as king (2 Chr 17:12-19). Here, too, the chronicles function as a hinge that opens our perception of the past while pointing us to the glory of what is ahead. Strengthened fortified cities, multiplied supplies, a growing army, and numerous men of valor not only pull the curtain back on the past, but they also reveal the coming reality that will accompany Christ's rise to his eternal resting place (Isa 11:10). Through the obedience of another, the Jews, along with Gentile believers, would one day enjoy the unrivaled strength of their eternal kingdom. The prophet Zechariah, who accompanied the exiles back to Jerusalem, also sought to comfort the people with this messianic vision for the future.

The LORD of Armies says this: "In those days, ten men from nations of every language will grab the robe of a Jewish man tightly, urging: Let us go with you, for we have heard that God is with you." (Zech 8:23)

Expanding military prowess would bring new temptations, however. Increased fortification and supplies left Jehoshaphat vulnerable to the enticements of the compromised tribes to the north who were suffering under the misguided leadership of their most spiritually obscene leader yet. As is always the case, divine blessings bring with them moral responsibilities. Jehoshaphat's failure to steward the outcomes of his obedience soon became an occasion for his stumbling.

The Subtleties of Weakness Are Problematic
2 CHRONICLES 18:1–19:11

After enjoying the strength that comes with obeying Scripture, Jehoshaphat's unholy alliance with Ahab is both jarring and unthinkable (18:1). As the sixth king in the north, Ahab sanctioned Baalism as the state religion of Samaria after marrying the wicked Jezebel (1 Kgs 16:31-33). How evil was she? The Lord would later personify the transgressions in the church at Thyatira by saying,

> But I have this against you: You tolerate the woman Jezebel, who calls herself a prophetess and teaches and deceives my servants to commit sexual immorality and to eat meat sacrificed to idols. (Rev 2:20)

Readers of the chronicle would have been familiar with the evil plight of these ungodly counterparts to the north. By allowing his son Jehoram to marry Ahab's daughter Athaliah, Jehoshaphat yoked himself and his kingdom together with Ahab and his kingdom in an unhealthy way.

The inserted detail of Ahab's kindness toward Jehoshaphat deviates from the Deuteronomistic historian slightly and likely represents the Chronicler's effort to expose his subtle manipulations (18:2 contra 1 Kgs 22:2). Both Ahab's true motivation and Jehoshaphat's naivete manifest when the two agree to battle together against Aram in order to regain Ramoth-gilead (vv. 3-4). More problematic is that these idolators to the north are not part of Judah, nor do they represent the true Israel.

Worse, though, is both the historical and theological ignorance and/or apathy shown by the southern king. In quite the ironic twist, Ahab duped Jehoshaphat into aiding his efforts toward undoing territorial lines won by his father, Asa. The Arameans claimed the territory through a treaty with Judah. Now, Jehoshaphat blindly partners with Judah's enemies due to his efforts to build goodwill and unity between the northern and southern kingdoms. Even if we assume the best intentions, the move was reckless and foolish, giving legitimacy to Samaria when there was none. Leithart explains,

> It is [Ahab's] war, and Jehoshaphat promises to throw his weight behind Ahab. The Chronicler highlights Jehoshaphat's theological error with subtle uses of names and titles. Ahab is not called "king of Israel" until he seduced Jehoshaphat into joining the military expedition (18:3). From that point, there

is a "king of Israel" and a "king of Judah." Ironically, the effort at united action reinforces the division of the two kingdoms. (Leithhart, *1 & 2 Chronicles*, 161)

These leadership weaknesses, while not overtly wicked, put Judah in a vulnerable position.

Similar gullible alliances plague many contemporary believers as well. Certainly, Christians should be wary of formal agreements with those who are unbelievers. The charge to avoid being unequally yoked (2 Cor 6:14) would not prevent simple acts of commerce, but avoiding intricate professional partnerships is wise. Also, Christians should only share the one-flesh union of marriage with those of equal commitment to Christ (Gen 2:24). While evangelistic friendships are a welcomed means to spread the gospel, followers of Christ must carefully avoid unintentional relational endorsements with those who teach falsehoods contrary to the gospel (2 John 10). Flirting with apostasy may increase our popularity, but in the end it ruins our spiritual credibility.

Thankfully, Jehoshaphat did not lack the courage to seek God, though his perception of what unfolds next remains puzzling (18:4). Though Ahab offered the support of four hundred prophets as affirmation of their next step (v. 5), the king of Judah wisely perceived these men were not true prophets of the Lord (v. 6). One cannot help but wonder why this was not enough to end this irresponsible pact before it caused further damage. Even Ahab's hatred for the one remaining prophet of the Lord who remained in Samaria (v. 7) should have been enough for Jehoshaphat to sever his support of the misguided war.

After the kings sent for the prophet Micaiah, Zedekiah and the false prophets of Israel doubled down on their prediction of victory (vv. 8-11). Like his father before him, Jehoshaphat heard from two prophets during his reign, and like his predecessor, he ignored one while heeding the counsel of the other. Despite the pleadings of Ahab's messenger, Micaiah refused to say anything that was not from the Lord (vv. 12-13). His sarcasm when questioned initially should not be interpreted as compromise (v. 14) because Ahab clearly knew Micaiah was not sincere in his initial claim (v. 15). Thus, God's prophet unloaded by predicting Ahab's death and Israel's defeat (v. 16).

Strangely, the northern king's hostility toward Micaiah was not enough to persuade Jehoshaphat to return home either (v. 17). Ahab's desire for teachers who spoke in accordance with his own desires revealed a heart eager to turn aside to myths and ears that were anxious to be tickled (2 Tim 4:3-4). In a vision that was surely for the benefit of Jehoshaphat, Micaiah explained in detail that Yahweh sent a lying spirit to deceive every false prophet that Ahab could employ (18:18-22). This act of judgment was a clarifying recollection that the Chronicler intended to reassure his postexilic readers that there was only one covenantal community.

How is it possible that God sent a lying spirit to lead Ahab astray? Before answering, we should first acknowledge that the scenario is not unique. Yahweh raised up Assyria as an aggressor against the northern kingdom and Babylon as an agent against the southern kingdom. Both acts of judgment were direct consequences for the rebellion of the people. Likewise, during a period of great tribulation on the earth, God will blind the minds of the unbelieving on the earth:

> For this reason God sends them a strong delusion so that they will believe the lie, so that all will be condemned—those who did not believe the truth but delighted in unrighteousness. (2 Thess 2:11-12)

Note, the hardening of these hearts is the outcome of previously rejecting the truth and taking pleasure in wickedness. Therefore, we should understand the plight of Ahab as the severe consequence of a lifetime filled with lawlessness and idolatry.

Enraged by what he heard, Zedekiah struck God's prophet, putting him in a long line of those who suffered unjustly for the Word of the Lord (18:23), even the Messiah himself (Isa 50:6; Matt 26:67; John 18:22). Micaiah responded with a pun (18:24), insinuating the seer who would not see would soon discover the veracity of his claims while hiding in a chamber equal to a modern bathroom (Thompson, *1, 2 Chronicles*, 286). Despite being thrown into prison by Ahab, the prophet remained faithful to speak the truth until he disappeared from the record (vv. 25-27).

Remarkably, Jehoshaphat remained undeterred in his support for Ahab and even tacitly responsible for the prophet's demise (v. 28). Even Ahab's plot to disguise himself so that Jehoshaphat appeared to be the only king in battle did not seem to alarm Judah's credulous leader (v. 29). In a powerful demonstration of God's determination to honor his revealed word, the Lord spared Jehoshaphat when he cried out for help, but he took the life of Ahab with what those on the battlefield perceived to be a random bowshot (vv. 30-34). No amount of human scheming can thwart the plan of God. Returning Jews anxious to rebuild Judah would have deduced themselves as the keepers of the covenant after reading this history. The apostasy of the north did not jeopardize Judah before the exile, and it certainly would not do so after their pilgrimage home.

Regardless of whether Jehoshaphat realized how close he came to falling, the Lord sent a second prophet to rebuke his carelessness (19:1-2). Because of his godly track record, there were fewer consequences than others might have experienced (v. 3). Unlike his father before him, Jehoshaphat received the rebuke by humbling himself before the Lord and leading his people to do the same (v. 4). The greatest sign of his repentance, though, was the judicial reforms that followed in the weeks afterward. He appointed judges in the fortified cities (v. 5) and admonished them with the fear of the Lord (vv. 5-7). Next, he assigned priests, Levites, and family heads to settle disputes among the people even as he cautioned them about incurring unnecessary guilt for promoting injustice (vv. 8-11). Despite his major missteps, Jehoshaphat was now providing a rich glimpse into the coming kingdom of the Messiah.

The Security of Worship Is Powerful
2 CHRONICLES 20:1-30

With the northern kingdom still at war with the Arameans and no alliance possible, outside enemies likely perceived Judah to be vulnerable. Sensing they had the upper hand, the Moabites and Ammonites, the descendants of Lot's incestuous relationship with his daughters, along with the Meunites, the offspring of Esau, came from every direction against Jehoshaphat (20:1-2). No matter the aggressors, the point here seems to be that the enemy encroached from every direction. Perhaps the most telling description of the threat is the admission that Judah's king was afraid (v. 3a). Yet in this same moment Jehoshaphat's most enduring quality rises as he sets his heart to seek the Lord while compelling the nation to join him through a national fast (vv. 3b-4). The prayer and praise that followed are instructive for believers in every age.

Our Praise Should Reflect God's Previous Works (20:5-9)

First, we learn to praise God for *who he is* as Jehoshaphat acknowledges the lordship, authority, power, and sovereignty of Yahweh (vv. 5-6). In other words, he sought peace by focusing on the greatness and majesty of the Lord. Imagine how encouraging these reminders must have been for the postexilic community as they faced the challenges surrounding Jerusalem's rebirth. Likewise, applying this practice today compels us to view our problems through the lens of God's glory rather than vice versa.

Second, we discover the value of praising God for *what he has done.* Jehoshaphat's familiarity with the history of the nation and Yahweh's provisions throughout gave the king confidence that the Lord would preserve his people again. Recalling God's past works likely shaped his awareness of who God is more than anything else. He remembered that God gave them their land (v. 7); he allowed Solomon to complete the temple (v. 8); and he promised to deliver those who sought him at the temple (v. 9). In fact, Jehoshaphat lifts his words directly from Solomon's dedication of the holy structure. With the splendor of the past looming large, the shadow of God's peace emerged over Judah's present dilemma. Similarly, though we do not always understand what God is doing (or not doing), praising the Lord for what he has already done helps us cope. A strong Christian walk requires a good memory!

Finally, our challenge is to praise God for *what he will do.* Again, Jehoshaphat highlights Israel's history but this time to anticipate Yahweh's response to the current predicament. By harking back to the time of the exodus, he poses a question rooted in the character of God (vv. 10-11). Despite Edom's refusal to allow the Hebrew sojourners to pass through their territory, Israel did not invade or destroy their nemesis (Num 20:14-21). The king could not fathom that God would allow these same peoples to destroy his chosen ones now. Therefore, without knowing *how* God might work, Jehoshaphat has tremendous trust that he *will* work. His admission of weakness was actually a confession of certitude that divine justice was coming (v. 12). With nowhere else to turn, all eyes were on Yahweh.

Though modern readers may find little relatability to the affliction that befell Judah, what will resonate is the overwhelming sense of desperation Jehoshaphat shouldered. Have you ever reeled knowing that unless God answered there was no hope? Did you know that unless he intervened there were no solutions? Did you despair that unless he provided there were no other options? Did you plead that unless he was strong on your behalf you were powerless to defend yourself? Moments like these constrain us to draw strength from God's past faithfulness. We will never praise God for what he will do if we do not intentionally, even strategically, remember what he has done.

And why should we praise God at all? Interestingly, for the same reason Jehoshaphat did. Judah's king called out to God based on the promise that Yahweh would hear and protect all who called out to him at the temple (v. 9). In doing so, he reminds new covenant believers that Jesus is the fulfillment of God's house. Because of his sacrificial death and resurrection, he is willing to hear us and protect us when we incline our hearts toward him and ask anything in accordance with his will. Thus, Jesus assured,

> *Whatever you ask in my name, I will do it so that the Father may be glorified in the Son. If you ask me anything in my name, I will do it.* (John 14:13-14)

Like the temple before him, Jesus gives us access to and hope in our God.

Our Praise Should Be Rooted in God's Prophetic Word (20:10-19)

After his heartfelt entreaty, the king and all of Judah stood humbly before the Lord (2 Chr 20:13). No sooner had Jehoshaphat prayed than God answered by sending a prophetic word through a Levite named Jahaziel (v. 14). His message was fourfold:

- Do not be afraid or discouraged (vv. 15,17).
- The battle belongs to the Lord (vv. 15,17).
- Position yourselves, stand still, and see the salvation of the Lord (v. 17).
- The Lord is with you (v. 17).

The language is similar to descriptions of God's initiative and protection during the exodus (Exod 14:13-14). In yet another instance of linking the past and the future, Yahweh's intervention on behalf of his people offers a beautiful depiction of the salvation that is coming in Christ, who took all initiative to save us. We are but spectators in the divine drama of redemption, realizing we could never add to the sacrifice of Jesus in any way. Faced with a battle we could not win, God fought it for us.

Could it be that we are less inclined to worship God as we should because we futilely attempt to control what only he can accomplish? Like Abraham sojourning with Lot as a backup plan for his family tree? Or his assuming that Eliezer would be an adequate heir? Or worst of all, his conspiratorial efforts to father Ishmael with Hagar? In our efforts to follow God on our terms, we often miss what only he can do for us and forfeit the basis of much adoration.

Not surprisingly, all the inhabitants of Judah bowed before the Lord in worship and praise after receiving his word (2 Chr 20:18-19). We should note that little had changed at this point, outside of God's revealed intent. Judah had the same problem and faced the same battle, yet praise illuminated the shadows of fear and dread that surrounded them. Today, Scripture affords us similar opportunities. Though living in a world of fallenness leaves much to despair, the God who reveals himself in the pages of Holy Writ compels our worship as we read of his attributes, his works, and his promises. Biblical praise is much more than mere emotionalism devoid of substance. We do not magnify God *despite* what we know but *because of* what we know. Scripture must inform our worship!

Another practical observation within the text is that Judah's worship of Yahweh preceded their deliverance. *Expressing* their faith was born out of *exercising* their faith. Many, though not all, will gladly honor God after receiving a miracle, but fewer still will revere him beforehand. Today, we rarely know how our trials will be resolved, but God calls us to worship nonetheless. Because of Scripture, we remain confident about *who* God is even when we do not fully comprehend *how* he will work on our behalf. When we feel alone (Isa 41:10), when our burdens are heavy (Rom 8:18), when we don't know what to do (Prov 3:6), and when we cannot articulate our pain (Rom 8:26), God's Word instills the hope of worship in our hearts.

Our Praise Should Be Regarded as God's Powerful Weapon (20:20-30)

As the moment of battle drew near, Judah's emboldened leader admonished his people to trust God's revealed word (2 Chr 20:20). In what can only be regarded as an unusual strategy, Judah is led by a convoy of worship leaders rather than military generals. Perhaps that is precisely the point. The apostle Paul later explained,

For although we live in the flesh, we do not wage war according
to the flesh, since the weapons of our warfare are not of the flesh,
but are powerful through God for the demolition of strongholds.
(2 Cor 10:3-4)

Praise is one of the more powerful weapons we have to fight against the enemy. Amy Carmichael wisely observed, "I believe truly that Satan cannot endure it [song], and so slips out of the room—more or less!—where there is true song" (Demaray, *Alive to God*, 51).

What was the result of these efforts? As the people lifted up their voices in song and devotion, Yahweh routed the enemy with a spiritual ambush (v. 22). Ironically, the enemies bent on destroying Judah helped to demolish one another (vv. 23-24). Just as promised, the Lord fought the battle for his people. All that remained was collecting the spoils of war (v. 25). Once more they worshiped after assembling in the Valley of Beracah, which means blessing (v. 26). The people returned rejoicing over their enemies, who feared the kingdom of God (vv. 27-30).

Again, the Chronicler reaches to the past in order to galvanize the postexilic community to prioritize worship due to the security it brings. Even so, he also elevates our perspective to the eternal power wrought by the worship of God's people as the enemies of heaven are put down by the strong hand of the Messiah again, just as they were during the days of Jehoshaphat. The prophet Joel predicted,

Let the nations be roused
and come to the Valley of Jehoshaphat,
for there I will sit down
to judge all the surrounding nations.
Swing the sickle
because the harvest is ripe.
Come and trample the grapes
because the winepress is full;
the wine vats overflow
because the wickedness of the nations is extreme.
Multitudes, multitudes
in the valley of decision!
For the day of the LORD *is near*
in the valley of decision. (Joel 3:12-14)

These visions of judgment will come to pass in the battle of Armageddon, just before Christ's millennial kingdom. And just as they did in the Valley of Beracah generations before, the twenty-four elders, the redeemed of the ages, the angels, and every living creature will worship the Lamb *before* he acts in righteousness (Rev 5:8-14; 7:9-12). Consequently, the enemies of God will again be routed. Revelation 16:13-16 describes the scene:

> *Then I saw three unclean spirits like frogs coming from the dragon's mouth, from the beast's mouth, and from the mouth of the false prophet. For they are demonic spirits performing signs, who travel to the kings of the whole world to assemble them for the battle on the great day of God, the Almighty. "Look, I am coming like a thief. Blessed is the one who is alert and remains clothed so that he may not go around naked and people see his shame." So they assembled the kings at the place called in Hebrew, Armageddon.*

Then God will defeat the forces of hell with just one word:

> *Then I saw heaven opened, and there was a white horse. Its rider is called Faithful and True, and with justice he judges and makes war. His eyes were like a fiery flame, and many crowns were on his head. He had a name written that no one knows except himself. He wore a robe dipped in blood, and his name is called the Word of God. The armies that were in heaven followed him on white horses, wearing pure white linen. A sharp sword came from his mouth, so that he might strike the nations with it. He will rule them with an iron rod. He will also trample the winepress of the fierce anger of God, the Almighty. And he has a name written on his robe and on his thigh: KING OF KINGS AND LORD OF LORDS.*
>
> *Then I saw an angel standing in the sun, and he called out in a loud voice, saying to all the birds flying high overhead, "Come, gather together for the great supper of God, so that you may eat the flesh of kings, the flesh of military commanders, the flesh of the mighty, the flesh of horses and of their riders, and the flesh of everyone, both free and slave, small and great."*
>
> *Then I saw the beast, the kings of the earth, and their armies gathered together to wage war against the rider on the horse and against his army. But the beast was taken prisoner, and along with it the false prophet, who had performed the signs in its presence. He*

deceived those who accepted the mark of the beast and those who worshiped its image with these signs. Both of them were thrown alive into the lake of fire that burns with sulfur. The rest were killed with the sword that came from the mouth of the rider on the horse, and all the birds ate their fill of their flesh. (Rev 19:11-21)

Conclusion
2 CHRONICLES 20:31–21:1

Overall, the reign of Jehoshaphat was a bright spot in the often dark history of the people of God. His example would have been a great encouragement for postexilic Jews to walk with integrity in their faith tradition (20:31-32). The king was far from perfect, though, as evidenced by the many high places that remained throughout the kingdom (20:33). Tragically, Jehoshaphat even repeated the same misstep as before by forming a new alliance with Ahaziah, king of the northern kingdom, after Ahaz died (20:35-37). As previously, the Lord chastised his leader so that there was no profit from the joint venture. God destroyed their fleet of ships designed for trade.

On the surface, Jehoshaphat repeated failures to rely on God by seeking human allies outside the covenantal community. Even the most committed followers of Christ struggle with the lust of the flesh and eyes along with the pride of life (1 John 2:16). A deeper analysis, though, reveals the admission that although Jehoshaphat was a good king, he was not *THE KING*. The challenge of life post-Babylon was to avoid the pitfalls of the past while continuing to look for the promised Son of David.

Reflect and Discuss

1. In what ways does the life of Jehoshaphat inspire and challenge you? How do you see yourself in his milestones and struggles?
2. What does Jehoshaphat teach us about the value of Scripture? How should we practically respond to his example?
3. How does the obedience of Christ bring blessings into our lives that exceed the favor Jehoshaphat enjoyed from the Lord?
4. In what ways do spiritual blind spots make us naïve to the dangers of sin? How can we protect ourselves?
5. What does it mean to be unequally yoked? What kind of unholy alliances should we avoid?

6. How should we respond to others who bring up the seeming contradictions of our faith?

7. What do Jehoshaphat's quick repentance and restoration teach us about God's eagerness to forgive when we stray?

8. In what way is worship a weapon? How can we establish a healthy rhythm of worship?

9. How does Scripture function like a guardrail that prevents our worship from moving into unhealthy extremes?

10. Why is it important for us to worship God before, or even without, his intervention in our lives?

Looking for Hope in the Dark Places

2 CHRONICLES 21–23

Main Idea: The full development of Jehoshaphat's previous entanglements provides both a warning against compromise and a greater motivation to worship. As always, understanding the missteps of the past better prepares us to be faithful in the present.

I.   **The Tragedy of a Wasted Life (21:1-20)**
II. **The Tactics of a Wicked Foe (22:1-10)**
III. **The Testimony of a Wonderful Promise (22:11–23:21)**

Have you ever wondered what happened to the prodigal son after the father welcomed him home? We know the wayward son came to his senses in the pigpen. We weep with joy over the details of the forgiveness of the father, who met his son while he was still a long way off in order to embrace him. And we celebrate the father's extravagant grace as he kills the fatted calf for a welcome-home party. But what happened to the forgiven son in the weeks and months that followed? Obviously, Jesus's fictional story never answered that question, but the scene does end with a jealous older brother who resents the father's compassion for his rebellious child.

In his book *Come Thirsty*, Max Lucado speculates about the pressure created by the older brother who wants to rain on the forgiveness parade:

> "If Dad won't exact justice on the boy," he thought, "I will."
>
> "Nice robe there, little brother," he tells him one day. "Better keep it clean. One spot and Dad will send you to the cleaners with it."
>
> The younger waves him away, but the next time he sees his father, he quickly checks his robe for stains.
>
> A few days later the big brother warns about the ring. "Quite a piece of jewelry Dad gave you. He prefers that you wear it on the thumb."
>
> "The thumb? He didn't tell me that."
>
> "Some things we're just supposed to know."
>
> "But it won't fit my thumb."

"What's your goal—pleasing our father or your own personal comfort?" the spirituality monitor gibes, walking away.

Big brother isn't finished. With the pleasantness of a dyspeptic IRS auditor, he taunts, "If Dad sees you with loose laces, he'll take the sandals back."

"He will not. They were a gift. He wouldn't . . . would he?" The ex-prodigal then leans over to snug the strings. As he does, he spots a smudge on his robe. Trying to rub it off, he realizes the ring is on a finger, not his thumb. That's when he hears his father's voice. "Hello, Son."

There the boy sits, wearing a spotted robe, loose laces, and a misplaced ring. Overcome with fear, he reacts with a "Sorry, Dad" and turns and runs.

Too many tasks. Keeping the robe spotless, the ring positioned, the sandals snug—who could meet such standards? Gift preservation begins to wear on the young man. He avoids the father he feels he can't please. He quits wearing the gifts he can't maintain. And he even begins longing for the simpler days of the pigpen. "No one hounded me there."

That's the rest of the story. (*Come Thirsty*, 29–31)

And what does Lucado base his speculation on? Galatians 1:6-7:

> *I am amazed that you are so quickly turning away from him who called you by the grace of Christ and are turning to a different gospel—not that there is another gospel, but there are some who are troubling you and want to distort the gospel of Christ.*

We all tend to stray from the simplicity and beauty of God's grace toward us, returning to the dead end of our deficient righteousness. The image reminds me of an Old Testament prodigal who never came home. In a sense, both Jehoram and Jehoshaphat abandoned the tremendous gifts Yahweh gave them. Though Jehoram benefitted greatly from God's favor and blessings during the reign of his father, Jehoshaphat, Judah's new king wasted his potential success in exchange for idolatrous paranoia and rage. One could also argue, though, that the seeds of reverting back to the pigsty of idolatry and compromise actually began with Jehoshaphat, who squandered the grace of God for carnal tactics.

This section of the chronicle is especially dark, demonstrating the generational spiral that resulted from the compromises of Jehoshaphat's reign. Johnstone astutely identifies the purpose behind the pericope as showing "how the poison introduced by Jehoshaphat's alliance with the royal house of the north, sealed by Jehoram's own marriage to Ahab's daughter, Athaliah, continues its deadly influence" by spreading "into the heart of the life of Judah itself" (*1 and 2 Chronicles, Vol. 2*, 108–9). At this historical juncture, the distinctions between the northern and southern kingdoms were slowly dissipating.

Though no hard break in messaging exists between 1 and 2 Chronicles, the former emphasizes inspiration more heavily while the latter prioritizes instructions for avoiding future judgment such as the exile. Fortunately for modern readers, the goals of reclaiming Jerusalem and renewing the Davidic covenant are not antithetical to efforts toward understanding what led to the exile in the first place. Also, contrasting the faithfulness of God with the wickedness of the people is clearly the Chronicler's intent.

For Jews looking to establish life after the exile, the resolution to the spiral of apostasy within the pericope focuses on rebuilding the temple cultus. Though the postexilic challenges were many, prioritizing renewed worship was the first and most important step toward covenantal renewal. These chapters inspire believers today to fear the Lord even as we worship him while also expanding our vision of his worthiness.

The Tragedy of a Wasted Life
2 CHRONICLES 21:1-20

After the death of Jehoshaphat, his eldest son, Jehoram, became king over Judah ahead of his six brothers (vv. 1-2). In an apparent effort to prevent any sibling rivalry that would undermine the strength of the crown, Jehoshaphat had given gifts of silver and gold, along with the leadership of fortified cities, to each of his sons. Presumably, these responsibilities would ward off any greater political ambitions that might exist among those not serving as king while also fostering Jehoram's genuine respect for them (v. 3). The stage was all set for a smooth transition. Tragically, though, Judah's fifth king after Solomon, whether due to his paranoia or his evil associations, killed all of his brothers and any other perceived threats to his throne (v. 4). Dillard rightly observes,

"There is both irony and retributive justice in that Jehoram sets in motion events that would ultimately lead to the near obliteration of his own line" (*2 Chronicles*, 165).

Though his reign was just eight years long, Jehoram's kingdom was a sign that Judah was becoming more like their wicked brothers to the north (v. 5). The newly installed king not only did evil according to the Lord, but he walked in the ways of Israel's kings, particularly the vilest of them all, Ahab (v. 6). Jehoshaphat's arranged marriage with the house of Ahab is still reeking with consequences, a reminder of how devastating our sins can be to others. The subtle deviances of one generation become the open rebellions of the next. Here now was a rightful son of David who cared nothing for Yahweh, his covenant, or his people. Rather than war against the northern kingdom, Jehoram aspires to be like them. Despite possessing the same promises given to David, Judah's king rebelled against all of them. Truly, he squandered every good thing God desired to give him.

And yet, remarkably, the Lord refused to forsake his commitment to the house of David. God, as he always does, remains faithful to us when we are unfaithful to him. His determination to provide a lamp for David is evidence of his deep resolve to win the war against the serpent (Gen 3:15). Using a metaphor to communicate the permanence of God's promises, the Chronicler celebrates that the "lamp" of David's house will continue to burn brightly even in the darkest moments of redemptive history (v. 7) (Selman, *2 Chronicles*, 453). Ironically, the lamp referred to here may be a reference to Jehoram because of his role as the only surviving heir within the Davidic family tree. Yahweh was committed to his chosen people, as he is to us, even when they strayed.

We should not assume, however, that God's assurances of preservation guaranteed protection from his retributive justice. Though the covenantal reality restrained the full extent of God's discipline, all of Judah suffered as their king forfeited the gains of Asa and Jehoshaphat. First, the Edomites in the south rebelled (v. 8), and despite his best efforts through a surprise attack, Jehoram was helpless to stop them because God was not with him (v. 9). In this instance, Esau usurped Jacob for a change. Next, the Libnahites revolted in the north as well (v. 10). All of this was the direct result of Jehoram abandoning the Lord, defined as his building pagan shrines and inciting his people to whore around with other gods, both physically and spiritually (v. 11).

Furthermore, a rare letter of rebuke from Elijah (not included in the Kings record) announced the severity of Jehoram's sins and the certainty of God's judgment against him (vv. 12-15). For the prophet known almost exclusively for his rebuke of the northern kingdom, this inclusion is yet another subtle example of the king's collaboration with and reflection of the spiritual apostates to the north. Additionally, Elijah also incorporates the language of spiritual prostitution two times (v. 13) in his effort to identify the sins of Judah with the transgressions of Samaria. Holding up Jehoshaphat and Asa as exemplars clearly indicates that a pattern of faithfulness is the standard rather than sinless perfection.

The language of the exodus pulls readers back to memories of Yahweh interceding on their behalf, but here the implication is the opposite, or what Leithart calls an upside-down exodus. "Jehoram and his land will suffer plagues, his own sons will be destroyed because Jehoram killed his brothers, and he himself, the firstborn will die an agonizing death" (*1 & 2 Chronicles*, 179). Most important for the postexilic community reading this history was the explicit explanation and warning that it was the Lord who stirred up the spirits of these enemies to attack Judah (v. 16) due to Jehoram's idolatry. Broadly, this recollection was a caution against viewing Yahweh as a passive spectator of their waywardness. Yahweh will not ignore idolatry. More specifically, the Chronicler earmarks prostituting with other gods as the single reason for the Babylonian exile (v. 11) by using the identical phrase ("roused the spirit"; v. 16) previously descriptive of the Assyrian captivity at the hands of King Tiglath-pileser (1 Chr 5:26). Although the Lord usually plays the role of our protector, he can also pose as our biggest threat when necessary.

Consequently, the judgment forecast by Elijah soon became a reality. In addition to their southern and northern opponents, the Philistines to the west and the Arabs to the east also come against them (2 Chr 21:16). Although David defeated the Philistines and Asa the Cushites, it was now apparent that the Davidic dynasty was shrinking. The plundering of the Lord's temple was but a forestate of what would soon befall both northern and southern kingdoms after God's patience ran out. In addition to these national crises, the personal health maladies predicted for Jehoram (v. 15) also came to pass (vv. 18-19). Sadly, no one grieved for the king who wasted his life and influence (v. 20).

Through all of this, Yahweh never wavered in his efforts to raise up a son to reign out of the house of David. Understanding the costly setbacks during this dark season would have been an invaluable perspective for the returning believers hungry to see Yahweh move among them again. Christians today must also learn that sin never occurs in a vacuum. Years of compromise are the usual backdrop to apostasy. As the old saying goes, sin will take you farther than you want to stray, keep you longer than you want to stay, and cost you more than you want to pay. How tragic would it be to die in such profound wickedness that no one cared to lament? Even more fearful is the thought of facing God's life-ending judgment and immediately answering to him for your downfall.

The Tactics of a Wicked Foe
2 CHRONICLES 22:1-10

Despite the abysmal leadership of Jehoram, the people of Judah still chose his son Ahaziah to be their next king (v. 1). Because confusion abounds when trying to distinguish between biblical characters in Judah and Samaria who share the same name, the following guidance is helpful:

> In order to make sense out of the events in this section, one
> must recognize the duplication of the names of the kings
> in the southern and northern kingdoms. In the northern
> kingdom of Israel, Ahab had two sons, Ahaziah and Jehoram.
> When Ahab died, his son Ahaziah succeeded him, and he in
> turn was succeeded by his brother, Jehoram (aka Joram). In
> the southern kingdom of Judah, Jehoshaphat was succeeded
> by his son Jehoram, and his successor was his son (and
> Jehoshaphat's grandson), Ahaziah (aka Jehoahaz). Thus
> the successions in the north were: Ahab, Ahaziah, Jehoram
> [i.e., Joram]; in the south the successions were: Jehoshaphat,
> Jehoram, Ahaziah. (*CSB Study Bible*, 673)

Ahaziah was contemptible like his father, in large part because his mother Athaliah was fully committed to Baal worship. Her influence was the primary reason for the short reign and early demise of her son (vv. 2-3). In addition to heeding the counsel of his ungodly mother, Ahaziah also surrounded himself with morally deficient advisors from the house of Ahab (v. 4). After the kingdom split due to Rehoboam's foolish counselors, now it was reuniting as Ahaziah's evil confidants convinced him to embrace the ways of Ahab throughout Judah (Leithart, *1 & 2 Chronicles*, 181). The result was his undoing.

Foolishly, like his grandfather before him, Ahaziah joined in the north's war against the Arameans in Ramoth Gilead (v. 5). Unlike Jehoshaphat, though, Ahaziah would not be fortunate enough to escape the conflict with his life. After the Arameans wounded Israel's King Joram in battle, he returned to Jezreel to heal (v. 6). Ahaziah went down to check on his uncle's condition, where he faced the fierceness of God's wrath against the house of Ahab (v. 7). With Jehu as God's chosen instrument, the divine intent was to wipe out the iniquitous seed of the northern kingdom's most corrupt king. As his execution of justice unfolded, however, Jehu overzealously slew Ahaziah along with the princes of Judah, all of whom had ties to Ahab, nearly eliminating any heirs to sit on David's throne (vv. 8-9).

While Jehu receives thorough attention in the Deuteronomistic history, the focus of the Chronicler is the southern kingdom and the lack of an heir to the throne of David. For postexilic readers, the account was a reminder and a warning against their religious compromises, even with their northern brothers who were part of a unified Israel. No matter what the future held or how many tribes participated in the nation's rebirth, avoiding the deterioration of their cultic commitments was pivotal going forward.

Additionally, in his efforts to demonstrate the tactics of the serpent against David's house, the Chronicler highlights the absence of a worthy heir to assume Judah's kingship and power (v. 9). The need of the moment corresponded to the desperation Jews after Babylon must have felt when they saw no evidence of a Davidic dynasty. Dillard notes,

> Surely the lesson was not lost on his post-exilic audience: even in adversity the royal line was preserved and would eventually regain the kingdom. Davidic hopes did not die at the time of Ahaziah, Athaliah, and Joash; they should not die in the post-exilic period. The flame from the promise of God that David would never lack a descendant to rule Israel (1 Chr 17:11-14; 2 Chr 21:7) may have become little more than a smoldering wick—but it could not be extinguished. (Dillard, *2 Chronicles*, 175)

The historical drama only increased as the writer segued to Athaliah's repugnant shenanigans.

After Ahaziah's downfall, his mother, the daughter of Ahab, strategically sought to destroy all royal offspring in order to assume Judah's throne herself (v. 10). Despite centuries of time and space, we must not overlook that these victims were Athaliah's grandchildren. Herein lies the chief tactic of the devil, namely, to destroy any familial lines leading to the Messiah.

> Ahab is not only an idolater, but also an oppressive king who arranges for Naboth's death and seizes his ancestral vineyard. Jehoram's wife Athaliah, daughter of Ahab, takes cues from her father and husband: when she takes the throne, she wipes out the whole royal seed to ensure the stability of her kingdom. In the house of Ahab, violence and idolatry go together. (Leithart, *1 & 2 Chronicles*, 178)

The driving force behind these events was part of a much greater battle that has raged since the garden of Eden.

As evidence of the enmity between the seed of the woman and the seed of the serpent, Cain rose up to kill Abel (Gen 4:8). In his efforts to put down Moses, Satan moved Pharoah to kill all the firstborn Hebrew sons in Egypt (Exod 1:22). During the days of Esther, the entire Jewish nation faced extermination at the hands of Haman (Esth 3:1-15). Likewise, King Herod ordered all Jewish sons born in and around Bethlehem at the time of Jesus's birth to be put to death (Matt 2:16). Perhaps Revelation gives us the most graphic picture by casting the devil as a dragon ready to destroy Israel's (portrayed as a woman) promised child,

> *Its tail swept away a third of the stars in heaven and hurled them to the earth. And the dragon stood in front of the woman who was about to give birth, so that when she did give birth it might devour her child.* (Rev 12:4)

For six long years it seemed as though Athaliah succeeded. For the first time in history, it seemed as though no one remained to lead the Davidic kingdom for God's people. The only qualified leaders from David's house were lying in Jerusalem tombs. The mighty Yahweh seemed defeated after promising so much.

Can you imagine how godly Hebrews would have tried to process these developments when they unfolded? And can you see how Jews after the exile would have shared similar concerns as they looked around and saw no king? When we pan out further, we learn that in the fullness of time God sent forth another son of David who was not like those who preceded him (Gal 4:4). After years of waiting, the disciples finally realized that this was their Messiah, the Son of the living God (Matt 16:16; Mark 8:29; Luke 9:20)! And then, as their ambitions for the kingdom soared, Jesus died a brutal death and was laid in a Jerusalem tomb. And while the Bible is not explicit about how the disciples felt after Jesus's crucifixion, it seems likely that their reaction would have been much like the crowd of people who mourned and lamented on the way to the cross (Luke 23:27).

In that moment the serpent appeared to be victorious. The death of Christ appeared to be more than a bruised heel; it seemed as though the Savior had a crushed head. The disciples' hopes died with Jesus that day. Why? Because just like during the days of Judah while Athaliah reigned, no qualified descendant of David existed. Or so it seemed.

The Testimony of a Wonderful Promise
2 CHRONICLES 22:11–23:21

But God. Not only does the text go to great lengths to illustrate how God intervened in order to preserve the Davidic dynasty, but the priority of the temple also emerges as a theme. Perhaps this was a subtle reinforcement for the postexilic community to focus on their cultic commitments while entrusting the seat of David to Yahweh. Because the Lord used his temple to maintain his covenant previously, Jews released from the grip of the Persian Empire should focus their efforts on God's house first. As always, only God was capable of building the house of David.

Here, the daughter of King Jehoram and sister to King Ahaziah, Jehoshabeath (possibly a daughter to the queen as well), rescued Joash from the grip of death (22:11). Just as Jochebed rescued Moses from Pharoah before, and Mary and Joseph would later do the same to protect Jesus from Herod, God through Jehoshabeath spared the chosen son of David. His salvation came by hiding in the temple for six years (v. 12). Finally, trusting in the promises of God, Jehoiada the priest forms a coup against Athaliah (23:1-2).

In bold declaration, Jehoiada insists that the king's son, the rightful heir, will reign from the seat of David as the Lord instructed (23:3). The captains, Levites, and heads of households joined in solidarity by surrounding Joash in the temple for his protection (vv. 4-7). These leaders carried out their orders exactly (vv. 8-10) as they crowned Joash as Judah's king (v. 11). The ensuing celebration had its desired effect, successfully wooing Athaliah into the temple (v. 12). When the unwanted queen sees the king standing in the temple, it is as though one had risen from the dead (v. 13). God successfully brought life out of seeming death.

Despite Athaliah's protesting, Jehoiada's coalition seized her, and not wanting to take her life within the temple, executed her at the Horse Gate of the king's house (23:14-15). With the stain of Ahab's influence finally purged, the people renewed their commitment to be the Lord's people by renewing the covenantal realities of the temple and a son of David on their throne (v. 16). In addition, they tore down the house of Baal, killed Mattan the false priest, renewed the cultic expressions under the authority of the Levitical priests, and stationed gatekeepers at the entrance of the temple (vv. 17-19). Clearly, the faithfulness of the nation would rise and fall with their worship priorities. Finally, they placed Joash on the royal throne as the people of Judah rejoiced (vv. 20-21).

The festive scene here is but a shadow of another celebration for a son of David who overcame death when all appeared hopeless.

> But no one in heaven or on earth or under the earth was able to open the scroll or even to look in it. I wept and wept because no one was found worthy to open the scroll or even to look in it. Then one of the elders said to me, "Do not weep. Look, the Lion from the tribe of Judah, the Root of David, has conquered so that he is able to open the scroll and its seven seals." Then I saw one like a slaughtered lamb standing in the midst of the throne and the four living creatures and among the elders. He had seven horns and seven eyes, which are the seven spirits of God sent into all the earth. (Rev 5:3-6)

A similar celebration of singing and rejoicing breaks out among the saints of God when Christ one day rules over us:

> When he took the scroll, the four living creatures and the twenty-four elders fell down before the Lamb. Each one had a harp and golden

bowls filled with incense, which are the prayers of the saints. And they
sang a new song:

> *You are worthy to take the scroll*
> *and to open its seals,*
> *because you were slaughtered,*
> *and you purchased people*
> *for God by your blood*
> *from every tribe and language*
> *and people and nation.*
> *You made them a kingdom*
> *and priests to our God,*
> *and they will reign on the earth.* (Rev 5:8-10)

Ultimately, all of creation will extol the one who sits on the throne of his
father David in power and blessing for all in his kingdom.

> *I heard every creature in heaven, on earth, under the earth, on the sea,*
> *and everything in them say,*
>
> > *Blessing and honor and glory and power*
> > *be to the one seated on the throne,*
> > *and to the Lamb, forever and ever!* (Rev 5:13)

We should also note that the victory in this pericope begins at the temple as the people gather around their king. Then, it flows out to the far
reaches of the kingdom as they defeat the counterfeit religion of the serpent. The same will be true in the new heaven and earth when the Lamb of
God dwells among his people as king. Revelation 22:1-3 explains,

> *Then he showed me the river of the water of life, clear as crystal,*
> *flowing from the throne of God and of the Lamb down the middle*
> *of the city's main street. The tree of life was on each side of the river,*
> *bearing twelve kinds of fruit, producing its fruit every month. The*
> *leaves of the tree are for healing the nations, and there will no longer*
> *be any curse.*

The testimony of these wonderful promises proved to be true during the days of Joash, and they will confirm God's coming intentions for
us in eternity. The Chronicler not only challenges postexilic Jews to lean
into the promises of God despite what they saw with their eyes, but he
also casts a vision for future believers to put all our hope on the one who

holds the government on his shoulders and reigns in glory from David's throne forever and ever.

Reflect and Discuss

1. In what ways do the continuing consequences of Jehoshaphat's previous sins challenge you to turn from wickedness? How do you see your sins hurting others?
2. What does God's judgment of Jehoram teach us about God's faithfulness when we rebel?
3. What does our tendency to repeat the sins of the past teach us about the value of Scripture in our lives?
4. In what ways can God become our enemy? What does this concept teach us about the holiness of God?
5. What does the preservation of Joash teach us about God's determination to redeem?
6. How has the serpent worked to kill the reign of Christ in your life?
7. What does God's judgment on the house of Ahab teach us about God's holiness?
8. How is Joash a picture of Christ's future resurrection from the dead?
9. What does Jehoiada's prioritizing the temple teach us about the role of worship in restoring us to God?
10. What does Judah's restoration teach us about the coming kingdom of God?

Stumbling at the Finish Line

2 CHRONICLES 24–26

Main Idea: As Judah drifted further and further toward the exile, three of their most promising kings stumbled in the latter part of their lives, effectively forfeiting their previous blessings from Yahweh. Their stories provide corrective directives for the postexilic community as well as for followers of Christ today.

I.   Joash: A Lesson on Accountability (24:1-27)
II. Amaziah: A Lesson on Apathy (25:1-28)
III. Uzziah: A Lesson on Arrogance (26:1-23)

The year was 1949. CIA operative Douglas Mackiernan fled for the border of Tibet as Mao Tse-tung's communist army swept through China. Though the national boundary was a treacherous twelve hundred miles away, getting there was the only hope for survival. For seven months he endured the elements. First, he needed to cross the desert. Going without water for three days at one point left Doug and his companions nearly dead. A seeping spring saved their lives.

Next, Mackiernan faced the Himalayas in the dead of winter. As they traversed the jagged terrain at sixteen thousand feet, the air was so thin and cold that speaking was simply too painful. Speaking only through hand signals, Doug and his comrades pressed on. The piercing winds threatened frostbite. Mounds of snow obscured the path. Losing his horse made the trek more difficult. But Mackiernan pressed on, never veering too far off the centuries-old path marked by large piles of stone.

What were the large mounds? They were the graves of those who had endeavored to make the arduous journey before. With the ground frozen solid, local residents did not attempt to dig graves. They simply pulled the deceased to one side of the trail and heaped piles of rocks over their bodies. These markers to the left and right of the path formed a natural map for those brave enough to keep pressing forward. Each grave was a visible reminder that no matter how far you moved along the trails you could not let your guard down until you finished.

The same is true for Christians today. No matter how long we serve the Lord, how faithful we've been, or how much distance we've covered, we can never let our guard down until we get to heaven. How we finish the race of faith is much more important than how we begin. As we age and mature in our walks with the Lord, our temptations may change, but they never go away. Finishing well requires as much discipline, if not more, in our final days as it does when we are new to the family of God. This pericope reminds us of our incredible propensity to stumble after years of faithfulness, when it matters most (Farrar, *Gettin' There*, 103–4).

As he continues to outline the events that ultimately led to Babylonian ruin and captivity, the Chronicler adds details and explanations omitted from the Kings record, especially about the sons of David who were the godliest. Despite their admirable leadership, Joash, Amaziah, and Uzziah all stumbled at the end of their lives and died out of step with Yahweh. Furthering his theme of covenantal retribution, the postexilic historian divides the reign of each aforementioned leader into positive and negative phases, reflecting righteousness and unrighteousness (Boda, *1–2 Chronicles*, 353). Serving as a measured warning, these accounts were to be a standard for those rebuilding Jerusalem. The goal was not simply to begin well but also to finish well. The glory of restoring the city would dissipate just as rapidly as before if God's people were not fully obedient and devoted to Yahweh.

This pericope also depicts the rebirth of the Davidic line after its near annihilation during the terror of Athaliah. The blessing of children meant that the chosen family would now continue for generations. Overall, there is a tone of both gratitude and regret for what was. Even during the best days of Judah with their finest kings leading, time and time again the people took their eyes off the Lord. As Leithart laments,

> The arc of Judah's history does not bend toward
> faithfulness. . . . This history is not a holding pattern. As Israel
> did during the time of the judges, Judah is declining, lurching
> toward the pure evil of King Ahaz. . . . Under the influence
> of the house of Ahab, Judah was made over into the image of
> Israel. (*1 & 2 Chronicles*, 191)

To forge a way forward after Babylon, they would need to correct the deviances of the past in order to enjoy Yahweh's continual blessings. Three protective lessons emerge that prove helpful for contemporary believers as well.

Joash: A Lesson on Accountability
2 CHRONICLES 24:1-27

After becoming king at the tender age of seven, Joash served the Lord faithfully for most of his life (v. 1). The Chronicler offers a qualifier, though, that is absent from the Deuteronomistic historian's record. The phrase "throughout the time of the priest Jehoiada" explained the idolatry that would stain the end of the king's reign (v. 2). In no way, however, is this new admission intended to diminish the significant accomplishments during the first half of Joash's kingship. The goal is to fill in gaps necessary for understanding the course of the exile and how to prevent it going forward.

With the new heirs secured in the line of David (v. 3), Joash turned his attention to restoring the temple structure (v. 4). To do so, he ordered the Levites to receive the temple tax throughout the kingdom in order to repair God's house annually (v. 5; see Exod 30:14). The king's command not only links the tabernacle and temple traditions but also establishes that the young ruler's desire reflects an old statute rather than an arbitrary command (Japhet, *I & II Chronicles*, 844). When these efforts did not transpire as quickly as he desired, Joash reprimanded the priest Jehoiada before commanding him to construct a chest for the collection (vv. 6-9). Rather than visit all the cities throughout the kingdom, Jehoiada places the offering box outside the temple and calls the people to give.

These recollections would have been as instructive as they were inspiring for the postexilic families eager to reestablish the cultus of the nation. Likewise, pastors have long used the concept of Joash's chest to call on God's people to support various projects within the church. We should note, though, that this ancient effort was not equal to leading a building campaign for a congregation, precisely because under the new covenant, God's house is not made up of bricks and mortar. The apostle Peter explained,

> *You yourselves, as living stones, a spiritual house, are being built to be a holy priesthood to offer spiritual sacrifices acceptable to God through Jesus Christ.* (1 Pet 2:5)

Just as God's presence came down and inhabited the temple, the Holy Spirit takes residence within every true follower of Christ (Rom 8:9). The closer equivalent for an offering of this kind, therefore, would be anything that builds up the body of Christ itself. That said, it is often necessary and right for God's people to support capital projects that will enhance the work and ministries of the church. The key is not equating the Old Testament temple and a church building.

The people of Judah not only gave at Joash's command, but they did so joyfully (v. 10) and sacrificially (v. 11). As a result of their generosity, the king successfully renovated the Lord's house according to its original specifications (vv. 12-13) while also restoring utensils pilfered during the reign of Athaliah (v. 14). As long as Jehoiada was alive, the people of Judah faithfully brought offerings to the Lord's house. Restoring temple worship was no small achievement for Joash, particularly against the backdrop of the Omride neglect and idolatry. As long as he was accountable to God's directions through the priest Jehoiada, this son of David prospered. Tragically, the story of the young, promising king does not end here.

The death of Jehoiada at the ripe age of 130 marks a major shift in the narrative (v. 15). The particular language ("he had done what was good in Israel") usually reserved for kings seems to be a nod to the godly priest as the true spiritual leader of Judah (v. 16b). In addition, the Chronicler notes Jehoiada's burial among the kings of the nation (v. 16a), while there is no mention of the royal cemetery after Joash's death (v. 25). At the very least, Jehoiada instigated the king's faithfulness.

If there is any doubt of these subtleties, note that Joash immediately embraces apostasy as his spiritual compass fades off the scene (vv. 18-19). In a remarkable turn of events, the same king who worked passionately to renovate the temple (vv. 4,12,13) is now abandoning the priority of its worship. Godless leaders in Judah—who were likely holdouts from the idolatrous years of Jehoram, Ahaziah, and Athaliah—negatively influenced Joash (v. 17). In addition to forsaking the Lord, Judah's backslidden king added to the wickedness of Baal worship by introducing Asherah poles in honor of the female Canaanite goddess. Guided by the whims of his own heart, Judah's king was accountable to no one but himself.

Though the Lord sent his prophets to woo the people of Judah back to himself, they rejected both the message and messengers (v. 19). Ironically, one of God's spokesmen was Zechariah, the son of Jehoiada the trusted priest. His words echoed a similar refrain: "Because you have abandoned the Lord, he has abandoned you" (v. 20). Instead of heeding the warning and abandoning idolatry, though, the people stoned the Lord's prophet. Lest we think the blame can somehow be shifted away from Joash, the text plainly states that the people stoned Zechariah "at the king's command" (v. 21). The Chronicler also adds that the king "didn't remember the kindness that Zechariah's father Jehoiada extended to him" (v. 22). Adding insult to injury, the site of Zechariah's stoning was the precise location where Jehoiada anointed Joash as king (v. 21; cf. 23:10-11).

The Lord's swift judgment for Joash's apostasy would have surely captured the attention of the postexilic believers. The invasion of the Arameans was part of a series of smaller judgments that preceded Judah's demise. God sent these judgments to turn their hearts and thereby prevent their captivity in a foreign land. All of Joash's restorative efforts on the temple were lost in an instant as this returning nemesis plundered the city and brought justice against the leaders whose counsel was wicked (v. 23). The Lord handed Judah over and fought to secure victory for the enemy despite the limited size of their army (v. 24). And just as Judah's foolish king chose to abandon the Lord, so he, too, felt the sting of abandonment when the Arameans left him behind wounded, only to be killed by his own servants (vv. 25-26).

Sins like these were part of the cumulative actions that sealed Judah's exile years later. How tragic would it be if they, like Joash, rebuilt the temple only to forsake Yahweh all over again? How could they ever make such an egregious mistake after enduring the severe consequence of exile? Tragically, this incident is a prophetic shadow that hints of future rejection of the Lord's temple and his prophets.

In his parable of the vineyard owner (Matt 21:33-44), Jesus rebuked the chief priests and Pharisees for their continued rejection of Old Testament prophets (servants in the vineyard) and God's promised Messiah (the son of the landowner), resulting in their deaths. Jesus is the rejected stone that became the chief cornerstone (Matt 21:42). The pattern of rejection illustrated by Zechariah's death continued up through the time of the Messiah's earthly ministry and years after. Jesus himself connected the hardness of Joash to the future rejection of God's servants:

> *This is why I am sending you prophets, sages, and scribes. Some of them you will kill and crucify, and some of them you will flog in your*

synagogues and pursue from town to town. So all the righteous blood shed on the earth will be charged to you, from the blood of righteous Abel to the blood of Zechariah, son of Berechiah, whom you murdered between the sanctuary and the altar. Truly I tell you, all these things will come on this generation. (Matt 23:34-36)

The historical chronicle that was meant to prevent another spiral into idolatry and apostasy actually forecast with laser accuracy what was coming when the Messiah came onto the scene. Joash died as judgment for his own sins as foreigners and his own people came against him. Jesus, though, died for the sins of others after being betrayed by those closest to him and then suffering at the hand of a foreign enemy. Even after their exile, God's people would kill his prophets again, not the least of which was our Prophet, Priest, and King. But, just as in the days following their Babylonian captivity, God determined not to cast his people aside forever.

Instead, the Lord used the temporary Jewish rejection as a means to bring Gentiles to faith. Because of the hardness of Jewish hearts after Babylon, God turned away from them in judgment (Rom 10:18-21). Yet the God of Abraham and David was not content to reject his people forever, so he preserved a remnant of Jews (Rom 11:1-5). With the curtain of redemptive history pulled back, the apostle Paul explains the purpose of Israel's spiritual exile:

I ask, then, have they stumbled so as to fall? Absolutely not! On the contrary, by their transgression, salvation has come to the Gentiles to make Israel jealous. Now if their transgression brings riches for the world, and their failure riches for the Gentiles, how much more will their fullness bring! (Rom 11:11-12)

No wonder the Chronicler extends such effort to warn the postexilic community not to fall away again. Regrettably, they never learned their lesson.

Just as lamentably, neither do we. Without accountability to God, his Word, and his people, we will repeatedly stray from our commitments to the Lord. Fortunately for Judah, and for us, the greatest Prophet they rejected not only pointed them to God's way, but he also incarnationally walked in total obedience on our behalf. Though his new covenant was also based on retributive justice, he absorbed the full punishment we deserved (1 John 4:10).

Amaziah: A Lesson on Apathy
2 CHRONICLES 25:1-28

Unlike his father Joash, Amaziah became king after he reached adulthood (v. 1). Where the two kings were similar, however, was in their unexplainable apostasy after starting so well as Yahweh's representatives. As before, the Chronicler offers a clue to the disappointment ahead with an addition to the Kings account. Though the king was known for doing what was right in the Lord's sight, the admission that he failed to do so "wholeheartedly" is jarring (v. 2). The statement is more than just a tragic revelation about the apathy of Amaziah's heart, though it is not less. Additionally, these words provided a stern warning concerning the postexilic renewal underway that is just as apropos today. Namely, it is impossible to serve or walk with the Lord half-heartedly. Jesus thus reduced the whole law to this Great Commandment: "Love the Lord your God with all your heart, with all your soul, and with all your mind. This is the greatest and most important command" (Matt 22:37-38). Apathy is the enemy of devotion.

Were it not for the hint about what is coming, we might feel better about the achievements Amaziah enjoyed during the early stages of his twenty-nine year reign. Despite the wickedness of his father's latter days, the king was right to put Joash's killers to death without punishing their children (vv. 3-4; see Deut 24:16). Even today, we should not bear consequences for the sins of others; neither will we be held responsible when standing before the Lord (2 Cor 5:10).

The first potential misstep for Amaziah takes the form of a massive army totaling three hundred thousand men from Judah who were fit for service (v. 5). Wanting to build a large coalition, he hired one hundred thousand supplemental warriors from the northern kingdom who were just as capable (v. 6). While on the surface these moves appear to be harmless, each was a subtle step toward greater reliance on human strength rather than on Yahweh. Much like David's census years earlier (1 Chr 21:1-5), numbering and assembling his troops left Amaziah vulnerable to pride instead of humility and to complacency in lieu of dependence.

Fortunately, an unnamed prophet confronted the king's inclusion of the Ephraimite army from the north for the liability that it was (v. 7). The unholy alliance was a precursor to certain defeat and doom due to the Lord's sovereignty over the battle's outcome (v. 8). Surprisingly, Amaziah yields to the prophet's wise counsel by releasing his acquired mercenaries to return home without recouping his previous payment (vv. 9-10). The malice of these Ephraimites echoed their foolishness years earlier when, after refusing to go to battle against the Midianites, they bemoaned their exclusion once Gideon's efforts were victorious (Judg 8:3).

Then, just as promised, the Lord rewarded Amaziah's humility with a substantial triumph over the Seirites in the Salt Valley (vv. 11-12). With little time to celebrate, though, the next challenge to his spiritual integrity was already underway. Not known for going away quietly, the Ephraimite militia killed and pillaged throughout the cities of Judah before returning home (v. 13). Would Amaziah respond in faith as he did previously? Or would these challenges result in his cynicism and apathy for the ways of God? The answer was just as shocking as it was far reaching.

In a move that can only be described as repugnant, Amaziah gathered idols of the enemy he just defeated and took them as his own (v. 14)! After reducing his army to comply with Yahweh's messenger and then benefiting on the battlefield, Judah's foolish ruler follows the same pattern of apostasy as his father Joash. If Amaziah intended to symbolize that the Edomite gods abandoned his enemy in order to support Judah, as was so common after successful military campaigns, the insult to Yahweh was even worse (Thompson, *1, 2 Chronicles*, 322–23). Even worse than crediting human strength or skill was to boast in pagan gods as the source of the victory.

Despite his anger, the Lord sent another messenger to question the ridiculous action (v. 15). Contrary to his past humility, Amaziah refused to listen and ignored the pronouncement of judgment against him (v. 16). Emboldened by his success against the Seirites, Judah's king foolishly sought revenge against the northern kingdom for the exploits of the Ephraimites (v. 17). When Israel's king, Jehoash, responded, he did so with a fable about a pompous thistle attempting to war with a cedar (vv. 18-19). In the most condescending way possible, Jehoash warns Amaziah to stay home so as not to hurt himself or Judah. Turning his arrogance against him, these events were a means from the Lord for retribution against Amaziah (v. 20). The resulting battle embarrassed Judah's king and damaged the kingdom.

In what could be described as a precursor to the exile, the north not only routed Judah but also tore down a portion of the wall around Jerusalem and plundered the treasures of the temple and the king's palace (vv. 21-24). Furthermore, despite living an additional fifteen years,

Amaziah eventually fell victim to a successful assassination plot that followed him to Lachish (vv. 25-28). Clearly, Amaziah was not the promised King that Judah was looking for. His life was a warning and example to the postexilic community, and to us, about the dangers of half-hearted commitment. When we are not drawing near to God, we will be moving away from him (Jas 4:8).

Uzziah: A Lesson on Arrogance
2 CHRONICLES 26:1-23

The rise and fall of Uzziah completes the trifecta of kings who show so much promise in the beginning but stumble in their latter years. From this point forward, the chronicle divides without nuance between those who are pleasing to the Lord and those who are not. As previously, new material expands the Deuteronomistic record significantly, with Uzziah's achievements and shortcoming becoming much more prominent. Ultimately, pride was the kryptonite that brought down Judah's king after a fifty-two-year tenure.

With a reign marked primarily by peace and restoration, Uzziah began his kingship at age sixteen and did what was right in the eyes of the Lord (vv. 1,3-4). His pattern was symmetrical with Joash in that he sought God throughout the lifetime of Zechariah, the primary voice of God to the people in those days (v. 5). Obviously, this was not the son of Jehoiada who was executed at Joash's command, but the similarities are eerie nonetheless, and they demonstrate our propensity to repeat the mistakes of the past. For Jews immediately after the exile, Uzziah's obedience and resulting blessings reaffirmed the need for a renewed cultic experience at the temple and through the priesthood.

Rebuilding the city of Eloth (v. 2) at Judah's most southern point, likely made possible by Amaziah's victory over the Edomites, meant access to prosperity not known since the days of Solomon (8:17). This port town on the Gulf of Aqaba gave access to the Red Sea and opened significant trade opportunities with Africa, India, and Asia (Boda, *1–2 Chronicles*, 366). The doorway of wealth created by increased commerce allowed for much greater exploits.

The expanse of Uzziah's success included military victories to the west against the Philistines (26:6) and to the south and east against the Arabs (v. 7). In addition, the Ammonites brought tribute from the east as God caused Uzziah's fame to spread and his power to grow (v. 8).

Outside of these offensive successes, he fortified Jerusalem's defenses by repairing its walls and adding watchtowers (v. 9). Because he developed an extensive agricultural economy, Uzziah added towers in the desert after irrigating the land (v. 10). Numerous allusions back to the glory of David and Solomon during this time restored hope that had been missing for generations. With great prosperity came a powerful army ready to fight defensively or offensively as directed (vv. 11-15). No matter the endeavor, God was helping Uzziah as long as he feared and obeyed him (v. 7). All of that changed, however, when the king became proud and strong in his own eyes (v. 15).

To avoid ambiguity, the Chronicler states clearly that Uzziah's arrogance led to unfaithfulness—specifically, burning incense in the temple contrary to Mosaic law (Num 16:40; 18:1-7)—resulting in his ultimate destruction (2 Chr 26:16). As throughout the chronicle, God responded to all acts of unfaithfulness with severe consequences. Pratt observes,

> Achan (Achar) died (1 Chr. 2:7). The half-tribe of Manasseh went into exile (1 Chr. 5:25). Saul died (1 Chr. 10:13). Rehoboam suffered Shishak's attack (2 Chr. 12:2). Uzziah contracted a skin disease (2 Chr. 26:16-19). Ahaz was subjected to Assyrian domination (2 Chr. 28:19, 22). Manasseh was exiled (2 Chr. 33:19). (Pratt, *1 & 2 Chronicles*, 59)

The king lived out the pithy reality later recorded in Proverbs 16:18: "Pride comes before destruction, and an arrogant spirit before a fall." The lesson here is not primarily about the arrogance of idolatry, though, but about the presumptuousness of worshiping God on our own terms.

A similar transgression occurred during the days of the exodus when the Hebrews pretentiously bowed down and worshiped a golden calf while Moses was on Mount Sinai. This was not, as some assume, paying homage to a different god. Exodus 32:4 clarifies, "This is your god, Israel, who brought you up from the land of Egypt" (NASB). In other words, the golden calf was a depiction not of strange gods but of Yahweh himself. The problem was not idolatry but approaching God in a way that he found offensive. Likewise, Uzziah was not worshiping the wrong God when he burned incense in the temple; he was arrogantly worshiping on his own terms. The problem was bad worship, not misdirected worship.

Are we not guilty of the same dangerous pattern when we ignore God's commandments as if they were trivial? Or when we define God in ways that are contrary to what he has revealed about himself in the Bible?

Or when we dismiss gathering with the body of Christ and embrace the individualism of modern Christianity? Or when we reverse the priority of Scripture by living as if God existed primarily for us rather than vice versa? As strange as it may sound, arrogance soils much of what passes for worship in many spaces.

God's judgment against Uzziah was swift. The godly priest Azariah led an additional eighty inside the temple to rebuke and correct the king (vv. 17-18). The episode narrowly defines the role of the Levitical priests as the sole bearers of incense within God's temple. This restriction would have been a fundamental priority after Babylon. Despite the priests' pleading, Uzziah became enraged and defiant rather than repentant, causing a skin disease (not the same as modern Hansen's disease) to break out on his forehead (v. 19). Whatever the nature of this disease, the symptoms were clear evidence of God's chastening.

Because the king was now ceremonially unclean (Lev 13–14), Azariah and the other Levites rushed him out of the temple. With the Lord's hand so heavy against him, Uzziah was anxious to comply (2 Chr 26:20). Now unable to approach God or interact with those in his kingdom for the rest of his life, the king lived out his remaining days in quarantine (v. 21). Even in death, the stain of Uzziah's arrogance remained. Though his burial ground was in the City of David, this was likely a field belonging to the monarchy but separate from the royal tombs of his fathers (vv. 22-23). Technically, the duration of his throne was fifty-two years, but a co-regency with his father Amaziah during the early days of his reign and then the same arrangement with his son Jotham over the course of his final decade at Judah's helm significantly reduced his leadership footprint. The text makes plain that Jotham was in the king's palace overseeing the leadership of the nation during his father's final years (v. 21).

Uzziah's arrogance was as old as the Hebrew exodus, where the people moved from the desperation of slavery to the pride of self-reliance remarkably fast. Their tendency to boast appeared again as one of Judah's most promising kings wavered in his commitment due to his perceived strength. Because of Uzziah, Moses's admonition as the wilderness wandering neared its conclusion was just as important to postexilic readers as it had ever been.

> *Be careful that you don't forget the LORD your God by failing to keep his commands, ordinances, and statutes that I am giving you today. When you eat and are full, and build beautiful houses to live in, and your*

herds and flocks grow large, and your silver and gold multiply, and
everything else you have increases, be careful that your heart doesn't
become proud and you forget the LORD your God who brought you out
of the land of Egypt, out of the place of slavery. (Deut 8:11-14)

Sadly, followers of Christ need these words just as much today. The same exaggerated self-perception that plagued ancient Israel is still afflicting the Laodicean church today. While saying that we are "wealthy and need nothing," we do not realize that we are "wretched, pitiful, poor, blind, and naked" (Rev 3:17). Our churches often give the appearance of starting well due to the purity of our doctrine, but we are stumbling when it matters most because we expect of others what we do not require of ourselves.

Conclusion

Three kings with promise. Three lessons in compromise. With so many pitfalls that could hinder their rise from beneath the shadows of judgment, the Chronicler calls the tribes returning to Judah to remain accountable to God's law and covenant, to follow the Lord with their whole heart, and to humble themselves as they remember Yahweh's goodness. With every misstep in the past, the southern kingdom moved closer to exile. Now, with a chance to understand the cumulative force of their generational wickedness, postexilic Jews could potentially avoid the sins of their past as they continued to look for the promised Son of David.

Modern readers possess an even greater opportunity now that a much fuller picture of God's dealings with his people make up a complete canon of Scripture. Israel's failure to heed the Chronicler's guidance and their eventual rejection of their Messiah is not a challenge for us to do better, for, alas, we cannot. Instead, we cast ourselves more fully on the mercy of God through his new covenant of grace, realizing that the best way to avoid falling is realizing that we are unable to stand on our own (1 Cor 10:12). Seeking to love God more fully while remaining accountable to the body of Christ is the best strategy for overcoming the boastful pride of life that tempts all of us to stray (1 John 2:16), especially as we near the finish line.

Do you remember Douglas Mackiernan? After seven months he finally made it to the Tibetan border. The week prior he radioed the US embassy requesting that they inform border guards of his arrival. When he was finally close enough to see the crossing between the two nations, Doug's exhaustion turned to joy and he began running fero-ciously toward freedom. When he was only one hundred yards away, tragedy struck when shots rang out. Doug Mackiernan was hit, and he fell dead on the path. The guards never received his message, and they mistook him for a renegade bandit.

Soon, they pulled his body to the side of the trail and covered it with stones. The man who labored a lifetime for his country became another boundary on the trail. His ending was a tragic warning for those that fol-lowed in search of freedom (Farrar, *Gettin' There*, 118). You and I don't have to be another spiritual casualty in the kingdom of God if we will heed the warnings of those whose falls instruct us. Though dead, Joash, Amaziah, and Uzziah still speak, admonishing us to learn from their mistakes. The freedom we find in Christ will be worth the discipline finishing well requires.

Reflect and Discuss

1. What do the Chronicler's added details about these Old Testament heroes reveal about them? About us?
2. What does the rebirth of the Davidic line through Joash reveal about God's redemptive goals for Judah? For us?
3. In what ways did Joash refuse covenantal accountability after Jehoiada's death? How are we sometimes guilty of the same?
4. How would the missteps of these kings increase the lament of the Jews after Babylon? How would these details inspire them?
5. Is obedience really possible if our efforts are half-hearted and apathetic?
6. What is most offensive about Amaziah's embrace of Edomite idols? How do we follow similar patterns in our lives?
7. In what ways does pride manifest itself in your life? How does arro-gance rob us of God's blessings in our lives?
8. How does forgetting past blessings increase the likelihood of arro-gance and self-reliance in our lives?
9. What do Uzziah's priestly ambitions reveal about our desire to walk with God on our own terms? How have you displayed unhealthy ambitions?
10. How do Jesus's comprehensive obedience and example free us and inspire us to finish our race for the Lord well?

The Good, the Bad, and the Better

2 CHRONICLES 27–32

Main Idea: Imperfect Judean kings leading imperfect people were inching closer and closer to exile. By examining each king's successes and failures along with his separation from or synergy with his citizens, we learn much about the faith and obedience that please the Lord. God holds every follower responsible for his or her actions.

I.   **Good Leadership Does Not Diminish Our Personal Responsibility (27:1-9).**
II. **Bad Leadership Does Not Dismiss Our Personal Accountability (28:1-27).**
   A.   Our detestable conduct (28:1-8)
   B.   Our dulled consciences (28:9-27)
III. **Great Sin Does Not Destroy Our Personal Revivability (29:1–31:21).**
   A.   Humiliation (29:3-10)
   B.   Consecration (29:11-36)
   C.   Invitation (30:1-12)
   D.   Celebration (30:13-27)
   E.   Preparation (31:1-21)
IV. **Great Success Does Not Deter Our Personal Vulnerability (32:1-33).**
   A.   From without (32:1-23)
   B.   From within (32:24-33)

Our ability to identify the shortcomings of others with pinpoint precision while ignoring our own ought to alarm us. Oliver Crangle typified the reckless energy we sometimes spend condemning others. If that name is unfamiliar, it should be. Crangle was a fictional character in a 1962 episode of *The Twilight Zone*. This harsh man lived alone with a parrot named Pete, imprisoned by his belief that most of the world deserved to die.

The show began, as all others, with Rod Serling narrating the important details. "That's Oliver Crangle," he said, "a dealer in petulance and poison. He's rather arbitrarily chosen four o'clock as his personal Götterdämmerung, and we are about to watch the metamorphosis of a twisted fanatic, poisoned by the gangrene of prejudice, to the status of an avenging angel, upright and omniscient, dedicated and fearsome."

Crangle rages against everyone. In his view, everyone is a communist, thief, or murderer. He demands that employers fire their evil employees. He berates a doctor as a killer due to his inability to save a patient in the ER. He files formal complaints again and again to no avail. Frustrated that the world has fallen prey to a secret conspiracy, he concocts a plan to purge the world of its wickedness through extraordinary means. He informs the FBI that at 4:00 pm, through a sheer force of his will, all the world's worthless riffraff will shrink to a height of just two feet, making them easy to identify and imprison. Finally, justice will prevail.

As the moment of reckoning approaches, Crangle gushes with enthusiasm. He rushes to his apartment window to celebrate the demise of his enemies. But, as the clock strikes four, the old crank realizes that he cannot peer out at street below because he now stands a mere two feet tall. As the episode concludes we hear the voice of Rod Serling again, "At four o'clock, an evil man made his bed and lay in it, a pot called a kettle black, a stone-thrower broke the windows of his glass house."

More than likely, there were a few Oliver Crangles who returned to Jerusalem after the seventy-year exile. As they read the Chronicler's history, more than a few might have been tempted to blame others rather than accept personal responsibility for the downfall of the nation. Wicked king after wicked king surely signaled the primary reason the people had suffered so much. It was the foolishness of others, after all, that led to their suffering. Thus, in an effort to push back against the victim mentality that still plagues our world today, the chronicle takes a deliberate turn toward personal responsibility. The broadened evaluation of the years leading up to exile now sets its gaze squarely on the capitulation of the common Israelite.

From this point forward, the chronicle focuses less on the nuances of kings who embody both positive and negative characteristics in exchange for a more monolithic approach. The reign of Jotham, for example, is entirely positive, while the throne of Ahaz represents the nation's lowest point for the Chronicler. What emerges is the consideration of the role Judah's citizenry played in their national decline.

Lest we think that only the kings of Judah were responsible for the seventy-year Babylonian captivity, the history shifts its focus a bit to the deplorable actions of the people in this pericope. Granted, each historical king provided spiritual leadership for the nation, whether for good or for bad, still each resident of Judah also bore responsibility for their allegiance to Yahweh or the lack thereof. This lesson was particularly relevant during the Persian reentry because the people, without a king on David's throne, would have to decide for themselves to resist idolatry and adhere to God's law.

Good Leadership Does Not Diminish Our Personal Responsibility
2 CHRONICLES 27:1-9

Jotham became king in Israel at twenty-five and reigned for just sixteen years (v. 1). The text emphasizes his righteousness with the standard phrase, "He did what was right in the LORD's sight" (v. 2). The comparison to Uzziah is entirely positive because of the caveat that Jotham did not enter the sanctuary like his father. Though some interpret the description negatively, as if the king refused to enter the temple for prayer and worship (Johnstone, *1 and 2 Chronicles, Vol. 2,* 171), the better understanding is that Jotham refused to assume the priestly function of burning incense like his predecessor. This king embodies the best of Uzziah without any of the baggage. In fact, Jotham is the first king since Abijah about whom the Chronicler has nothing critical to say.

The view that God's people always followed their kings without delay or deviance, avoiding any spiritual responsibility for the health of the nation, is far too simplistic. At Jehoram's funeral, it was the people who withheld the typical honors (21:19-20); the people organized a coup and rejoiced together after ousting Athaliah (23:1-21); the servants of Joash conspired against him (24:25); and the people rose up to kill Amaziah (25:27) (Wilcock, *Message of Chronicles,* 234). Repeatedly, God-fearing citizens rose up against their wicked leaders. Here, we encounter the first instance where evil constituents dismissed the godly example of their king.

To highlight their personal responsibility, first, the Chronicler deletes any reference to the worship of Baal through sacrifice and incense at the high places (2 Kgs 15:35) in order to avoid the perception that Jotham was to blame. Next, he places the burden of compromise solely at the feet of the people by simply stating "the people still behaved corruptly" (2 Chr 27:2). The same root, *shakhath*, used to describe Uzziah's destruction (26:16) is now identifying the nation as a whole (Boda, *1–2 Chronicles*, 372). The problem that besieged Judah, in other words, was not exclusive to the throne. The people were marching toward exile even when their kings were not. The downward spiral of the monarchy was often a reflection rather than the cause of the spiritual vacuum throughout the kingdom.

For postexilic Jews, the broad obligation of this revelation was a call to live in personal holiness and accountability. The cover of good leadership was not a license to live oblivious to God's expectations. The same is true for twenty-first-century disciples. Those in authority may point us to Christ, but we are responsible for walking with him. Modern readers must accept responsibility for our role in preserving the unity of our bond (Eph 4:3) and refusing to quench the Spirit (Eph 4:30). Knowing that false teachers will creep into the church (2 Pet 3:1-3), God calls every Christian to test all doctrine to determine what is good (1 Thess 5:21), along with the spirits behind the teaching we hear (1 John 4:1-3). Under no circumstance are believers excused for being tossed about by the winds of heresy (Eph 4:14). When necessary, our spiritual obligations demand that we rebuke wayward elders who continue in sin (1 Tim 5:20). The structures of leadership that God provides were never intended to substitute for the personal responsibilities that accompany our place in the family of God.

The rebelliousness of the people notwithstanding, Jotham served the Lord faithfully and prospered the kingdom tremendously. Specifically, building projects (vv. 3-4) and military success (v. 5) were the unambiguous evidence of God's blessing. His work on the temple and Jerusalem's wall, along with his fortresses and towers in the forest, further fortified the strategic city of David and the surrounding hill country. Furthermore, Jotham's victory over the Ammonites guaranteed tribute from his enemies for three years. Though the king became powerful, he, unlike his father Uzziah, did not waver in his obedience (v. 6).

Despite their recognition of these accomplishments, Jews after Babylon certainly realized that Jotham was not the eternal Son of David. For one thing, the godly leader had long since been in the grave when the Chronicler penned these words. Reading about his reign of righteousness was not equal to experiencing it personally (vv. 7-9). Also, though the people of Judah certainly benefitted from the king's blessed obedience, Jotham lacked the power to impute his integrity to them. They remained in their sins as this son of David communed with Yahweh. Jotham was a good king, but he was not *THE KING*.

All these years after the exile, the people would have to keep looking for the promised messianic ruler. As they rebuilt their temple and kingdom, though, every citizen would bear the individual responsibilities of avoiding corruption and living in holiness. Without a king on the throne, the blessings of the Davidic covenant would be tied to their personal walk in a more visible way. As they waited for the final heir to David's throne, God expected his people to humble themselves, pray, seek his face, and turn from their wicked ways as they reestablished the temple cultus (7:14).

Bad Leadership Does Not Dismiss Our Personal Accountability
2 CHRONICLES 28:1-27

For the sake of Jotham, God persisted in his blessings to Judah even though the people continued to sin without punishment until, as Wilcock observes, "[T]he one who now holds it back . . . is taken out of the way (2 Thes. 2:7) and the accession of Ahaz reveals the bankruptcy of throne and people alike" (*1 and 2 Chronicles*, 413–14). The deficiencies of Judah hidden by the righteousness of Jotham were now dancing out in plain view. Later we discover that there was a lack of restraint throughout the southern kingdom (v. 19).

Just as all the people bore a responsibility to resist compromise when a righteous king reigned over them, so also all of Judah remained accountable to the Lord when a scoundrel lived in the king's palace. As stated previously, the rise of Ahaz marks the lowest point in the nation's history for the Chronicler. His tenure is a stark departure from the faithfulness of his father, without one positive contribution recorded.

Our Detestable Conduct (28:1-8)

For sixteen years, Ahaz displeased the Lord, defined specifically as walking in the ways of the kings of Israel (vv. 1-2). The Deuteronomistic historian used the phrase "the sins of Jeroboam" to personify the consistent pattern of idolatry in the north that the writer references here. So severe were these transgressions that their final outcome was the irreversible fall of the northern kingdom (Boda, *1–2 Chronicles*, 374).

> *The Israelites persisted in all the sins that Jeroboam committed and did not turn away from them. Finally, the LORD removed Israel from his presence just as he had declared through all his servants the prophets.* (2 Kgs 17:22-23)

Because Ahaz settled into this pattern, his defilement is difficult to overstate. He created molten images of Baals, burned incense in Ben-hinnom Valley, and sacrificed his children in the fire (vv. 2-3). Located just south of the temple, Ben-hinnom was a landfill used to burn sewage, waste, and corpses. The sight of maggots crawling through the ruins and the sickening smell of the simmering smoke caused it to become known as the perfect symbol of hell and its agonies, so much so that Jesus used its Aramaic name, *Gehenna*, to refer to hell (eleven times in the Gospels). The clear implication is that this king was an instrument of hell as he offered the sweet smells of incense and his own children to his pretend gods in Jerusalem and surrounding areas (v. 4).

God forbade these egregious acts within his law, even calling for the death of those who violated these decrees (Lev 18:21; 20:1-5; Deut 18:10-11). Detestable practices like these were more closely aligned with nations dispossessed from the land of promise. Contrary to what revisionists sympathetic to the former residents of Canaan try to depict, their culture was so vile that God ordered its elimination (Lev 18:28; 20:23; Deut 7:22-26; 12:2-4; 18:9-14) (Thompson, *1, 2 Chronicles*, 335). Is there any wonder God began to displace Judah when they embraced these atrocities as well? The Lord handed Judah over to the Arameans, resulting in a miniature exile to Damascus (2 Chr 28:5a). Next, the last king of Israel, Pekah, struck Ahaz with such force that twenty thousand brave warriors, all apostate, fell dead in one day (vv. 5b-6). Ahaz lost his son and members of his royal court to the hands of an Ephraimite warrior named Zichri (v. 7). Finally, the Israelites took two hundred thousand people of Judah captive, another wave of exile, along with great plunder from Jerusalem (v. 8).

These words would have leaped off the page for Jews seeking to understand the exile and avoid it in the future. When Manasseh later followed the same offensive pattern, it settled the certainty of the Babylonian invasion (33:2,6). Those looking to rebuild Jerusalem could not afford to hide behind bad leaders as if they had no accountability to the Lord. Those who fell victim to God's retribution against Ahaz were just as guilty of idolatry as their king.

Our Dulled Conscience (28:9-27)

To further illustrate the nefariousness of Judah at this point, the Chronicler breaks his pattern of ignoring the historical situation in the north. Once more he highlights the value of the prophetic word by detailing the message of and the response to a prophet named Obed. Speaking to the victorious Israelite army, God's messenger admits Judah's guilt and the Lord's anger toward them while also confronting the rage and overreach of the conquerors (v. 9). In addition to the excessive slaughter of their brothers to the south, now the Samaritan leaders were planning to subjugate their captives to slavery (v. 10). This clear violation of God's law (Lev 25:39-55) added to the devastating guilt that had the northern kingdom on the verge of extinction already. Therefore, the only honorable way to avoid God's wrath was to return the prisoners (v. 11).

Remarkably, the leaders of Israel heeded the prophet's words and opposed those returning from battle with what appears to be a straight-forward recognition of guilt and genuine repentance (vv. 12-13). In what amounts to an effort of restitution, the Israelites released, clothed, fed, anointed with oil, and returned the abductees to Jericho. Readers are not accustomed to such compassion and humility from the northern kingdom. In fact, the chronicle repeatedly demonstrates them to be enemies of the house of David. Yet at this juncture Ahaz walked in the ways of Israel more than Israel did. With the demise of the north immi-nent, this is a declaration that Judah is not far behind. At least in this instance, the north, not the south, is sensitive to a word from the Lord.

Rather than respond with brokenness and gratitude, Ahaz called for Gentile help to overcome his enemies. Additional attacks from the Edomites and the Philistines intended to humble Judah's king for his unfaithfulness actually had the opposite effect (vv. 17-19). Instead of seeking the Lord, Ahaz enlisted the Assyrians as allies (v. 16), only to be betrayed afterward (v. 20). Whereas David and Solomon received tribute from surrounding nations, this king was content to give it away by plundering the temple and royal palace himself (v. 21).

Ahaz's spiral deeper into idolatry only accelerated as he became more desperate (v. 22). Assuming the Aramean gods were the cause of his downfall, the Judean king further angered Yahweh by choosing to worship these pagan deities (v. 23). In moves that can only be described as irrational, Ahaz emptied the temple of its treasures in order to refashion them as incense altars for other gods (vv. 24-25).

These spiritual deficiencies were even more tragic when one considers the phenomenal opportunities Ahaz had after the prosperity of Jotham. In addition, he had received Isaiah's messianic prophecy about the arrival of the promised Son of David (Isa 7:14). Had he seized this moment, he could have called the people back to their covenantal hopes and commitments, eliminating the high places of Baal in the kingdom.

More significant, though, was the fall of Samaria to the Assyrian Empire on Ahaz's watch. This strategic development effectively ended the divided monarchy, presenting an opportunity to reassimilate under one throne the godly from the northern kingdom, many of whom realized all the descendants of Jacob were still family (v. 11). At the very least, the sobering trauma of Assyrian invasion should have ignited a flame of revival in Judah lest they suffer the same fate. Blinded by his idolatry, though, Ahaz pushed the southern kingdom one step closer to their own exile.

And the people of Judah blindly followed their leader without hesitation, fulfilling the prophecy Moses spoke years before:

> *Future generations of your children who follow you and the foreigner who comes from a distant country will see the plagues of that land and the sicknesses the LORD has inflicted on it. All its soil will be a burning waste of sulfur and salt, unsown, producing nothing, with no plant growing on it, just like the fall of Sodom and Gomorrah, Admah and Zeboiim, which the LORD demolished in his fierce anger. All the nations will ask, "Why has the LORD done this to this land? Why this intense outburst of anger?" Then people will answer, "It is because they abandoned the covenant of the LORD, the God of their ancestors, which he had made with them when he brought them out of the land of Egypt. They began to serve other gods, bowing in worship to gods they had not known—gods that the LORD had not permitted them to worship. Therefore the LORD's anger burned against this land, and he brought every curse written in this book on it. The LORD uprooted them from*

their land in his anger, rage, and intense wrath, and threw them into another land where they are today." (Deut 29:22-28)

Tragically, the warnings from God's Word were not enough to prevent the rebellion and idolatry that became common throughout Judea. In his efforts to promote the postexilic renewal, the Chronicler is promoting covenantal accountability.

These lessons from the past are just as instructive today about the dangers of living without restraint, oblivious to the standards of holiness laid out in Scripture. God calls every Christian to forsake the ways of those who do not know God.

> *Therefore, I say this and testify in the Lord: You should no longer walk as the Gentiles do, in the futility of their thoughts. They are darkened in their understanding, excluded from the life of God, because of the ignorance that is in them and because of the hardness of their hearts. They became callous and gave themselves over to promiscuity for the practice of every kind of impurity with a desire for more and more.* (Eph 4:17-19)

These inclinations not only described ancient Israel, but they also typify us when we stray from God.

Great Sin Does Not Destroy Our Personal Revivability
2 CHRONICLES 29:1–31:21

The reforms of Hezekiah were so important that his reign occupies more space in the record than any king other than David and Solomon. Like the Deuteronomistic historian's, the Chronicler's recollection is positive, but new evidence of Hezekiah's faith and impact surfaces. Ascending the throne at age twenty-five, this king not only did what was right in the eyes of the Lord, but he was also compared to David, the highest compliment given to any king since the division of the kingdom (29:1-2). His rise could not have been timelier, with Judah being far from God and Assyria growing in power. For the postexilic historian, Hezekiah's contribution represents the zenith of Judah's history after Solomon (Japhet, *I & II Chronicles*, 936). His rule is a reminder that despite the great sin in Judah's past, the Lord was willing to revive his people.

Three key emphases from this historical period guide the narrative concerning Hezekiah's significance:

(1) Hezekiah's actions to reunify Israel after the fall of the
northern kingdom to Assyrian aggression, (2) Hezekiah's
affinity with the values and action of David and Solomon
(union of the kingdoms, reforms of worship, accumulation
of great wealth, attention by Gentiles, royal practice of
prayer), and (3) Hezekiah's demonstration of the validity
of the Chronicler's theology of retribution. (Boda,
1–2 Chronicles, 382)

Though one concluding detail about Hezekiah's rule cannot be understood as positive (32:25), overall his leadership is commendable to the
point of emulation. These reforms translated well for those eager to
reestablish Israel's place as the people of God because they demonstrated that revival and renewal were possible. The first step in reform
was a recognition of how far they had drifted as a nation.

Humiliation (29:3-10)

Quite the opposite of his father Ahaz (28:24), Hezekiah opened the
doors of the temple in order to repair it (29:3). At this point, the Judeans
were living under the judgment of God for their idolatry. Because they
had high places in every city of the southern kingdom, the anger of the
Lord burned against them (28:25). Therefore, Hezekiah assembled the
priests and the Levites to enlist their help (29:4). His undivided loyalty
takes center stage as he recalls the wickedness of both his father and the
people in order to accentuate the deserved wrath of God that fell on
them (vv. 5-9).

Here we should pause to reflect on the magnitude of Hezekiah's
commitment. For him, following Yahweh meant exposing his father for
the evil king that he was. Likewise, believing Jews after the exile had
to grapple with the transgressions of their forefathers before enjoying
the blessings of restoration. Revival does not come when we ignore the
offenses of the past. Even today, walking with Christ often requires us to
separate from practices or people that have long been part of our lives
as we seek to offer the Lord our undivided loyalties.

Surely this is what Jesus called for when he insisted, "If anyone
comes to me and does not hate his own father and mother, wife and
children, brothers and sisters—yes, and even his own life—he cannot
be my disciple" (Luke 14:26). As much as we care for our families, the
people we love are sometimes obstacles to experiencing a revival with

the Lord. Hezekiah deliberately chose Yahweh over his familial heritage, and so should we.

Also of importance within Judah's humiliation is the lack of generalities. Phrases like *if I sinned* or *if I offended God* are noticeably absent. Instead, there is a thorough acknowledgment (29:6):

- Our ancestors were unfaithful.
- Our ancestors did what was evil in the sight of the Lord.
- They abandoned . . .
- They turned their faces away . . .
- They turned their backs . . .

The Aramean and Israelite captivities along with the Edomite and Philistine attacks were direct consequences of Judah's prolonged evil (vv. 8-9).

Thankfully, the humiliation of the past stirred within Hezekiah a desire to turn away from sin in order to renew the nation's walk with God (v. 10). He believed, as Ezekiel would later prophesy in Babylon, that the nation was not destined to repeat the sins of their fathers, and a new start was realistically possible (Ezek 18:1-32). Neither are we irreparably bound to the shame of our pasts, but believers today must also be willing to humble ourselves by weeping and mourning over the humiliation of our sins (Jas 4:9).

Consecration (29:11-36)

Realizing the need to reconsecrate both the Levites and the temple for service, Hezekiah assembled his leaders with a reminder of their calling and privilege (v. 11). The list of those who responded undoubtedly cast the vision for new leaders to rise up and serve during the reentry to Jerusalem (vv. 11-14). These spiritual servants were casualties of Ahaz's reign of terror, being unused and even apathetic to the worship of Yahweh themselves. Yet with a new sense of purpose, they gathered their kind, purified themselves, and set out to cleanse the temple of its abominations (v. 15). All totaled, it took sixteen days to rid the house of God of its idols and pagan collections (vv. 16-17). When they finished, the temple once again resembled Solomon's original design (vv. 18-19).

Because the goal was greater than outward conformity, Hezekiah ordered a festival of sacrifices as an act of rededication. Their sin offerings totaled twenty-eight animals and were an admission of the people's guilt (vv. 20-24). The phrase *all Israel* indicated Hezekiah's inclusion of the northern kingdom, which had fallen to Assyria at this point, in his atonement for the nation (v. 24). For the first time since Solomon there was a realistic opportunity for all twelve tribes to unite under one Davidic king, an opportunity available after Babylon as well.

Next, in the tradition of David, Hezekiah stationed vocalists and instrumentalists throughout the temple area (vv. 25-26). As offerings were sacrificed, the musicians played and singers sang as acts of worship (vv. 27-28). All who were present, even Hezekiah himself, joined in worship in recognition that Yahweh was the true King in Israel (vv. 29-30). With the temple dedicated and the people purified, Hezekiah invited all Israel to bring sacrifices and thanksgiving offerings of their own (vv. 31-33). Because the gifts were many and the priests were too few, consecrated Levites assisted them (v. 34). Through sacrifice and praise, the people rejoiced that the spiritual pulse lost during the reign of Ahaz was finally beating again (vv. 35-36).

For postexilic Jews wondering if God would bring restoration and healing after so much loss, their previous revival under Hezekiah would have been a tremendous motivator. Though the sins leading to exile were great, so were those that sent Judah into partial captivity when Ahaz reigned. If God heard their repentance before, surely he would again. Similarly, as modern Christians see evidence of Yahweh's eagerness to forgive repeatedly throughout Israel's history, we can recommit ourselves to the Lord with full confidence that he will forgive and cleanse us (1 John 1:9).

Invitation (30:1-12)

In further demonstration of his commitment to unify the kingdom under one throne, Hezekiah sent letters to *all Israel*, represented by Ephraim and Manasseh, to join at the temple for a Passover celebration (v. 1). The same feast that marked their beginning as a nation was also a reminder of God's willingness to be merciful by not imposing his wrath. The decision to observe the festival in the second month instead of the first was entirely pragmatic. Without enough consecrated priests and citizens, they simply were not ready earlier (vv. 2-3). Fortunately, a provision in the law allowed for such a delay in the case of uncleanliness (Num 9:1-14). Delaying the observance for one month was the best possible solution (2 Chr 30:4).

The broad appeal to the farthest-reaching tribes to the north was, at its core, an invitation for God's people to unify under a Davidic vision (vv. 5-9). Contextually, the repeated admonishment to *return to the Lord* (vv. 6,9) is a call to repentance.

- Return to God so that he will return to you (v. 6).
- Do not be like your ancestors and brothers (v. 7).
- Do not be obstinate (v. 8).
- "Serve the Lord your God so that he may turn his burning anger away from you" (v. 8).

The king's messengers made a broad appeal to any who were willing to humble themselves before the Lord. Today, God's invitation remains the same. Though he resists the proud, he gives grace to the humble (Jas 4:6). When we resist the devil, he flees; when we draw near to God, he draws near to us. The doorway to Christ swings on the hinges of humility, and the road to remain with him is a narrow road. All who will come are welcome, but few will choose to do so (Matt 7:13-14).

Thus, the response to Hezekiah's invitation is disappointing but not surprising. Most mocked and ridiculed the royal couriers (2 Chr 30:10), but a humble remnant chose to accept the extended grace (v. 11). Also, the Lord worked powerfully in Judean hearts to foster a spirit of unity as the northern tribes returned to the covenantal fold (v. 12). Truly, the revival that ensued was entirely a work of God's Spirit among his people. Similarly, God was just as willing to breathe life into weary Jewish exiles as they came back to him in repentance. Hezekiah's inclusion of the northern tribes in his celebration bears similarity to the chronicle's concluding invitation, spoken by King Cyrus of Persia:

> The LORD, the God of the heavens, has given me all the kingdoms of the earth and has appointed me to build him a temple at Jerusalem in Judah. Any of his people among you may go up, and may the LORD his God be with him. (36:23)

All who will humble themselves are free to join in covenantal commitment to Yahweh. The same is also true for all believers today. Christ is eager for us to accept his invitation to worship him in Spirit and in truth (John 4:23). In fact, the New Testament concludes with a corresponding invitation:

Both the Spirit and the bride say, "Come!" Let anyone who hears, say, "Come!" Let the one who is thirsty come. Let the one who desires take the water of life freely. (Rev 22:17)

Celebration (30:13-27)

When we are far from God, it is difficult to imagine a celebratory revival that reconnects us to the Lord. Yet those who turned away from their sins in response to Hezekiah's invitation found more joy than they likely envisioned. Large crowds gathered (Scripture uses "Festival of Unleavened Bread" and "Passover" interchangeably) (v. 13). They tore down the altars and high places constructed under Ahaz (v. 14). As the festivities got underway, priests yet to consecrate themselves moved quickly due to their embarrassing lack of preparation (v. 15). In light of the priestly shortage, Levites joined the efforts to prepare blood sacrifices for the people (vv. 16-17).

Because people from the northern tribes had seldom or never observed the feast, they ignorantly ate their Passover feast while ritually unclean (v. 18). Sensing their obliviousness and pure motives, Hezekiah interceded to the Lord on their behalf (v. 19). Christians today will easily relate to the innocent misstep because of the numerous sins of omission that often characterize new believers. Yahweh's gracious response is further evidence that God looks primarily at our hearts when we obey (v. 20; see 1 Sam 16:7). Though not always in dichotomy, outward conformity is no substitute for heartfelt devotion. Oppositely, neither is simple sincerity an acceptable replacement for mature obedience. Of note is Hezekiah's request for atonement after the error (v. 18). The key is showing grace as a *means of* growth instead of an *obstacle to* growth. We should not live as if ignorance is bliss, but neither should we suppose that knowledge is maturity.

The picture that unfolds is one of joyful exuberance (vv. 21-27). There were joy and praise (v. 21) along with encouragement, sacrifices, and thanksgiving (v. 22). In another irregularity, after seven days of celebration, the people decided to continue for an additional seven days (v. 23). Hezekiah provided additional offerings for the Lord, and the number of priests who consecrated themselves continued to grow (v. 24). With the north and south together rejoicing after years of dysfunctional wickedness (v. 25), Israel was finally functioning as she did during the days of Solomon (v. 26). The blessings and prayers pleased the Lord as they rose up to heaven (v. 27).

Again, the Chronicler's history is strategic. Because the Kings account focuses primarily on Sennacherib's invasion (the subject of chapter 32 here), the emphases on the temple's restoration and worship reforms is all new material. The celebrative festivals were a challenge to the postexilic Jews to go beyond rebuilding cultic structures to prizing genuine passion for Yahweh as their first priority. The goal after Babylon was more than a believing culture; it was heartfelt commitment. Jesus later rebuked the Pharisees for appearing to be righteous while inwardly reeking of hypocrisy (Matt 23:27-28). Believers today must also be on guard against having a form of godliness while denying its power (2 Tim 3:5).

Preparation (31:1-21)

Realizing they were just one generation removed from full-blown idolatry, Hezekiah took active steps to reestablish regular worship so as to prevent another moral slide in the future. He removed the high places, altars, and idols throughout the kingdom (v. 1). Next, he reassigned priestly duties for the sons of Aaron according to their divisions (v. 2). Out of his own riches, Hezekiah provided enough morning and evening sacrifices until it became routine for his people (v. 3). Understanding that a healthy priesthood was essential for the spiritual vitality of the nation, the king commanded collections be taken for the care of the priests to protect their focus on God's law (v. 4). The people responded with such generosity that their produce, flocks, oil, and wine began to pile up because the abundance satisfied the priests with plenty left over (vv. 5-10). To accommodate the plenitude that was regularly given, Hezekiah prepared for its storage and distribution (vv. 11-19). A final summary statement demonstrates just how far-reaching these reforms and the blessings that accompanied them were (vv. 20-21).

Unlike during the days of Jotham, the obedience of the king and the citizenry were aligning for the good of the nation as a whole. Part of correcting the wrongs of the past was constructing new, healthier rhythms for living. Surely this example motivated Jews after the exile to steward their resources so that the worship of Yahweh would flourish again. In addition to rebuilding the temple, these regular contributions helped reinstate a robust priesthood.

Though new covenant Christians do not find an equivalency between church buildings and the Old Testament temple, there should be great joy in funding the work of the ministry, including compensation for those who serve as pastors or elders. In fact, there does seem to be correlation between the care for the Old Testament priest and the New Testament pastor according to the apostle Paul:

> *Don't you know that those who perform the temple services eat the*
> *food from the temple, and those who serve at the altar share in the*
> *offerings of the altar? In the same way, the Lord has commanded that*
> *those who preach the gospel should earn their living by the gospel.*
> (1 Cor 9:13-14)

With Christ as our example of sacrificial giving (2 Cor 8:9), we give cheerfully, believing God will use us so that we can, in turn, invest in others (2 Cor 9:7-8).

Great Success Does Not Deter Our Personal Vulnerability
2 CHRONICLES 32:1-33

One should not fall for the deception that faithfulness is a one-time or seasonal exercise. Because arriving spiritually is impossible, we never move beyond the vulnerabilities that plague us in a fallen world. Usually, when God works on our behalf or provides abundantly, a test of some kind will come to measure our ability to handle the Lord's blessings. These pressures take many forms, but all irritants come either from without or within.

From Without (32:1-23)

After claiming Samaria and Damascus under Sargon II, the Assyrian Empire had a new leader named Sennacherib who was anxious to make a name for himself by capturing the territories of Judah (v. 1). Knowing that the real prize was Jerusalem, Hezekiah, like the other righteous kings before him, put three defensive measures in place to protect his capital city. First, he stopped up the water supply in the region to make any enemy offensive measures more difficult (vv. 2-4) while building a tunnel to give Jerusalem access to a reliable water supply (v. 30). Second, he rebuilt the existing wall around the city, erected higher defensive towers, and added a second outer wall for protection (v. 5). Finally, he organized his army and prepared them for battle (vv. 6-8).

These preparations were not substitutes for Hezekiah's faith in Yahweh to deliver Judah but expressions of it. Hard work and depending on God are not necessarily mutually exclusive. After highlighting the faithfulness of his past actions, the Chronicler carefully extols Hezekiah's words as the fruit of covenantal faith. The fourfold command—Be strong! Be courageous! Don't be afraid. Don't be discouraged (v. 7).—mirrors the charge Moses passed on to Joshua (Josh 1:6-9) and David gave to Solomon (1 Chr 22:13). Furthermore, Hezekiah's strong belief that God would fight their battles (2 Chr 32:8) demonstrates spiritual leadership that had been lacking in Judah for generations. He understood, as postexilic Jews needed to, that the presence of God was the distinguishing factor between Israel and other nations.

Soon, Sennacherib sent messengers to Jerusalem blaspheming Yahweh (vv. 9-19). Summarized significantly from the Kings account, the text captures the arrogance with which Assyria's king scoffs at assertions that are true. He mocks the notion that Yahweh Elohim will deliver Judah (v. 11). He laughs at the idea of a single altar before which Hezekiah permits the people to worship (v. 12). Beliefs like these would have been just as unpopular among the surrounding nations after the exile.

Modern examples of basic, Christian convictions that evoke the world's scorn are common:

- Do you actually think God will forgive you of sin and save you from hell?
- Do you really believe God will protect you from your enemies?
- Do you really trust that Jesus rose from the dead and that you will, too?
- Do you blindly conclude that God will punish the wicked and bring justice to the earth?
- Do you naïvely accept that Scripture is truth—and build your life around it?
- Do you foolishly assume that what some preacher told you is true?

On and on it goes. Biblical doctrine and conviction are dismissed as fanaticism in most places.

In his efforts to dissuade Judean believers, Sennacherib elevated himself as more powerful than any of the gods from the defeated nations who defied Assyria (vv. 13-14). From his perspective, the same outcome awaits Israel if they heed the spiritual conviction of Hezekiah (v. 15). Through messengers, letters, and even direct communication with the people in Hebrew (vv. 16-18), these pagans mocked the strength and glory of Yahweh as they would a wooden idol (v. 19). Yet as Hezekiah and Isaiah prayed, the judgment of the Lord was swift, and the fall of the enemy was great, even resulting in Sennacherib's death at the hands of his own children (vv. 20-21). The Lord heard his people just as he promised he would (7:12-16).

Hezekiah survived his vulnerable moment as God saved his kingdom and gave him rest on every side (32:22). His fame spread among the nations much as it did for Solomon years before (v. 23). Perhaps some even wondered if this was the promised son of David who would usher in the messianic age. Regardless, the underlying implication for the Chronicler's audience was the priority of the temple for the welfare of the nation. With worship and dependence interlocked, the cultic experience was the means to know God more deeply and to trust God more fully. Soon, though, Hezekiah's great success would expose another vulnerability that was much more difficult to overcome.

From Within (32:24-33)

While details regarding Hezekiah's sickness remain a mystery, the text does reveal a terminal prognosis (v. 24). Again, the Chronicler condenses the narrative, expecting his readers to be familiar with the record of the Deuteronomistic historian (2 Kgs 20:1-11). The miraculous sign of the reversal of the progression of the shadow on the steps (2 Kgs 20:11) affirmed the promise of the supernatural healing and the lengthening of Hezekiah's life. This was the reward for the king's dependence on and trust in the Lord (2 Kgs 20:3). Tragically, his physical deliverance became an occasion for pride and, for the first time, an ungodly independence that separated Hezekiah from Yahweh. Most likely, his inappropriate response to the wealth he enjoyed was a reference to his attempted treaty with envoys from Babylon (2 Chr 32:31; cf. 2 Kgs 20:12-13).

In what was his only failed test of leadership identified by the Chronicler, Hezekiah sealed the fate of Babylonian exile, though not in his lifetime (2 Kgs 20:16-18). His quick repentance was further evidence that, though he was not the messianic ruler, Judah's king had a tender heart impassioned to please the Lord (2 Chr 32:26). With Hezekiah's unparalleled wealth for his day (vv. 27-29) and unquestioned success in his kingdom (v. 30), the nation honored Hezekiah's faithfulness throughout his life and in his death (vv. 32-33).

The king's flawed testimony is a reminder of at least four biblical lessons regarding our inner vulnerability to temptations:

- No one is exempt from the deceptive lure of pride.
- A lifetime of integrity does not give one permission for even a moment of sin.
- Momentary disobedience can result in great, even eternal, consequences.
- The remedy for spiritual arrogance is humble repentance.

The New Testament echoes these principles for contemporary disciples. Even the great apostle to the Gentiles, knowing his personal weaknesses and flaws, remarked, "I discipline my body and bring it under strict control, so that after preaching to others, I myself will not be disqualified" (1 Cor 9:27). He then added, "So, whoever thinks he stands must be careful not to fall" (1 Cor 10:12). Indeed. Few men can rival Hezekiah's accomplishments or commitment. We are wise to learn from his mistakes even as we rest in the One who was in all ways tempted as we are yet remained without sin (Heb 4:15).

Reflect and Discuss

1. Why do Christians often prize individual blessings but shun individual responsibilities?
2. What responsibilities do Christians have for the overall health and vitality of the congregation they are part of?
3. Why should Christians resist the urge to blame spiritual leaders, even bad ones, for their disobedience?
4. How can we discern that our conscience has dulled?
5. Why are weeping and mourning necessary parts of experiencing genuine revival?
6. How can we consecrate ourselves before the Lord after we stray from him?

7. How can we move past cultural Christianity to deeper, more sincere faith? What preparations do we need to make?

8. Why is cheerful giving such an important part of our spiritual growth?

9. How do outside pressures test our commitment to and maturity in the Lord?

10. How are you inwardly vulnerable in your walk with God? In what ways does pride prevent you from depending on the Lord?

Where Sin Did Abound

2 CHRONICLES 33

Main Idea: The remarkable history of Manasseh's repentance and restoration is a miniature shadow of the greater exile and renewal that awaited those who were part of the Persian restoration. For contemporary Christians, the text is a celebration of God's willingness to forgive even the vilest sinner who repents.

I.   **Compromise Always Leads to Rebellion (33:1-9).**
II. **Consequences Sometimes Lead to Repentance (33:10-13).**
III. **Contrition Often Leads to Restoration (33:14-25).**

When Jeffery Dahmer died by the hands of a fellow inmate in Wisconsin's Columbia Correctional Institute in 1994, not many people grieved. Though his crimes were committed more than three decades ago, a new generation still shivers at the name of one of history's most grotesque killers. Between 1978 and 1991, Dahmer raped, murdered, and dismembered seventeen young men and boys. The offenses his victims suffered remain unspeakably depraved.

But do you know what bothers me the most about Jeffrey Dahmer? Not his cannibalism or necrophilia, though both were horrifying. Not his lack of remorse throughout his lengthy trial, though I admit that angers me. Nor was it his life-without-parole sentence, though the death penalty certainly seemed more fitting.

What bothered me the most about the vile killer was his . . . *CONVERSION.* The admission embarrasses me, and it must seem strange coming from a pastor, but it is true nonetheless. Months before an inmate took Dahmer's life, multiple reports indicate that he repented of his sins and gave his life to Christ. It all began when an Oklahoman named Curt Booth began sending the criminal Bible literature. Soon thereafter, a local minister named Roy Ratcliff began visiting him and finally baptized him.

But how could a horrible monster claim God's forgiveness? How could he use words like *saved* or *redeemed?* Is it really possible that someone so vile could be cleansed of his sins after hurting so many people?

The fact that I struggle with questions like these proves I don't fully grasp the depth of my own sinfulness. The moment we assert that another does not deserve the grace of God, we erroneously imply that we do. Believe it or not, the Old Testament presents another unlikely candidate for grace that must have shocked the entire nation of Judah. The Deuteronomistic historian records none of the redemptive details found here, perhaps because they were so difficult to believe. The story of Manasseh is not only one of great sin and transgression but also one of tremendous grace and restoration.

Despite the comprehensive reforms Hezekiah instituted, his inability to sustain Judah's devotion to Yahweh beyond one generation testifies to how wicked the southern kingdom had become. In our continued search for understanding of the factors that ultimately led to the Babylonian exile, the abiding impression is that Judah is living on borrowed time at this point. For modern readers, the story of Manasseh is a subtle warning about how far our depravity often takes us and how quickly we sometimes spiral out of control. More explicit, though, is the principled message this record offers us about God's willingness to forgive even though we stray.

Examples of Yahweh's continual faithfulness to the Davidic covenant were the written means of reinforcing the postexilic hope that a future son of David would reign and the fortunes of the nation would be restored. By this point, the glory of Judah's past was a distant memory that only few had experienced for themselves. Notions of future greatness seemed to be nothing more than wishful thinking. Thus, the Chronicler penned the remarkable history of Manasseh's repentance and restoration as a miniature shadow of the greater exile and renewal that awaited those now free from Persian rule. By arguing from the lesser to the greater, this pericope celebrates the magnanimity of God's grace toward his people then and now.

The absence of these events in the Deuteronomistic history should not be viewed as evidence of their fabrication. On the contrary, because of his unique purposes for writing, the Chronicler often abbreviates, edits, deletes, or adds to material from his original sources. Without these changes, there would be no need for an additional history to encourage God's chosen people. Consequently, within this expanded account of Manasseh's forgiveness, there are three lessons about falling away from God and finding your way back to him, all of which were relevant to the postexilic community and are equally pertinent today.

Compromise Always Leads to Rebellion
2 CHRONICLES 33:1-9

Manasseh could not stand in sharper contrast to his father, Hezekiah. In fact, this wicked leader was so vile that the entire nation followed him into apostasy. With a tenure longer than any king in Judah's history, decades of spiritual damage characterized Manasseh's reign (vv. 1-2). The history in 2 Kings presents him as the worst king on record. The Chronicler, though, has a much different goal for his readers. Without denying his detestable leadership, the Chronicler provides a word of hope for anxious Jews who regathered in Jerusalem after the exile by detailing the miraculous repentance of this evil man. To truly appreciate how remarkable Manasseh's change was, we must first survey the depths of his rebellious compromise.

As a demonstration of the unified accuracy of the two accounts, we should note that 33:1-9 is nearly identical to 2 Kings 21:1-9. The recollection begins and ends by associating Manasseh with the defilement of the Canaanites who previously had possessed the promised land (vv. 2,9). Only Ahaz merited an equally damning assessment (28:1-3). The specificity that follows is jarring, precisely because, as Thompson notes,

> If Manasseh had searched the Scriptures for practices that
> would most anger the Lord and then intentionally committed
> them, he could not have achieved that result any more
> effectively than he did. (*1, 2 Chronicles*, 368)

His actions read like a checklist of Deuteronomy 18:9-14, which surveys the idolatries and sins of the Canaanites (vv. 3-8). Manasseh reconstructed high places, altars for Baal, and Asherah poles while worshiping the stars (v. 3). He burned incense to stars (vv. 4-5), burned his children alive as sacrifices, practiced witchcraft, and consulted mediums—all of which provoked the Lord's anger (v. 6).

Worst of all, Manasseh's desecration of the temple was a line no king before him dared cross (vv. 7-8). By placing a carved image in the holiest place, he was effectively replacing Yahweh with Baal. In essence, Manasseh foolishly sought to dethrone Israel's God and thus repudiated all the promises tied to the Davidic line of which he was a part. Consequently, after the tremendous revival of Hezekiah, Judah sank once again into reprehensible evil.

These acts were so atrocious that the Deuteronomistic historian sees not just correlation but causation for the Babylonian captivity:

Since King Manasseh of Judah has committed all these detestable acts—worse evil than the Amorites who preceded him had done—and by means of his idols has also caused Judah to sin, this is what the Lᴏʀᴅ God of Israel says: "I am about to bring such a disaster on Jerusalem and Judah that everyone who hears about it will shudder. I will stretch over Jerusalem the measuring line used on Samaria and the mason's level used on the house of Ahab, and I will wipe Jerusalem clean as one wipes a bowl—wiping it and turning it upside down. I will abandon the remnant of my inheritance and hand them over to their enemies. They will become plunder and spoil to all their enemies, because they have done what is evil in my sight and have angered me from the day their ancestors came out of Egypt until today."
(2 Kgs 21:11-15)

Though the full destruction of the nation did not come until after his death, Manasseh is clearly held responsible for the events of the exile. Two times we read the same historical interpretation within the Kings record (2 Kgs 23:26-27; 24:3-4), and both evaluations place the blame for Judah's judgment at the feet of their longest-serving king.

For those returning to Jerusalem, the compromises of Manasseh were a strong warning against following a similar plight. Future rebellion against God's covenant would result in the same condemnation Judah experienced long ago. Believers might find difficulty relating to the specific deviations within the text, but the pattern of compromise leading to rebellion against God rings true even today. The apostle Paul warns against our conforming to the world, knowing that doing so makes it impossible to know and live the will of God (Rom 12:2). Small compromises of one's faith can lead to monumental spiritual damage and even apostasy.

The cultural pressure to capitulate to the ecumenical spirit of our day places many professing Christians outside the boundaries of orthodoxy much more quickly than they realize. Accepting the exclusivity of Jesus as the only way to heaven, for example, is not one of many valid responses to the gospel; it is the only scriptural response (Acts 4:12). For some, the redefinition of marriage is nothing more than a different point of view under the umbrella of Christian faith. But biblically, homosexuality is not just unnatural, though it is, but it is also key evidence of an idolatrous heart that no longer acknowledges God (Rom 1:24-28). Prosperity teaching subtly justifies insatiable materialism as normative and even a sign of God's blessing, when the Scripture warns that the love of money leads to the destruction of pulling people away from the faith (1 Tim 6:9-10). These examples are far from comprehensive, but they do illustrate that the spirit behind Manasseh's compromise still leads many to rebel today.

Consequences Sometimes Lead to Repentance
2 CHRONICLES 33:10-13

Despite the Lord's warnings, neither Manasseh nor his people heeded the gracious call (v. 10). Therefore, Yahweh raised up the king of Assyria, likely Esarhaddon, to come against Judah, bind Manasseh, and lead them to Babylon as captives (v. 11). The descriptive language of this small-scale exile foreshadows the same outcomes larger in scope when the nation later crumbled into captivity under the leadership of Jehoahaz and Jehoiakim. Here, modern readers might ask why God delayed the full-blown exile predicted during the reign of Hezekiah (2 Kgs 20:16-18). Clearly, Manasseh and his people were ripe for judgment because of their evil deeds. Additionally, the Deuteronomistic tradition firmly identified this king as the antecedent to the coming Babylonian invasion.

So, why did God delay? In what is surely the most unexpected change of heart in Israel's history, Manasseh repented for his atrocities. Because of his distress, the king humbled himself, prayed, and sought the Lord. God in his graciousness heard and answered Manasseh's royal prayer to bring him back to Jerusalem (vv. 12-13). Our initial reaction to what unfolded might be suspicion because the burden of consequences was obviously behind this dramatic repentance. Yet the text makes plain that Manasseh came to know Yahweh as the true God through the ordeal.

The possibility of redeeming consequences was just as important for the postexilic community, if not more so, as it is for believers everywhere today. The plight of Babylon was an unquestionable outcome of decades, even generations, of idolatry in Judah. These penalties were not, however, evidence that God had washed his hands of his people forever. On the contrary, the chastening burdens heaped on the nation were merciful efforts to turn the people's hearts back to the Lord. In this sense, the exile was an act of compassion, not condemnation, precisely because these were God's people forever, bound by his covenantal promises. Consequences are meant to bring us back, not keep us away.

Earthly parents discipline their children for one reason: to correct their bad behavior. As a father of five, my goal for discipline is not that my children will cease to be mine but that they will thrive because they are. The writer of Hebrews used the same analogy when he spoke of the Lord's chastisement:

> *And you have forgotten the exhortation that addresses you as sons:*
>
> > *My son, do not take the Lord's discipline lightly*
> > *or lose heart when you are reproved by him,*
> > *for the Lord disciplines the one he loves*
> > *and punishes every son he receives.*
>
> *Endure suffering as discipline: God is dealing with you as sons. For what son is there that a father does not discipline?* (Heb 12:5-7)

Furthermore, when severe repercussions bring about a change in their behavior, I rejoice rather than resist my children. The writer goes on to explain,

> *For they disciplined us for a short time based on what seemed good to them, but he does it for our benefit, so that we can share his holiness. No discipline seems enjoyable at the time, but painful. Later on, however, it yields the peaceful fruit of righteousness to those who have been trained by it.* (Heb 12:10-11)

In other words, the consequences wrought by God often bring us to repentance, produce holiness in our lives, and yield the peaceful fruit of righteousness. We should celebrate these outcomes rather than question them. Jews coming out of exile needed to believe that the severity of God's past retribution was a doorway to starting over again. So do we.

Thankfully, those who yield to God's correction by humbly seeking him and calling out to him can receive grace and mercy from the Lord. **No person is beyond the grace of God.** Consider the testimony of God's missionary to the Gentiles. Paul wrote,

> *I give thanks to Christ Jesus our Lord who has strengthened me, because he considered me faithful, appointing me to the ministry— even though I was formerly a blasphemer, a persecutor, and an*

arrogant man. But I received mercy because I acted out of ignorance in unbelief, and the grace of our Lord overflowed, along with the faith and love that are in Christ Jesus. This saying is trustworthy and deserving of full acceptance: "Christ Jesus came into the world to save sinners"—and I am the worst of them. But I received mercy for this reason, so that in me, the worst of them, Christ Jesus might demonstrate his extraordinary patience as an example to those who would believe in him for eternal life. (1 Tim 1:12-16)

Even when the consequences for past actions remain, those trained by God's chastening hand can still bear the fruit of righteousness. It is never too late to turn to God. It is never too late to do the right thing. The Lord will give grace to the humble.

Contrition Often Leads to Restoration
2 CHRONICLES 33:14-25

Remarkably, the Lord chose to restore Manasseh to his throne in Jerusalem (v. 13). Once there, Manasseh began rebuilding the city and eliminating the idolatry he previously sanctioned. Williamson observed, "Manasseh furnishes the most explicit and dramatic example of the efficacy of repentance in the whole of the Chronicler's work. . . . Even in [his] dire circumstances, it is implied, restoration remains a possibility" (*1 and 2 Chronicles*, 389). Therein lies the heartbeat of this pericope's importance. Believing that Yahweh would forgive them was a stretch, but trusting him to restore them after so much spiritual treachery seemed too good to be true. The path forward for the postexilic community depended entirely on God's willingness to heal and restore.

Manasseh took all the necessary steps of restitution to place Judah in a position for God to renew them. The text indicates that he focused on three specific reforms in his efforts, effectively undoing all that he had forced on the nation previously. He continued work started by Hezekiah on the west side of Jerusalem's outer wall in an effort to make it higher (v. 14a). Next, he reorganized Judah's army to include the nation's fortified cities (v. 14b). Finally, and perhaps most critically, he revived temple worship by removing his idol from the most holy place, as well as the many altars to false gods he had constructed (v. 15). He not only rebuilt the altar of the Lord but also made sacrifices on it while instructing the people to do so as well (v. 16)—though many refused, as evidenced by the next two Davidic reigns over the kingdom. In the immediate wake of Manasseh's rehabilitation, the high places remained but were repurposed for sacrificing to Yahweh (v. 17).

Lest we doubt the legitimacy of his repentance, even the record of Manasseh's death has a reconciliatory tone to it. Whereas 2 Kings 21:17-18 emphasizes his great sin, 2 Chronicles 33:18-20 lead with the king's prayer and God's receptive forgiveness without denying his shameful years. Furthermore, the brief, backslidden reign of Amon concludes the passage as further evidence of Manasseh's genuine change (vv. 21-25). Already influenced by the dark years of his father's throne, Amon did evil in the sight of the Lord and made sacrifices to idols carved by Manasseh (v. 22). His guilt grew because he refused to humble himself before Yahweh (v. 23). Yet in what appears to be a dramatic step backward, we also read that his reign ended after two years when his servants put him to death (v. 24). Though not reflective of the entire nation, those closest to the king were unwilling to tolerate his renunciation of Manasseh's reforms. At the very least, an influential minority bore the fruit of renewal even after the former king's death.

Why are these developments included in the chronicle? Put simply, to demonstrate Yahweh's faithfulness to the covenant he made with David even when his people fall short. To remind the postexilic community that where sin increased, God's grace abounded even more (Rom 5:20). The same God who brought Manasseh out of his personal captivity was passionately solicitous toward his people who needed similar deliverance now. If he restored after the lesser exile of Judah's wicked king, he could do so now as the entire nation awaited to reinhabit and recultivate the land of promise. Not only do these verses demonstrate that Manasseh's repentance bore the fruit of good works, but they also showcase the blessings of God again through his rebuilding efforts. Though much was lost in Babylon, God was willing to restore what the locusts had eaten during Israel's years of shame (Joel 2:25).

The joy of restoration should not, however, be interpreted as a license to slide back into idolatry. The swift removal of Amon was as much a warning to Judah as the forgiveness of Manasseh was an encouragement. God's forgiveness should never be used as a license to sin. Continuing to rebel does not increase the grace of God; it forfeits it (Rom 6:1-2).

Christians today also live as exiles on the earth, awaiting our return to the Edenic paradise that was lost. Because our citizenship is in heaven

(Phil 3:20), we join Abraham in looking for a city whose architect and builder is God (Heb 11:10). Until that time comes, we look for a greater King who is coming. Postexilic believers looked backward only to realize none of their leaders, who were now in the grave, qualified for the messianic role foretold. We look for the return of a future son of David who will sit on the eternal throne of his father. Until he comes, we, like our Jewish forefathers, must dwell in exile, making the best of each fallen moment, just as the prophet Jeremiah instructed:

> *This is what the LORD of Armies, the God of Israel, says to all the exiles I deported from Jerusalem to Babylon: "Build houses and live in them. Plant gardens and eat their produce. Find wives for yourselves, and have sons and daughters. Find wives for your sons and give your daughters to men in marriage so that they may bear sons and daughters. Multiply there; do not decrease. Pursue the well-being of the city I have deported you to. Pray to the LORD on its behalf, for when it thrives, you will thrive."* (Jer 29:4-11)

Even more immediately, we know that God is available and willing to forgive those who come to him with genuine humility and repentance. Oftentimes, cleansing washes over us with the same profound restoration Manasseh experienced. Christ brings us out of our personal exiles that keep us far from him. And we similarly stand amazed by his grace and mercy.

- Like Joseph's brothers, our fellowship with God can be renewed when we turn away from wickedness (Gen 50:19-21).
- Like Gomer, we can find love from a heavenly bridegroom even after we stray (Hos 3:1).
- Like the woman at the well in Samaria, we will find living water for our souls despite our sins when we drink deeply from Christ (John 4:14).
- Like Peter, we can be repurposed for service despite having denied the Lord in numerous ways (John 21:15-17).
- Like Onesimus, we can receive a fresh start from God when we face the consequences of our actions (Phlm 17-21).

Reflect and Discuss

1. What types of sin leave us feeling unredeemable? What transgression in your life left you wondering if God could love and forgive you?

2. How should we treat those who repent after egregious, abhorrent sin? What signs of sincerity should we look for?

3. How does the record of Manasseh's repentance and forgiveness change our perception of the 2 Kings history? In what ways are these two accounts difficult to synthesize?

4. How do small compromises make us more vulnerable to great rebellion?

5. How can the consequences for our sin have a positive impact on our lives? What do our consequences teach us about our relationship with God?

6. When people repent after experiencing painful consequences, how do we typically respond to them? In what ways are our responses unbiblical?

7. How did their years in Babylon help the Jews reacclimate themselves to the covenantal realities they experienced in Jerusalem?

8. Does God's restoration of us guarantee the removal of all the consequences created by our sin? Why or why not?

9. How can we avoid minimizing sin when we experience the abundant grace of God in our lives?

10. As we look for the final restoration of all things, how can we remain faithful to Christ while we are exiles on this earth?

The Tipping Point

2 CHRONICLES 34–36

Main Idea: Spiritual renewal is possible when we respond obediently to God's revelation of truth. Yet we should never confuse the Lord's patience toward us as a license to sin. Eventually, there will be a reckoning for disobedience.

I. **There Is a Lifeline for God's People (34:1–35:19).**
   A. Removing Judah's wickedness
   B. Reestablishing God's worship
   C. Rediscovering God's Word
   D. Remembering God's works
II. **There Is a Lesson about God's Priority (35:20-27).**
III. **There Is a Limit to God's Patience (36:1-23).**
   A. Joahaz (36:1-3)
   B. Jehoiakim (36:4-8)
   C. Jehoiachin (36:9-10)
   D. Zedekiah (36:11-21)
   E. Appendix (36:22-23)

Many behaviors are contagious. Little adjustments can have big effects. Monumental changes happen in one dramatic moment, called a tipping point, rather than gradually. These three premises guide Malcolm Gladwell's best-selling book, *The Tipping Point*, in which he explains how change occurs.

Consider, for example, the ebb and flow of new technology. In the mid 1980s, Sharp introduced and sold about eighty thousand fax machines in the United States. By 1987, the concept of a fax became commonplace, forcing a tipping point as sales reached one million that year. Just two years later, in 1989, two million devices were in operation. For most of the 1990s, the technology was as ubiquitous as commerce itself. After two decades of the twenty-first century, however, momentum in the other direction has left fax machines nearly obsolete, proving that tipping points can work for or against you. Cell phones followed a similar trajectory as they got smaller and cheaper in the 1990s, leading to a commercial tipping point of dramatic proportions. Today, one out of every two people possesses a mobile phone of some kind (*Tipping Point*, 7–12).

After years of spiritual highs and lows, there were more subtle compromises than recommitments in Judah. Idolatry was just as contagious as yawning among the people, and the tipping point of God's judgment was near. With the exile looming on the horizon, this pericope records the dramatic renewal of Judah under the leadership of Josiah, as well as his complicity in the eventual demise of the nation. The movement toward God's disciplinary correction, which began as far back as Ahaz and progressed during the reigns of Hezekiah and Manasseh, picks up remarkable speed with the final preexilic generation. For the Chronicler, who writes to help the recovering community understand what led to the exile, the rapid conclusion accentuates the broad responsibility of many failed generations. Japhet correctly points out that the entire nation and history bear the weight of the consequences ahead (*Ideology*, 364–65).

For the postexilic restoration efforts, these chapters also prominently prize the word of the Lord as the key to future renewal while also contrasting the devastation of ignoring what God reveals. Also, the urgency of responding quickly to God's compassion and invitation motivates the generation seeking to rebuild Jerusalem. Believers today can be similarly challenged by the same message as we wrestle with and seek to avoid the consequences of our disobedience under the lordship of Christ.

There Is a Lifeline for God's People
2 CHRONICLES 34:1–35:19

Though the fall and restoration of Manasseh provided postexilic believers with a path forward from their national exile by means of repentance, overall his kingship was a failure that left generational consequences behind. His son, Josiah, was a mere eight years old when he ascended David's throne, yet he received glowing reviews from the Chronicler for his thirty-one-year reign (34:1). Much like his grandfather Hezekiah, Josiah was a reformer who sought the Lord, repaired the temple, and reestablished the cultic tradition of the nation. Without deviation, the young king walked in integrity before the Lord (v. 2). Along with Hezekiah, he is only one of two kings in the chronicle that compare favorably with David. His reign highlights the importance of Scripture, which functions as the lifeline for the covenantal community. Even believers today should appreciate a renewed commitment to God's Word after reading this passage.

Removing Judah's Wickedness

At the age of sixteen, Josiah began seeking the Lord for himself (34:3). Likely more a reflection of his personal piety and development, the statement signals that Josiah's godly leadership grew out of his genuine commitment to Yahweh. Four years later, as an adult, the king is ready for the monumental task of purging the land of its idolatry. In a dramatic display of devotion to the Lord, Josiah not only tore down the high places, Asherim, and molten images, but he also ground them into powder that he then sprinkled on the graves of idolaters (v. 4). He also burned the bones of false priests on their wicked altars (v. 5). The Deuteronomistic historian reveals that Josiah dug up the bones of previous idolatrous leaders (2 Kgs 23:16) and executed those who were living (2 Kgs 23:20). In addition to purifying Jerusalem and Judah, these far-reaching reforms extended to Simeon and into the former northern kingdom to cities in Manasseh, Ephraim, and even as far as Naphtali (2 Chr 34:6-7). Josiah's purging of the land was unlike any since the days of Joshua.

Reestablishing God's Worship

After cleansing the land of its wickedness, Josiah, now twenty-four years old, focused his efforts on repairing the temple by commissioning Shaphan, Maaseiah, and Joah to lead its renovations (34:8). Details about the collection to fund the work are reminiscent of Joash's leadership.

By adding greater specificity about those who participated in the offering (cf. 2 Kgs 22:4), the Chronicler communicates his priority of uniting all of Israel under the direction of Yahweh, a foundational theme established by Hezekiah that was essential for the postexilic community (34:9). In fact, all the renovation details are considerably more thorough, and understandably so, than the older history. This pericope functioned like an instruction manual for those rebuilding the temple after the exile (vv. 10-13). Accepting personal responsibility for their national decline was also key, and would be in the future, to forging a path forward (v. 11). Both the integrity and the skill of the workers made the effort successful (v. 12).

Rediscovering God's Word

During the work's execution, the priest Hilkiah discovered the book of the law and delivered it to King Josiah (34:14-16). The identity of this scroll has been the source of debate, with some claiming it is the entire Pentateuch (Williamson, *1 and 2 Chronicles*, 402; Japhet, *I & II Chronicles*, 1030), but the majority recognizing it as the book of Deuteronomy (Boda, *1–2 Chronicles*, 414; Dillard, *2 Chronicles*, 280; Merrill, *A Commentary*, 581; Pratt, *1 & 2 Chronicles*, 483; Selman, *2 Chronicles*, 552). Regardless, after Shaphan gave a progress report concerning the temple, he began reading from the book of the law in the presence of Josiah (vv. 17-18). Devastated panic filled the king's heart as he realized the nation was vulnerable to the judgment of God (v. 19).

Therefore, with a determination to obey all that God revealed in his Word, Josiah sent his servants to inquire of the Lord on behalf of the people (vv. 20-21). The king's priority alone would have been instructive to those rebuilding after the exile, even as it is for readers today. The fact that Hilkiah immediately went to Huldah the prophetess for direction from Yahweh reveals her established reputation for accurately communicating the words of God (v. 22).

For some, particularly those who interpret gender roles in a complementary way, the presence of a female voice in this historical situation raises practical questions. For example, why does God restrict the role of pastor to men if he chooses to speak through females in a prophetic role (1 Tim 2:12-14)? What differences are there, if any, between God's prophets and his pastors? With numerous prophetesses in the Bible, including Miriam, Deborah, Isaiah's wife, Huldah, and Anna, how can we reconcile the apparent contradiction?

To answer, we must first appreciate the distinction between a prophet and a preacher of Scripture. The former delivered on behalf of the Lord a message or direction without additional explanation or application. A prophet was never free to add to or take away from the revelation received from Yahweh. The latter, however, does not espouse new revelation but explains existing revelation. The modern equivalent would be the difference between reading Scripture and explaining Scripture. A New Testament pastor is more like an Old Testament priest, none of whom were women, than a prophet from either dispensation. Throughout the Bible, God encourages women to prophesy, but there is no example of his placing them in the role of pastor or priest (see DeYoung, *Men and Women in the Church*, for a concise theology of biblical complementarianism).

Unfortunately, the word revealed through God's messenger was a detailed explanation for Judah's coming exile (34:23-25). Their idolatry wrought irreversible consequences, providing a valuable lesson about presuming on the grace of God as license to sin. One silver lining, though, was a reward for Josiah's humility and eagerness to obey the precepts of the Lord: these judgments would not become reality until the years after Josiah's leadership ended (vv. 26-28). The recognition of and appreciation for the king's brokenness over the spiritual broken-ness of the nation provided a path forward for those who returned from Babylon. God remains enthusiastic to forgive all who turn from their sins with a pure heart even today (Ps 24:3-5).

Gripped by what he heard, Josiah accepted spiritual responsibility for the nation by gathering all its inhabitants around him and reading from the book of the law (2 Chr 34:29-30). Then, leading by example, the king pledged his personal commitment to God's covenant while also compelling the people of Judah to do the same (vv. 31-32). Though Josiah's influence resulted in the people's cooperation, there is a hint ("he made all who were present," NASB) that the entire citizenry did not share his conviction from or enthusiasm for the directives of God's Word. The abrupt departure from these national priorities immediately after Josiah's death would seem to suggest so as well. Nonetheless, the Chronicler paints a picture of comprehensive renewal as the standard of faithfulness for the covenantal community going forward (v. 33).

Remembering God's Works

Again, we see Josiah's commonality with Hezekiah through his obser-vance of Passover in order to celebrate God's past faithfulness, pro-vision, and grace (35:1). Through the king's preparations of both priests and Levites, his attention to cultic protocol and biblical wor-ship remains clear (vv. 2-6). The goal is the correct use of the tem-ple. His Levitical charge to teach all Israel alongside the priests again underscores the emphasis and priority of Scripture at the heart of the nation (v. 2).

Because there is no mention of the ark's removal from the tem-ple, though some suggest Manasseh replaced it with an idol, the com-mand to return it is problematic (v. 3). Perhaps Josiah's reading of

Deuteronomy caused confusion among the Levites, and Josiah was merely explaining that their previous transportation duties were no longer needed now that the ark had a permanent resting place. Or maybe the pagan ritual of carrying deities around on poles had infiltrated the practices of Judah, requiring correction. Regardless, Josiah delineated the assignments and functions of the Levitical order, and the Chronicler preserved the instructions for the postexilic efforts. His lasting protocol was dividing duties according to ancestral families and divisions (v. 4) established by the authority of David, Solomon, and Moses (v. 6) (Boda, *1–2 Chronicles*, 418). These orderly procedures carefully aligned with the newly discovered book of Deuteronomy.

King Josiah and his officials gave liberally so that there were enough sacrifices for the Passover celebration (vv. 7-9). Once all was ready, the ceremony that followed divided into two parts. First, the priests and Levites prepared and offered the sacrifices (vv. 10-12). Next, the people shared the Passover meal together (vv. 13-14). Musicians carried out their assignments according to the divisions laid down by David, as did the gatekeepers (vv. 15-16). The ensuing celebration was unlike anything previously experienced during Israel's monarchial period (vv. 17-19). Covering a span of seven days in recognition of the Festival of Unleavened Bread, the unparalleled event marked what could be in the kingdom just before the nation fell into judgment. The resulting message is that the difference between consequence and blessing is the distance between faithfulness and disobedience.

For contemporary believers, reading Josiah's reforms ought to deepen our love for and devotion to Scripture. The Bible's clarity to tell us what is right and wrong, as well as how to course correct and remain faithful, is essential for our sanctification and growth in the Lord (2 Tim 3:16-17). Because the deceptions of our hearts pull our priorities away from what is right and true (Jer 17:9), individual Christians must use God's Word as both an anchor for and measure of faithfulness. A daily devotional time to read Scripture and respond to it prayerfully is essential for maintaining a vibrant walk with Christ.

Likewise, the church that does not read and teach the Word corporately will soon find itself drifting from the faith that was once for all handed down to the saints (Jude 3). Sadly, the American church often jettisons the agenda of Scripture in exchange for the whims of culture. Affirming the inerrancy of Holy Writ falls flat if we do not appropriate the sufficiency of the same. Our days are not all that different from the compromises that plagued Israel and Judah long ago as described by the prophet Amos:

> *Look, the days are coming—*
> *this is the declaration of the Lord GOD—*
> *when I will send a famine through the land:*
> *not a famine of bread or a thirst for water,*
> *but of hearing the words of the LORD.*
> *People will stagger from sea to sea*
> *and roam from north to east*
> *seeking the word of the LORD,*
> *but they will not find it.* (Amos 8:11-12)

The Bible should define when we worship, how we worship, who leads us in worship, and how we respond to worship. Scripture offers wisdom that leads to salvation through faith in Christ (2 Tim 3:15); it, through its commands and instructions, illuminates and empowers sanctification in the lives of believers (2 Thess 4:1-2); and it points to the coming glorification of all the saints (1 John 3:2-3).

The fallacy of felt-needs preaching is the assumption that a preacher is wise enough to put his finger on the greatest spiritual needs and priorities of a congregation. A steady diet of biblical exposition evokes responses similar to those who heard the word for the first time during Josiah's reign in Judah. Hebrews 4:12 explains:

> *For the word of God is living and effective and sharper than any*
> *double-edged sword, penetrating as far as the separation of soul*
> *and spirit, joints and marrow. It is able to judge the thoughts and*
> *intentions of the heart.*

The Holy Spirit convicts, confronts, corrects, and comforts through the proclamation of Scripture, addressing issues that need attention. Simply put, God uses his Word to do his work.

There Is a Lesson about God's Priority
2 CHRONICLES 35:20-27

The priority of obedience takes center stage as Judah's faithful king stumbles at the end of his memorable reign. Whereas the Deuteronomistic record elevates Josiah to the highest status after Solomon, the Chronicler writes to connect his personal demise to the downfall of the entire nation. In this sense, Josiah's reign was the beginning of the end for Judah. The pattern of the king's downfall follows a predictable pattern within Chronicles.

- Despite God's previous protection and favor, the king fears an outside threat.
- The king ignores a warning about his military actions.
- The king stumbles at the end of his life.
- Death is the immediate consequence for the king's disobedience. (Begg, "Death of Josiah," 1–8)

Through Josiah's abrupt decline we learn again about the priority of obedience for the Davidic kingdom. To enjoy the blessings of God, the king on Yahweh's throne had to hear and heed the directives of the law.

Assyria, Babylon, and Egypt were the three superpowers battling for supremacy at this point of Josiah's tenure. To overcome their common enemy, Assyria and Egypt formed an alliance to defeat Babylon. Though Judah was uninvolved, Josiah recklessly inserted himself into the controversy by opposing Neco, who was not an enemy to Judah at this point (35:20). Remarkably, words from the lips of a pagan king carry a prophetic warning against the chosen king (vv. 21-22). With no textual evidence that God prompted his involvement, Josiah's interfering with Egyptian affairs was equal to interrupting Yahweh's design for history.

Though we cannot pinpoint his underlying motive, this is the first example we have of Josiah ignoring the word of the Lord. Most likely, the maneuver was a misguided attempt to find favor with the Babylonians, but regardless, Leithart wisely identifies the incident's greatest failure as theological:

> The king of Judah is Yahweh's prince, the prince of the Creator of heaven and earth, who is enthroned in Jerusalem. Judah's kings should approach the world from a position of strength. They are not called to be involved in the power struggles of other kings. They are called to be agents of Yahweh's kingship. (*1 & 2 Chronicles*, 240–41)

Even more egregious, God already promised to preserve Judah during the lifetime of Josiah. Due to his ill-advised efforts, Josiah effectively shortened his life and endangered his people much sooner than necessary by making his death premature. Like the disguised Ahab who led the northern kingdom astray, one of Judah's most treasured kings died in disobedience to God (vv. 23-24). Because his effective reign ended with a tragic fall, Josiah's life was a powerful reminder that even the nation's best kings could not fully protect God's people. Only the coming son of David would successfully do so. Though many before him served up until their deaths, only he would be obedient even to the point of death (Phil 2:8).

Josiah's life is also a vivid warning about our tendency to make matters worse when we act independently of God while seeking to do his work. Abram's wife Sarai is an earlier example of the unrighteous solutions we sometimes offer when God does not work according to our timetables or plans. Years after receiving Yahweh's promise, at the age of seventy-five Sarai suggested that her handmaiden, Hagar, bear God's promised child for her husband (Gen 16:2). The result was a boy named Ishmael, leading to immediate jealousy and rage in Sarai's heart (Gen 16:4-6). Miraculously, God was gracious to all involved by reaffirming his intention to raise up Israel through Isaac while also promising that a great nation would rise from Ishmael as well (Gen 21:12-13). The resulting schism, though, could fill oceans with blood as modern Jews and Arabs war with each other. Scars from human reason and independence litter the landscape of redemptive history.

With this passage in mind, modern readers should renew their Christian commitment of walking in truth and obedience. Though Christ secured for us the blessing of eternal life through his perfect observance of the law, expressions of obedient faith serve as the evidence of genuine salvation. Even under a new covenant of grace, our commission is to let our light shine through good works that glorify our Father in heaven (Matt 5:16). Every disciple saved by grace through faith lives with the spiritual purpose of adhering to God's desires (Eph 2:10). Indeed, because faith without works is dead, the goal is to be doers of the word and not merely hearers who delude ourselves (Jas 1:22; 2:26). Consequences for disobedience remain even if they do not undermine the security found in Christ.

Despite the unfortunate compromise surrounding Josiah's final acts as king, the Chronicler remembers him fondly as the fulfillment of Huldah's prophetic word (35:25-27). Buried in the tombs of his fathers, the people mourned the loss of their king significantly. Ironically, Babylon was rising while Judah was falling. The same nation Josiah sought refuge from would soon become the means of the nation's destruction through exile.

There Is a Limit to God's Patience
2 CHRONICLES 36:1-23

As with any leadership transition of national importance, acting quickly to fill a vacancy preserves a sense of stability and confidence in the people. Joahaz was the clear choice of the common people in Judah (v. 1). Initially, it seems odd that the Chronicler would eliminate the Deuteronomistic detail that this king was also evil in the sight of the Lord (2 Kgs 23:32). Yet in his efforts to highlight the unnecessary interference and sin of Josiah, along with its lingering consequences, the omission seems prudent.

> Instead of treating Josiah's successors as rulers in their own
> right, the Chronicler places their reigns within the shattering
> aftermath of Josiah's death. That literary device italicizes
> the actual political situation: after Josiah, only Joahaz rules
> independently, and that for only three months. Otherwise,
> the final Davidic kings rule under the oversight of Gentile
> rulers, who install and replace them for their own purposes.
> (Leithart, *1 & 2 Chronicles*, 244)

This final pericopal division makes up the chronicle's concluding chapter. It presents Judah's four final kings and three waves of exile that result in a complete reversal of the nation's exit from Egypt.

Joahaz (36:1-3)

At just twenty-three years old, Joahaz only ruled from David's throne for three months before being deposed by the king of Egypt (vv. 2-3a). On the heels of Josiah's unpredicted and unexplainable intrusion into his national affairs, Neco sought to ensure that no Judean king would interfere in his military efforts again. His solution was to shut Joahaz away in Egypt forever (Jer 22:11-12). Adding insult to injury, Neco levied a fine on Judah for silver and gold that surely came out of the temple treasury (2 Chr 36:3b). As further evidence of Egyptian hegemony, he also chose the next king over Judah: Joahaz's brother Eliakim (v. 4).

Jehoiakim (36:4-8)

By asserting the authority to change Eliakim's name (to Jehoiakim), Neco was clear from the outset that this king was there to do the bidding of Egypt rather than of Yahweh. Despite reigning for eleven years, the text reports that Jehoiakim did evil in the sight of the Lord (v. 5). As time passed, Nebuchadnezzar's Babylon grew strong enough to overthrow Egypt, and one force of tyranny replaced the other. Like Manasseh before him, Jehoiakim committed detestable acts reminiscent of the Canaanites in the land previously. Though the means of God's judgment shifted away from Egypt to Babylon, nothing could diminish the force of Yahweh's anger against his unfaithful king (v. 6).

In what was truly the beginning of the end, a first wave of deportation to Babylon included Daniel and his friends (Dan 1:1-2), fulfilling the words of Jeremiah the prophet (Jer 25:1-11). Though the text seems to include Jehoiakim in this initial exodus, correlating it with Jeremiah 22:18-19 gives the impression that he was merely bound in bronze chains but died before leaving Jerusalem. Because his concluding formula is the only one of its kind in the chapter (v. 8), it could be a further indicator that Jehoiakim died before his personal exile (Selman, *2 Chronicles*, 568). The lack of burial information reinforces the detestable nature of his reign.

In any case, the emphasis is that God's judgment has begun to fall on Judah. Boda has astutely noted that the phrase used to describe Jehoiakim's capture (v. 6) is identical to the language of Manasseh's previous reckoning (33:11), which could serve as a hint for the reemergence of the disgraced yet chosen line (*1–2 Chronicles*, 425). While he is the only king in the chapter with a concluding formula (36:8), there is no mention of his death.

Also interesting is the absence of Jehoiakim's provoking Nebuchadnezzar three years after the Babylonian invasion of Jerusalem (2 Kgs 24:1). As with other omissions in the chronicle, the goal is to help the reader see the cause and effect of the king's and the nation's evil and God's resulting discipline. While the aforementioned episode does not contradict the Chronicler's conclusion, it does distract from it. While Neco and Nebuchadnezzar were evil in their own right, this history positions them as the agents of God's justice for the chosen line.

Plundering the temple was yet another indicator of Babylon's dominance over Judah (v. 7). These items were physical connections back to the monarchy of Solomon, and their loss demonstrated Judah's forfeiture of covenantal blessings, at least in the foreseeable future.

Jehoiachin (36:9-10)

Like the brevity of Joahaz's reign, Jehoiachin (also spelled Jeconiah) only ruled in Jerusalem for three months and ten days (v. 9). Despite his young age, the text indicates that he, too, was evil in the sight of the Lord. This short period represents the second wave of deportation as Nebuchadnezzar deports both the king and additional temple treasures (v. 10). Clearly, the momentum of God's judgment against his people is building, reaching its maximum repercussion after Zedekiah assumed the throne in Jerusalem.

Interestingly, the royal genealogy that opens the chronicle traces Jehoiachin's line into the postexilic existence (1 Chr 3:17). The Chronicler does not record his release from prison in Babylon (2 Kgs 25:27-30), but even in exile the people likely viewed Jehoiachin as their king. The line of David would continue despites the abysmal consequences of Judah's rebellion.

Zedekiah (36:11-21)

Zedekiah serves as the nineteenth and final king of Judah for eleven years (v. 11). Josiah's third son was Nebuchadnezzar's second enthroned puppet. His only assignment was to yield to his Gentile overlord, which is a possible explanation for the length of his reign. He, too, was evil in the sight of God, refusing to heed the instruction of the prophet Jeremiah (v. 12). In fact, Zedekiah's subsequent rebellion against Nebuchadnezzar may be the carnal result of his defying the Lord's prophet (v. 13). As in the early days of Manasseh, the nation resembled the detestable pagans previously driven out of the land more than the chosen people of God.

Amazingly, in his compassion for the people, Yahweh continued to show patience with them by sending his messengers to correct them (v. 15). Yet because of their continual rejection, God's long-suffering ended, and he gave his people over to the consequences of their actions. Even today, the Lord continues to show patience toward those who ridicule his truth, but his forbearance is not limitless. Far too often we mistake God's slowness to judge sin as his approval of it. Tragically, we foolishly boast of the Lord's compassion as a justification for our waywardness.

Do you despise the riches of his kindness, restraint, and patience, not recognizing that God's kindness is intended to lead you to repentance?

Because of your hardened and unrepentant heart you are storing up
wrath for yourself in the day of wrath, when God's righteous judgment
is revealed. (Rom 2:4-5)

When the tipping point comes, though, judgment is unavoidable.
For Judah, the moment of truth came when Nebuchadnezzar finally
led the Babylonians to overcome them. He massacred those hiding
in the temple (v. 17), plundered its remaining valuables (v. 18), then
burned the entire structure to the ground, and tore down the city's wall
(v. 19). Finally, the Chaldean ruler deported the remaining survivors to
Babylon (v. 20).

Today, with the birth of the Messiah behind us and second coming before us, God again demonstrates his patience toward those who
remain in unbelief. Despite the mockers who scoff at his physical return
(2 Pet 3:3-4), the Lord is not eager to judge, not wishing for any to
perish (2 Pet 3:9). Yet at some point, Yahweh's patience will run out
again as he makes his rulership not just over one nation but over the
whole world (2 Pet 3:10-13). The kings of the earth will not be able to
hide when the day of his wrath comes (Rev 6:12-17). The scenes of his
judgment will be piercing (Rev 14:9-11; 16:1,17-21). With the time of
repentance ended, the Lord will deal with his enemies once and for all:

> *A sharp sword came from his mouth, so that he might strike the*
> *nations with it. He will rule them with an iron rod. He will also*
> *trample the winepress of the fierce anger of God, the Almighty. And he*
> *has a name written on his robe and on his thigh:* KING OF KINGS AND
> LORD OF LORDS. (Rev 19:15-16)

Appendix (36:22-23)

The final two verses of the chronicle function as an appendix that sets
the stage for the restoration of Israel after the deportation. Quoting
from the opening of Ezra 1:1-3, the proclamation of Cyrus (the third
foreign king over the Jews during the exile) allows the people to return
to the land of promise to begin again (vv. 22-23). Still under Babylonian
hegemony, crowning a son of David to rule over them would have to wait
until later (we now join in their waiting as we anticipate the Messiah's
return). In the meantime, the people busied themselves with the work
of reestablishing their cultic identity through their rebuilding efforts.
Since this is the last book of the Jewish Old Testament, the next major

event on God's redemptive calendar was the birth of the promised King the Jews were looking for and that we celebrate.

The point for them, and us, is that the Davidic dynasty was not dead. God was still working his plan. The short-term postexilic gains were not the fulfillment of their realized hope. Life after the exile, as before, was but a shadow of the coming kingdom under the lordship of Jesus Christ. As the footprint of God's family grows to include Gentiles (Rom 11:25), we join the chorus of those who cry, "Amen! Come, Lord Jesus!" (Rev 22:20).

Reflect and Discuss

1. Why should we understand obedience as an expression of God's grace in our lives?
2. What role does Scripture play in our continued sanctification and growth?
3. In what ways will a church's commitment to Scripture be visible? What are nonnegotiables believers should look for when seeking a church home?
4. What ordinances of remembrance are just as meaningful to Christians today as Passover was to God's people who lived before Christ?
5. How will God respond to believers who repeatedly ignore his word and disobey his commands?
6. In what ways do we sometimes take advantage of God's long-suffering toward us?
7. What does the limit to God's patience with Judah teach us about how God will interact with us?
8. What does God's current delay in judgment teach us about his concern for those who do not know him?
9. How should we respond to those whose hearts are hardened toward the Lord?
10. How can we wait well for the Messiah's second coming?

WORKS CITED

Andrews, Andy. *The Butterfly Effect: How Your Life Matters.* Nashville, Thomas Nelson, 2010.

Archer, Gleason L. *A Survey of Old Testament Introduction.* Chicago: Moody, 2007.

Begg, C. T. "The Death of Josiah in Chronicles: Another View." *Vetus Testamentum* 37 (1987): 1–8.

Boda, Mark J. *1–2 Chronicles.* Cornerstone Biblical Commentary 5a. Carol Stream, IL: Tyndale House, 2010.

CSB Study Bible. Nashville: Holman Bible Publishers, 2017.

Demaray, Donald E. *Alive to God through Praise.* Eugene, OR: Wipf & Stock, 1976.

DeYoung, Kevin. *Men and Women in the Church: A Short, Biblical, Practical Introduction.* Wheaton, IL: Crossway, 2021.

Dillard, Raymond B. *2 Chronicles.* Word Biblical Commentary 15. Nashville: Thomas Nelson, 1986.

ESV Study Bible. Wheaton, IL: Crossway, 2008.

Farrar, Steve. *Gettin' There: How a Man Finds His Way on the Trail of Life.* Sisters, OR: Multnomah, 2001.

Geiger, Eric. *Identity: Who You Are in Christ.* Nashville: B&H Books, 2008.

Gladwell, Malcom. *The Tipping Point: How Little Things Can Make a Big Difference.* New York: Little Brown and Company, 2002.

Grudem, Wayne. *Systematic Theology: An Introduction to Biblical Doctrine.* Grand Rapids: Zondervan Academic, 1994.

Hill, Andrew E. *1 & 2 Chronicles.* NIV Application Commentary. Grand Rapids: Zondervan Academic, 2003.

Hunter, Trent, and Stephen Wellum. *Christ from Beginning to End: How the Full Story of Scripture Reveals the Full Glory of Christ.* Grand Rapids: Zondervan, 2018.

Japhet, Sara. *I & II Chronicles.* Louisville, KY: Westminster John Knox, 1993.

———. *The Ideology of the Book of Chronicles and Its Place in Biblical Thought.* Winona Lake, IN: Eisenbrauns, 2009.

Jeremiah, David. *Captured by Grace: No One Is Beyond the Reach of a Loving God.* Nashville: Thomas Nelson, 2006.

———. *Life Wide Open: Unleashing the Power of a Passionate Life.* Nashville: Integrity, 2003.

Johnstone, William. *1 and 2 Chronicles, Volume 1: 1 Chronicles 1–2 Chronicles 9: Israel's Place among the Nations.* Sheffield, UK: Sheffield Academic Press, 1998.

———. *1 and 2 Chronicles, Volume 2: 2 Chronicles 10–36: Guilt and Atonement.* Sheffield, UK: Sheffield Academic Press, 1998.

Kalimi, Isaac. *The Retelling of Chronicles in Jewish Tradition and Literature.* Winona Lake, IN: Eisenbrauns, 2009.

King's Business, The. "Illustrated Daily Text." August 30, 1928: 511. https://online.flippingbook.com/view/642411/56. Accessed April 14, 2023.

Klein, Ralph. "David: Sinner and Saint in Samuel and Chronicles." *Currents in Theology and Mission* 26/2 (2006): 104–16.

Knoppers, Gary N. *1 Chronicles 10–29.* Anchor Bible. New York: Doubleday, 2004.

Kuruvilla, Abraham. *Genesis.* Eugene, OR: Resource Publishing, 2014.

———. *Privilege the Text! A Theological Hermeneutic for Preaching.* Chicago: Moody, 2013.

Leithart, Peter J. *1 & 2 Chronicles.* Brazos Theological Commentary. Grand Rapids: Brazos, 2019.

Levenson, Jon D. "The Temple and the World." *The Journal of Religion* 64 (1984): 275–98.

Lewis, C. S. *The Silver Chair.* Middlesex, England: Puffin, 1977.

Longman, Tremper, III, and Raymond B. Dillard. *An Introduction to the Old Testament.* 2nd ed. Grand Rapids: Zondervan Academic, 2006.

Lucado, Max. *Begin Again: Your Hope and Renewal Start Today.* Nashville: Thomas Nelson, 2020.

———. *Come Thirsty.* Nashville: W Publishing, 2004.

Mabie, Frederick J. "1 and 2 Chronicles." Pages 23–335 in vol. 4 of *The Expositor's Bible Commentary.* Edited by Tremper Longman III and David E. Garland. Grand Rapids: Zondervan Academic, 2010.

MacDonald, William. *Believer's Bible Commentary, 2nd ed.* Nashville: Thomas Nelson, 2016.

Merrill, Eugene H. "1 Chronicles 17: The Davidic Covenant (II)." Pages 425–36 in *The Moody Handbook of Messianic Prophecy.* Edited by Michael Rydelnik and Edwin Blum. Chicago: Moody, 2019.

———. *2 Chronicles.* Bible Knowledge Commentary. Vol. 1. Edited by J. F. Walvoord & R. B. Zuck. Wheaton, IL: Victor Books, 1985.

———. *A Commentary on 1 & 2 Chronicles.* Grand Rapids: Kregel Academic, 2015.

Newton, John. "Amazing Grace: The Scripture Texts." JohnNewton.org. https://www.johnnewton.org/Groups/231009/The_John_Newton /new_menus/Amazing_Grace/Texts/Texts.aspx. Accessed October 8, 2022.

Nix, Elizabeth. "6 Infamous Imposters." *History.* August 19, 2014. https://www.history.com/news/6-infamous-impostors. Accessed January 22, 2023.

NIV Biblical Theology Study Bible. Grand Rapids: Zondervan, 2018.

Olley, John W. *1–2 Chronicles.* Pages 899–1294 in *1 Samuel–2 Chronicles.* ESV Expository Commentary 3. Edited by Iain M. Duguid, James M. Hamilton Jr., and Jay Sklar. Wheaton, IL: Crossway, 2019.

Payne, J. B. "1, 2 Chronicles." Pages 303–564 in vol. 4 of *The Expositor's Bible Commentary.* Edited by Frank Gaebelein. Grand Rapids: Zondervan, 1988.

Pratt, Richard. *1 & 2 Chronicles.* Mentor Commentary. Ross-shire, UK: Christian Focus, 2020.

Sailhamer, John. *First and Second Chronicles.* Everyman's Bible Commentary. Chicago: Moody, 1983.

Schrock, David. "Jabez and the Soft Prosperity Gospel." *The Gospel Coalition.* June 18, 2015. https://www.thegospelcoalition.org/article /jabez-and-the-soft-prosperity-gospel1. Accessed January 4, 2023.

Selman, Martin J. *1 Chronicles.* Tyndale Old Testament Commentaries. Downers Grove, IL: IVP Academic, 1994.

———. *2 Chronicles.* Tyndale Old Testament Commentaries. Downers Grove, IL: IVP Academic, 1994.

Spurgeon, Charles. "Honest Dealing with God." https://ccel.org/ccel /spurgeon/sermons21/sermons21.xxxii.html. Accessed August 22, 2023.

Swindoll, Charles. *Simple Faith: Discovering What Really Matters.* Nashville: W Publishing, 2003.

Thomas, Heath, and J. D. Greear. *Exalting Jesus in 1 & 2 Samuel.* Christ-Centered Exposition Commentary. Nashville: Holman Reference, 2016.

Thompson, J. A. *1, 2 Chronicles.* New American Commentary 9. Nashville: B&H, 1994.

Tozer, A. W. *Knowledge of the Holy.* San Franscisco, CA: HarperOne, 2009.

Walton, John H. *Genesis.* NIV Application Commentary. Grand Rapids: Zondervan Academic, 2001.

———. *Genesis 1 as Ancient Cosmology.* Winona Lake, IN: Eisenbrauns, 2011.

Wenham, Gordon. "Sanctuary Symbolism in the Garden of Eden Story." Pages 399–404 in *"I Studied Inscriptions from before the Flood": Ancient Near Eastern, Literary, and Linguistic Approaches to Genesis 1–11.* Edited by Richard S. Hess and David Toshio Tsumura. Winona Lake, IN: Eisenbrauns, 1994.

Wiersbe, Warren. *The Wiersbe Bible Commentary.* Colorado Springs, CO: David C. Cook, 2007.

Wilcock, Michael. *The Message of Chronicles.* The Bible Speaks Today. Downers Grove, IL: IVP Academic, 1987.

———. *1 and 2 Chronicles.* New Bible Commentary, 4th ed. Edited by D. A. Carson, R. T. France, J. A. Motyer, and G. J. Wenham. Downers Grove, IL: IVP Academic, 1994.

Williamson, H. G. M. *1 and 2 Chronicles.* Eugene, OR: Wipf & Stock, 1982.

SCRIPTURE INDEX